Teaching S
About the
World of Work

WORK AND **LEARNING SERIES**

Series edited by Robert B. Schwartz and Nancy Hoffman

OTHER BOOKS IN THIS SERIES

Teaching Students About the World of Work

A CHALLENGE TO POSTSECONDARY EDUCATORS

Edited by

NANCY HOFFMAN
MICHAEL LAWRENCE COLLINS

Harvard Education Press
CAMBRIDGE, MA

Copyright © 2020 by the President and Fellows of Harvard College

Paperback ISBN 978-1-68253-494-6
Library Edition ISBN 978-1-68253-495-3

Library of Congress Cataloging-in-Publication Data is on file.

Published by Harvard Education Press,
an imprint of the Harvard Education Publishing Group

Harvard Education Press
8 Story Street
Cambridge, MA 02138

Cover Design: Wilcox Design
Cover Image: SDI Productions/E+ via Getty Images

The typefaces in this book are Adobe Garamond, Milo OT, and Mundo Sans Std

CONTENTS

SECTION III—THEORY AND EVIDENCE: IMPLICATIONS FOR PRACTICE

SERIES FOREWORD

– ROBERT B. SCHWARTZ –

Since 2011, Harvard Education Press has published six books—beginning with Nancy Hoffman's *Schooling in the Workplace*—that have focused on the case for integrating work and learning in the high school years. In 2019 HEP brought these volumes together in an ongoing series called Work and Learning, for which Nancy and I are serving as curators. This latest entrant, *Teaching Students About the World of Work*, is distinctive for many reasons, most obviously because it is the first book in the series to deal primarily with the world of community colleges.

Why the attention to community colleges? While the school-to-work movement of the 1990s and its current successor, the career pathways movement—the subject of earlier books in this series—have focused on promising strategies for integrating academic and technical education and expanding work-based learning in the high school years, the reality is that virtually all of the good jobs that pay decent wages in tomorrow's economy will require something more than a high school diploma. While the *New York Times* and other publications that cater to a professional-class readership continue to behave as if "college" means only four-year institutions, nearly half of all undergraduates (and most students of color) in fact attend two-year colleges. More important, only one young American in three attains a four-year degree by age twenty-five, and for young people born in the bottom 40 percent of the wealth distribution, it's little better than one in ten. This last number suggests that if we are serious about providing economic opportunity and mobility for those young people and adults who are furthest behind, our community and two-year technical colleges have a critical role to play.

There are over 1,100 community colleges in America, currently serving 13 million students—adults as well as those just out of high school. Except for families in the most remote rural areas, nearly everyone lives within commuting distance of a community college. These institutions have multiple missions, serve multiple populations, and have enormous regional variation in how they define themselves. In northern cities, for example, some began life as "junior colleges," providing thirteenth and fourteenth years of mostly technical education under the umbrella of the local school district. In other states, most notably California, community colleges were explicitly designed to provide the first two years of higher education for students lacking the academic qualifications for admission to the state's four-year institutions. The premise was that those who successfully completed the two-year program would then be encouraged to transfer to a four-year institution. In other states, especially in the South, community colleges were created by governors and legislatures eager to recruit new industries to their state by providing a set of institutions primarily dedicated to developing a skilled workforce to meet the needs of employers.

The editors and contributors to this volume believe that, whatever their origins and priorities, all community colleges would serve their students well by paying more attention to the world of work and the role that work plays in human lives. They make a powerful case that work must move from the periphery and no longer be seen as solely the province of those running occupational degree or certificate programs and staffing career services offices. Rather, they argue that work must move to the center of the curriculum and be seen as a subject worthy of serious academic attention, as is the case with Guttman Community College's innovative Ethnographies of Work course, profiled in chapter 3 of this volume.

Editors Nancy Hoffman and Michael Lawrence Collins have brought together a thoughtful collection of practitioners and researchers not only to make the case for the inclusion of work as a central topic in the curriculum of community colleges, but to address the "what" and "how" questions as well. This is a book not only for community college educators but also for those who work with community college students in other settings, including the workplace.

FOREWORD

– GARRETT MORAN –

Today in America we have a full employment economy in which our employers are increasingly confounded by a scarcity of candidates adequately prepared for employment. At the same time, we know there are millions of ambitious young adults who struggle unsuccessfully to get the preparation needed to capture these opportunities. And this "opportunity divide" seems to keep getting worse each year.

Is there something our employers and educators are missing? Are young adults failing to seize sensible choices that would solve a lot of this problem? What should we expect from our employers, educators, and young adults in partnering to close this gap? How should we go about diagnosing this affliction and prescribing a cure? Approaching it from the supply side (young adults as career aspirants) and the demand side (employers who want to recruit talent and grow their businesses), we should ask three questions:

- What do the aspirants and the employers see when they approach the labor market from their respective sides of the field?
- What do they want or expect from the market? In the case of job aspirants, the "market" includes educators and trainers who help provide access to employers.
- And, finally, what do we know about what works, especially proven approaches that can readily be applied more broadly?

The demand side complaints are familiar: that the candidate pool of young adults is technically unprepared for work, and that their feeder colleges are failing to keep up with an evolving market and have been unsuccessful in forging effective business partnerships that are dynamic and durable. An even larger issue for most companies seeking young employees, however, is the social-emotional gap. This is most often described as a fundamental disconnect about what is expected in the employer-employee relationship. This includes simple things like punctuality and respectful workplace behavior and extends to having realistic expectations for personal advancement and being an effective project team member.

But as Nancy Hoffman and Michael Lawrence Collins's new volume argues, the answer on the supply side isn't just to get better and more up-to-date technical training, take part in a workshop about teamwork and collaboration, and complete your degree. Their book steps back to ask: What should college faculty know and help students understand about the world of work? The book synthesizes research in the sociology and psychology of work for an audience focused on promoting economic mobility of the many low-income students who see community colleges as a lifeline and who sacrifice so much to stay enrolled.

As a number of chapters suggest, students who have few professional connections and whose only work history consists of hourly-wage jobs will certainly need postsecondary education, but that won't be enough to launch a career. This volume proposes that community college faculty and students make the world of work a subject of study. Colleges should help students answer the big questions, such as: What satisfactions do people get from work beyond adequate compensation? What makes an employer a good employer? When is a job just a job and when is it a career? And what are soft skills and who defines them? If everyone knows it's good to network, how does one make valuable contacts and begin building useful relationships? The book also argues that the best way to learn about the workplace is through "real time" workplace experiences—if not paid internships, then job shadows, structured visits, and opportunities to interact with business leaders.

Everyone has a role to play in helping our young adults prepare for work, but educators have a central role in linking their students to careers. I know about the value of comprehensive preparation for the work world from my five years' experience as president of Year Up. Year Up serves low-income eighteen- to twenty-four-year-old high school graduates who are not sustainably in work or school. It's a high-expectations, high-support twelve-month program divided between six months of training in hard skills and soft/professional skills followed by a six-month paid internship with one of our corporate partners. We seek out ambitious young adults whom we believe can succeed in our program and in the white-collar jobs that follow. They have typically graduated from weak high schools and have undistinguished high school GPAs, but they have demonstrated that they have the brains, talent, and drive to thrive in jobs that are frequently reserved for four-year college graduates.

For our students, Year Up is transformative. Eighty percent of our graduates are in jobs earning an average of $40,000 per year within months of completing the program. We have over twenty thousand total graduates today and a growing roster of corporate partners who will offer our students over four thousand internships this year. Our success strongly supports the arguments made in this volume about the nature of the labor market today, the workforce of tomorrow, and the special steps that can be taken to prepare talented young adults.

In the simplest terms, we have a program that offers a big dose of what community colleges may aspire to but can't afford to provide—individual attention and support, including career training and guidance, academic counseling, and personal help that might otherwise be offered by a social worker or a parent with a mainstream career. A key to our program is effectively building in students that sense of excitement and confidence in a career path that is within their reach if they work hard and make important sacrifices.

Year Up, of course, is not the only program that provides the powerful mix of professional skills training, technical education, and internships. There are additional standalone programs as well as a good number associated with community colleges—often called "Learn and Earn" programs. But even with twenty thousand graduates over nineteen years of operation, Year Up and other programs are small and often have high per-student costs. Community colleges are, in effect, our nation's comprehensive workforce development system; they educate nearly nine million students a year, including the majority of low-income students and students of color. The challenge is bringing approaches like Year Up's to scale in these important institutions.

Young adults entering community colleges are presented with an overwhelming array of academic options with limited academic guidance or career planning to help them make good choices. This is no wonder because, as college budgets have been squeezed over recent decades, guidance resources have been crushed. Students also see low degree completion rates and may find out that the sacrifices required for degree completion do not yield a career payoff. At the same time, the world of work is rapidly evolving. Matching up academic degrees, industry certifications, and real job opportunities has become a bewildering challenge. And getting access to interviews and jobs without serious help too often seems like an impossible hurdle. Students want to understand potential career pathways and the training required. They need the information, support, and experience to navigate the choices and tradeoffs that present a big challenge even for a well-resourced, well-supported young adult.

Beyond choosing among technical programs, students want to fully understand the real world of potential career pathways. They can get exposure to these pathways through work-based learning, meetings with industry leaders, and coaching on the nuances of a career progression and the ups and downs of life in the foreign world that is the modern workplace. They want to know how to "walk the walk" because they understand that it is a competitive advantage, builds confidence, and will help them fit effectively into the workplace.

Ideally much of this learning would come in the form of one-on-one support, but failing the resources for that kind of investment, community colleges can integrate into courses the topics that prepare students for work, as well as encourage faculty to incorporate out-of-classroom experiences that introduce students to a variety of workplaces and professions. While developing paid internships at scale is an enormous challenge, colleges can provide job shadows, hold networking events, and facilitate group activities that provide much of the desired engagement.

As Pam Eddinger—the president of Boston's Bunker Hill Community College (BHCC)—and Richard Kazis explain in chapter 2: "The interest in and power of internships for community college students is evident in school after school. . . . Community college leaders and personnel are beginning to act on the recognition that their students need both stronger connections to employers and work experience—and that their institutions must develop programs that are better tailored to their students' needs." But, they also note, "the aspiration of placing every learner into an internship they would find attractive is remote, even impossible. But that does not mean that students cannot learn in a formal, structured way from the low-wage, part-time jobs they hold while in school, or dig deeply into how the professions operate." BHCC is integrating many of the topics in this book into its learning community courses. While not a substitute for a paid internship, the courses "provides students with analytical tools that are helpful in seeking entrance to new areas in the labor market."

We can't expect that students will gain all of this learning unless they are taught and actively supported. Thinking about my own children's and their friends' search for work, I recognize that they began with so many advantages: no college debt; access to internships and information about various professions and occupations; adults willing and eager to open doors; professionals whose behavior they have observed over years; and, perhaps most of all, the expectation that they could choose a career that would satisfy and challenge them while offering the prospect of a life of continuous learning. This volume supports the notion that our community colleges can take important strides toward replicating many of these advantages and more effectively provide the opportunities that their students so ardently desire.

Garrett Moran joined Year Up in 2013 after a year in Harvard's Advanced Leadership Initiative. Before coming to Year Up, he was COO of Blackstone's private equity business and prior to that held other positions in the finance sector.

Why This Book?

– NANCY HOFFMAN –

It is time for education institutions that serve the majority of low-income students to address the topic of work. This edited volume is about where "work" fits into formal education. Many students make enormous sacrifices to go to community and four-year colleges, too often with blind faith in the outcomes that will be theirs with a college degree—a good salary and work that provides at least some satisfaction. They go into debt, put their families at financial risk, and endure stress as they work and care for others while going to school. Far too many do so knowing little about what awaits them at the end of this journey, how difficult it may be to find a good job even with a degree, how long it will take to pay back loans, what the salaries are at entry level, and how important it is to leverage networks and professional friendships to have a chance. In a focus group I did recently with a colleague at a community college, the mostly young, male, and ethnically diverse students had only the vaguest ideas about the relation between college and the labor market. With unfounded conviction they believed they'd earn more money than in their current hourly-wage jobs—one even said "six figures"—if they had a degree. A fall 2018 report from the Georgetown Center on Education and the Workforce sums up the Center's research on the plight of working learners, the population community colleges serve:

> low-income working learners are going to school more and working more hours yet struggling to make it. They have been failed by an education system that perpetuates intergenerational inequality; a labor market that offers them fewer high-quality job opportunities with career-building work experience while they are in school; . . . poor information about education and career pathways and their outcomes; and a lack of sufficient support mechanisms and financial and social safety nets.[1]

All colleges give students massive amounts of information as they enter college, choose majors, and learn about general education requirements and prerequisites. They are told where pathways lead, and at best whether there are transfer, graduate, and internship opportunities. The push toward guided pathways and metamajors in community colleges emerged because research confirmed that "undeclared" students have higher dropout rates and that liberal arts two-year degrees add almost no value in the labor market. It is all to the good that more students are choosing a career pathway or area of interest early on, but even an early choice and good guidance cannot make up for the chasm between young people growing up in professional households and those whose families have had few opportunities for well-paid and engaging work.

For low-income students, getting financial aid forms filled out and admissions applications submitted can be daunting; just being admitted with all the right paperwork filed can seem a victory. Such students need answers to and help with immediate and practical questions once they arrive. A recent study for the Bill & Melinda Gates Foundation provides evidence of the class and race divide around "the aspirations people have and pathways they perceive as available to them for future employment." Among black and Latinx communities, the focus was on "near-term obstacles to access," such as costs of college, barriers of inequality, and need for persistence; among the general populations, it was on "future-oriented career success" and "dream jobs."[2] Information provided about careers and majors in the first weeks of college can do only part of the work. Colleges *can* address students' gaps in knowledge and aspirations, but this is a longer-term proposition.

Given these realities, the question this book raises isn't just in service of adding an engaging topic to the curriculum (although the topic of work *is* engaging), it is an ethical question: *Do public higher education institutions have an obligation to help students understand the world of work?* For the authors of this collection, the answer is yes. As a Labor Day article in the *New York Times* asserts: "It's easy for most people to find a job in America on Labor Day 2019. The unemployment rate is very low; store windows are plastered with help wanted signs. But for millions of Americans, one job is not enough." We don't want students who work so hard and give up so much to join the ranks of the 8 million Americans, roughly 5 percent of workers, who hold full-time jobs that pay so little that they are obliged to work a second job to support themselves and their families. The average adult spends ninety thousand hours in paid employment over the life span, and that's with average eight-hour days. Thus, it is extremely important that young adults entering the labor market are equipped to choose how that one-third of a lifetime is spent. A decade from now, when many of today's jobs will likely be unrecognizable, we want students to say that their postsecondary education prepared them for that future with careers that left them time for healthy and balanced lives.

For the several reasons stated here, and for broader questions plaguing American society, the moment seems right to engage questions about work. A society of haves and have-nots predicted in the apocalyptic reports on the future of work will not serve anyone well. Indeed, many such reports argue that poorly paid service jobs will proliferate and will be filled by the poorly educated while the well-connected and highly educated will do even better than they are today, exacerbating economic inequality. That is why a major argument in chapter 1, "Putting Work at the Center of Community College Completion Reform," by Michael Lawrence Collins, is that colleges must go beyond focusing on degree completion, the goal of much reform over the last decade. Collins notes that "the college mobility narrative is more complicated than we have imagined. . . . Earnings data show that factors such as socioeconomic status, race, ethnicity, gender, institutional selectivity, type of degree, and social capital influence who benefits from college completion." He adds:

> The fact that over 80 percent of community college students say that they want to earn a bachelor's degree or higher suggests that they are not merely interested in getting a job. They are interested in the premium in wages that is available to bachelor's degree holders and people with advanced degrees. In short, they are interested in doing well economically.
>
> Surprisingly, for all of community college students' interest in good jobs associated with careers, there is little to no consideration of work in the college experience.

The emphasis on careers as an outcome of education does not mean that this book advocates abandoning the liberal arts for technical education;

rather, the authors agree that colleges should incorporate a range of questions about work into their programs of study, many of them exactly the stuff that makes liberal arts education engaging. Here are two: *What is the role of work in human lives? Why do most people want to work?* Additional questions are helpful if the goal is student economic mobility: *How are careers created and developed? What are the characteristics of a good job? Who defines "soft" or "professional" skills, and how does one develop them?* And, particularly for low-income students and those of color, this vital question: *What barriers and sorting systems must students recognize, understand, and overcome in a labor market that favors the well connected?* The authors also agree that the best way to learn about work is by experiencing a variety of workplaces. So a theme in this book is that students who study work, including their own jobs, and hold internships that introduce them to possible careers, are best equipped to move into satisfying work. This is the topic that Bunker Hill Community College President Pam Eddinger and researcher Richard Kazis take up in chapter 2, "Reimagining Experiential Learning and Internships for Community College Students."

A PERSONAL NOTE ABOUT THE BOOK

This book owes much to the thinking behind the Ethnographies of Work (EOW) course at Guttman Community College of the City University of New York (CUNY). The course is described briefly in this introduction and in chapter 3, by Mary Gatta and Niesha Ziehmke, "Ethnographies of Work: A Transformative Framework for Career Learning." I had a role in advocating for a course about work when Guttman was in the planning phase a decade ago. The topic has long been a preoccupation of mine for personal reasons. I went to college in the 1960s when college-going women thought about their BAs in conjunction with what was commonly called their "Mrs. degrees." Thinking back, I realize I did not have a single woman professor—not one—from undergraduate education through graduate school, and no women authors were on the syllabus. By graduation, many of us were married. If women from middle-class families like mine prepared for work, it was generally to be a secretary, teacher, nurse, or social worker—jobs that you could do if you had to, and that were extensions of women's "natural" role as caregivers or guides for the young. Many women gave little thought to the result of this gendered social arrangement until private life became too constraining or a divorce or spouse's death made work a necessity. I watched many of my contemporaries—with college degrees and without—try to enter the labor market in their thirties and forties with kids at home and no marketable skills. In the 1970s, I taught at a college designed for older adults. Our students were struggling women without degrees, and ours was a very early career-focused institution. I have always liked my work, and it's a personal mission to help others find work that satisfies needs both basic and human.

Fast-forward to 2019 and to practical realities. Eighteen years ago, I stopped being a full-time professor to join a national nonprofit, Jobs for the Future (JFF). JFF redesigns education systems and institutions as well as workforce programs to help more people gain the credentials that will earn them a reasonable living and, at best, well-being. My particular team works with high schools and community college systems that should serve as scaffolds into good jobs that meet employer demand, but too often don't work that way. Even with a college degree in a full employment economy, many low- and middle-income young people are still disadvantaged. They are more likely than their advantaged peers with similar education credentials to land in lower-wage jobs without security, benefits, and opportunities for promotion, the dream of upward mobility lost.[3] After many years at JFF learning from colleagues in high schools, community colleges, nonprofit organizations, and businesses, and reading incessantly about the growing gaps in family assets and access to social capital, I know even more than I did in my twenties not only about why work is so important, but also about how perilous the journey is to find a good and satisfying job.

THEMES

On June 25, 2019, the authors of this book came together in Boston to share ideas and attempt to make an edited collection into a coherent book. The authors are practitioner leaders who focus on improving community colleges, nonprofit senior staff who work to improve education and workforce outcomes across the US, and professors committed to seeing their research applied. Some of us are currently playing or have played several of these roles. The result is a book that speaks to a variety of audiences: faculty, higher education leaders, policy makers, those responsible for career advising and services, as well as a broader public interested in education and economic mobility. To address these multiple audiences, the book is divided into three sections: Beyond College Completion: Why Work Belongs in the Curriculum; Good Jobs, Good Careers; and Theory and Evidence: Implications for Practice. We do not offer specific recommendations or solutions for how higher education institutions should go about putting work at the center of learning; instead, our goal for this project is to begin a conversation and provide resources to inform a dialogue in the field on the role of work in postsecondary education.

Beyond College Completion: Why Work Belongs in the Curriculum (Chapters 1–3)

The chapters in this section set out the problem from the perspective of community college leaders and reformers. As luck would have it, not only have colleges begun to rethink career advising, but Guttman Community College, a new member of the CUNY system now in its eighth year, developed the innovative yearlong required course and lab mentioned earlier, Ethnographies of Work, which demonstrates one powerful way that colleges can integrate topics related to work and careers into the curriculum. A number of community colleges are adapting EOW to suit their populations and their structures of learning. For example, Bunker Hill Community College, the institution that chapter 2 coauthor Pam Eddinger leads, is infusing the key concepts of EOW into its learning communities and other courses.

EOW challenges the ways that colleges traditionally deliver career advising. As chapter 3 authors Mary Gatta and Niesha Ziehmke explain, the course operates on this simple theory of change: "Students who understand the meaning of work in human lives and who have a critical understanding of work experience will have greater agency in entering and navigating the labor market than those who believe they need only a credential." The chapter explores how this theory of change plays out in the classroom and fieldwork experiences of Guttman students as well as in their ability to navigate further education and work. Along with discussion of assignments including the fieldwork component, chapter 3 includes students' thoughts as they reflect on their learning in EOW. This statement from a Guttman alum now in graduate school provides a window into one young woman's perceptions:

> One of the things that I learned was that our careers are kind of created and built. It's not just something that you just—you get your degree, you learn a set of skills, and you just get a job and you apply it; it's not given to you that way. So, I learned more of like career dynamics and how we're always learning and navigating through different stages. It's not as clear-cut as, you know, learning how to do one thing and then there's a clear definition and task description for a specific thing that you'll do.

This young woman entered the course with a mental image of a future of routine or repetitive work—"you get the skills and you apply it . . . you learn . . . how to do one thing." She left the course with an idea of a non-routine work, a career where she would grow and where she had agency. "I learned more of like career dynamics and how we're always learning and navigating through different stages." As Gatta and Ziehmke argue, EOW "offers a paradigmatic shift in career learning," helping students both master professional skills or "soft skills" in lab while fortifying themselves through their field experiences. They can use new social science insights to face and manage the inevitable societal inequities they will confront as they search for satisfying work in today's labor market.

Good Jobs, Good Careers (Chapters 4 and 5)

These two chapters provide practical insights into the labor market with the goal of improving the choices and outcomes for low-income job seekers. The authors believe this information is badly needed even for students in career-focused programs. For example, students often choose human services fields, wanting to give back to their communities, but they may not know that the median salary for social and human service assistants with two-year degrees is $33,120.[4] Neither might they be aware that a master's of social work (MSW), the preferred degree, requires one to two years of schooling beyond the bachelor's degree with the median salary rising to around $62,000. Then this information should be contextualized against living wage information for a region. (MIT's Living Wage Calculator defines a living wage as two and half to three times the minimum wage in any locality.[5]) According to the Calculator, a single parent with two children would need $58,000 in Columbus, Ohio, but community and social services jobs pay a median wage of $45,000, and an MSW pays about $62,000, the national average. Thus, supporting a family in Columbus would require an MSW, more years of schooling, and greater cost than many community college students would anticipate.

WHEN CAN A JOB LAUNCH A CAREER? In chapter 4, "When Can a Job Launch a Career?," Sara Lamback and Charlotte Cahill explore what students need to know as they look ahead to careers in a shifting, complex labor market—and how faculty, advisors, career services, and other staff can support students' career planning and development. They answer the following questions: Which jobs have the potential to lead to careers with opportunities for advancement, and which may lead to dead ends? What sources of information illuminate the skills and educational credentials students should earn in order to be competitive job applicants? What strategies are useful to ensure that students' postsecondary choices and options set them up for career success?

The chapter first demonstrates how labor market information can be used to better understand the relationship between jobs that lead nowhere and careers with advancement opportunities and to identify which industries offer an array of career possibilities. These possibilities include middle-skill work, which does not require a four-year college degree. Drawing on an analysis of nearly 4 million résumés of middle-skill job seekers across the country from a database developed by Burning Glass Technologies, Lamback and Cahill highlight a subset of middle-skill jobs in health care, IT, business, and manufacturing that promote career advancement and income growth based upon four metrics: job stability, career stability, advancement, and pay. (The chapter includes a framework for identifying three distinct types of middle-skill jobs: lifetime jobs that *are* careers, springboard jobs that *lead* to careers, and static jobs characterized by low pay, low stability, and low advancement potential.)

The authors also discuss what labor market information can tell us about the skills and credentials most frequently sought by employers—and how educators can support students in making sense of this information in the context of a changing labor market. With the automation of job tasks once performed by human workers, employers are increasingly seeking workers who possess skills—such as critical thinking and problem solving—that are difficult to automate. The chapter also explores research related to credentials and the role they can play in supporting both advancement and career/job stability for workers. Finally, the authors offer suggestions about how what we know about the labor market can and should inform students' educational choices. For example, how might what we know about different types of middle-skills jobs in the health-care industry—and the continuing importance to health-care employers of skills such as thinking critically and making decisions under pressure—factor into the decision-making process of a student choosing among several programs of study in the health sciences?

WHAT MAKES A GOOD JOB? In chapter 5, "What Makes a Good Job?," Katie Bach and Sarah Kalloch, both staff members at the nonprofit Good Jobs Institute, delve into the resources available publicly to job seekers as they ask questions about what might be a good company or a good employer. The Good Jobs Institute was developed to work directly with companies to improve their practices in ways that enhance both worker satisfaction and productivity. While the organization's tools, resources, and Good Jobs Scorecard are designed for employers, job seekers or students preparing for careers can use these resources to evaluate a potential employer. This is the chapter students and advisors might turn to for a framework and tools for assessing a job opening in a corporate or nonprofit entity.

Bach and Kalloch start from the premise, confirmed in a number of chapters in this book, that *work* is not working for millions of Americans. They note that 42 percent of Americans make less than $15/hour, and many have partial to no benefits, unstable schedules, and limited career growth—hence the many people who hold several jobs at one time to make ends meet. Low-wage jobs often also disrespect worker time and knowledge, which further diminishes the dignity of people living on the margins. A unique contribution of the Good Jobs Institute is to foreground qualities that make a job satisfying and engaging, what most people aspire to when queried about their ideal careers.

Using an employee pyramid based on Maslow's Hierarchy of Needs, the chapter describes how companies can meet basic needs—fair pay, stable schedules, career growth, and security and safety—as well as higher needs, including belonging, recognition, achievement, and personal growth. The chapter sets out a list of questions, external data sources, and considerations that students should review before taking a job, as well as strategies to help make a job better once they are hired. For example, readers learn about crowdsourced worker reviews of companies and organizations like B Corp that certify corporations that meet standards of social and environmental performance. The Good Jobs framework also allows job seekers to make tradeoffs between different elements of the framework, and addresses how those considerations might change with life circumstances.

Theory and Evidence: Implications for Practice (Chapters 6–9)

The four chapters that make up the final section of this book draw on the extensive social science research literature about work. The authors of the chapters are steeped in the data related to economic inequality as well as in the social science literature on systemic and structural barriers that are its root cause. As in the two previous sections, the writing in this section employs an equity lens that sheds light on and proposes solutions to inequality, particularly in regard to employment. We chose these respected scholars for this section because they are eager to apply their research in the service of economic mobility strategies that lead to better life outcomes for low-income youth and adults.

Many of the readers of this volume go home from work most days feeling that they have made a useful contribution to their worlds. They are relatively satisfied with the choices they have made about how to earn a living. But this is not the experience of the majority of people on the planet. We know that not working—unemployment—is destructive to most adults. Extended periods of unemployment result in low self-esteem, loss of agency, increases in rates of depression, and damage to close relationships. Divorce rates rise and domestic partnerships are less likely to form when those who wish to work are unemployed. But if absence of work can be destructive, having work does not mean that workers are satisfied or engaged. Herein lies a sad paradox—for many, work is the lesser of two evils. It provides the wherewithal to pay the bills, gives a structure to one's days, and puts one into a community of coworkers, but the cost may be diminished humanity, dignity, agency, and even health.

On August 29, 2018, the *Wall Street Journal* reported that according to the Conference Board, 51 percent of workers said they were satisfied with their jobs.[6] This is the highest rate since 2000. The same month, the *Wall Street Journal* reported on a Gallup Poll showing that only 34 percent of workers claimed to be engaged.[7] And a 2016 Gallup worldwide poll showed even lower numbers: a sample of 250,000 people from 150 countries yielded the fact that only 13 percent of workers say they are engaged in their jobs.[8] Not all of these unsatisfying jobs pay low wages; anecdotal evidence supports the notion that one can sell one's soul for a big salary. Some workers find basic living-wage jobs satisfying. Community college students often hold unsatisfying low-wage jobs, since they must take what employment they can get to earn money and get by while going to school. Their choices are often not based on what they can learn from a job or with whom it will connect them if they wish to move up. The entitlement to choose satisfying work may not have been something a low-wage working student ever considered.

The world of student aspirations is segmented by class and race: young people from families in the top 20 percent income group are accustomed from childhood to think they are entitled to work that is fulfilling, pays well, and will earn them status and respect. And many fulfill their aspirations. This outcome is confirmed by research studies showing that family income is associated not only with level of education, but also with postgraduation earnings. As a number of researchers have documented, young people benefit from their family's affluence and the mainstream social skills they learn while growing up; they also have access to elite education institutions and valuable connections and networks. The high-wage jobs they enter are a growing segment of the labor market. But the economy is also proliferating low-paying service jobs in fast food restaurants, hotels, home health care, retail, or gig work like driving for Uber and Lyft. These jobs have few benefits or opportunities for advancement and generally fall to those without other choices.

THE PSYCHOLOGY OF WORKING THEORY In chapter 6, "The Psychology of Working Theory" (PWT), David L. Blustein and Maureen E. Kenny propose a revised framework for the academic disciplines of career counseling and vocational psychology to make them more inclusive. As the chapter notes, "By the end of the twentieth century, most career choice and development theories focused on individuals with relative volition in their lives. In effect, the career development world morphed into a field focusing on the lives of those with career choice privilege—the capacity to create and implement a career based on one's interests, values, and aspirations." The guiding principles of the psychology of working theory shift the narrative from emphasizing the psychological makeup of an individual as responsible for barriers that impede her success to putting greater emphasis on influential contextual factors. In PWT, these barriers fall into two categories: "economic constraints" and "marginalization." It is these barriers that shape "work volition" and "career adaptability" among low-income populations. Here, a further word is useful about work volition, which the authors define as "one's perception of the capacity to actually implement decisions and choices in one's work life."

Applying this theory to practice, Blustein and Kenny suggest that, with a critical understanding of the power of social and economic factors, individuals can equip themselves to become proactively engaged in managing, if not overcoming, barriers. Taking action against structural inequality, they argue, is a responsibility of both the privileged and the marginalized. But the authors also recognize that "for equitable access for all to decent work," it is not just individuals who must struggle and adapt, but systems that must change as well. In this regard, PWT moves beyond career counseling and advising to serve as a framework for the massive policy changes needed to enable more people to choose how they spend their ninety thousand hours.

WORK-RELATED BARRIERS EXPERIENCED BY LOW-INCOME PEOPLE OF COLOR AND INDIGENOUS INDIVIDUALS Few readers will need to be convinced that structural and systemic barriers impede the labor market success of marginalized populations. In chapter 7, "Work-Related Barriers Experienced by Low-Income People of Color and Indigenous Individuals," Gloria McGillen, Lisa Flores, and Gregory Seaton document the lived experience of low-income people of color who are identifiably different from their prospective or current employers. At the outset, they make a useful distinction between "obstacles" and "barriers"; everyone, they note, faces obstacles or bumps in the road to achieving their goals, but barriers are "structural challenges that are more difficult to overcome, prevent access to fulfilling one's goals, or shape one's path in such ways that individuals may avoid or abandon some work opportunities altogether." Drawing on a wide range of research studies, they describe the labor market barriers faced by those who speak a language other than English, or those who are Latinx, African American, or members of another identifiable nonwhite group. The authors show how these barriers are manifested across developmental stages, including childhood, in postsecondary education, during the transition from school to work, and within work settings. They also highlight how the experience or anticipation of academic and work barriers impacts the mind-set of individuals and affects their vocational development and work-related outcomes. The academic and work barriers that youth of color face are deep-rooted and long-standing within US institutions. The authors argue for an ecological or systems perspective in tackling these barriers but are realistic in saying that it will take individuals committed for the long term to *changing the educational and work systems* to reduce and eliminate the structures and policies that sustain these barriers and allow them to operate.

The authors emphasize the need to equip students of color with strategies for coping with workplace stressors. They conclude by discussing how professionals can intervene at the institutional level to reduce barriers for students, providing recommendations for working with students to manage the effects of these barriers. They make a case for the importance of helping students and job seekers develop self-efficacy so they are able to advocate for themselves as well as identify allies who will tackle barriers with them. Echoing an important theme from chapter 6, they also set the expectation that the privileged must advocate on behalf of less privileged people of color in the workplace as well as educate companies about the challenges that marginalized people experience.

"IMPLICIT" SKILLS: MEETING THE CHALLENGE OF THE TWENTY-FIRST-CENTURY WORKFORCE A theme throughout the following two chapters is the increasing importance of soft skills or, particularly for a book focused on economic mobility in the labor market, the ability of an employee to "perform" the professional behaviors appropriate to a specific work setting. The topic of "soft" or "professional" or "twenty-first century" skills is a complicated one. Brent Orrell (chapter 8) and Nancy Hoffman and Mary Gatta (chapter 9) come at the growing importance of these skills in two different ways. Orrell attempts a challenging endeavor—to define these behaviors or capacities, using fresh language to do so. Hoffman and Gatta ask, Who defines the behaviors or capacities called soft skills, and how do these skills function to include or exclude people from the labor market? Both of these chapters, however, encounter similar challenges: How do we define, talk about, and teach qualities so subjective and difficult to assess—from self-awareness and empathy to leadership and creativity?

Chapter 8, "'Implicit' Skills: Meeting the Challenge of the Twenty-First-Century Workforce," provides depth and insight into this issue. Orrell observes that, based on employer feedback, the biggest challenge in the US labor force is not employees' lack of technical skills. While employers value and seek to develop the technical skills of their workforces, they routinely list *nontechnical*, or what Orrell calls "implicit," skills as the main deficit in the US workforce—a deficit that appears to be growing. Orrell defines "explicit" skills as related to specific business or mechanical processes (e.g., how to use tools on a factory floor, build code for a software product, or design and populate a complex spreadsheet), while "implicit" skills—also known as noncognitive or soft skills—are overarching "master" skills that form the capacity for learning, on-the-job training, and professional advancement as well as managing relationships with managers, coworkers, and customers.

Orrell also argues that, paradoxically, demand for such skills is growing even as technologies like artificial intelligence and robotics spread within the workforce, a fact recognized even by the major high-tech firms who increasingly prioritize implicit skills over technical skills in their hiring and promotion policies and practices. In the STEM fields, a similar trend is apparent. Orrell reports on a new AEI Reuters-Ipsos interview study of STEM workers showing that strong interpersonal skills are associated with rising income as well.

Taking on a sensitive topic that many people tiptoe around, Orrell traces possible sources of the implicit-skills gap to the acceleration of divorce and unmarried births over the last several decades, noting that children born in stressed families face challenges that can last into adulthood. While the chapter does not go into depth to explain the sources of growing family fracture among both white and African American families, Orrell notes contributing factors such as fewer constraints of single parenthood, declining job opportunities for middle-skill males, opioid addiction, and the legacy of racism. Finally, the chapter includes summaries of a number of interventions that have promise for increasing the stock of implicit skills in the US workforce to better position workers for an economy that prizes such capacities as automated processes take over much of the routine cognitive and physical work of business and industry.

SOCIAL CAPITAL AND THE SOCIAL CONSTRUCTION OF SKILLS As numerous authors in this book assert, just getting a college degree does not guarantee economic mobility. One of the least tangible but most important aspects of preparing for good jobs is learning to access and mobilize the relationships and networks that open opportunity. In the final chapter, "Social Capital and the Social Construction of Skills," Mary Gatta and I take on soft or professional skills, those skills that employers assess as they sort résumés posted online or judge candidates in a "blink" moment during an interview.[9] The chapter begins with the concept of social capital, defined as resources embedded in one's social networks. Capital, of course, implies monetary value, but is used metaphorically in the phrase *"social" capital* to suggest that networks and the people within them have value in the connections, recommendations, and introductions they provide. In network theories of social capital, social networks are the vehicles through which social capital is accrued; belonging to a social network is demonstrated through social behaviors or social skills that characterize that network.

The question the chapter raises, then, is, How do job seekers learn the "right" soft skills for the network that will help them find and land a new job? The second section of the chapter asserts that, contrary to popular opinion, skills are neither "natural" (i.e., you are born with them) nor ascribed or learned. As the chapter notes, "Sociologists have suggested that skills cannot be so neatly and objectively conceived. Instead, we must understand the circumstances by which occupations become socially constructed as 'skilled,' and the ways skills are inextricably tied to social categories such as race, class, and gender." An aspect of skills about which there is little said is that they are enacted in social settings. Unlike technical skills, professional or soft skills are context-dependent and judgments about them are highly subjective. In her own neighborhood, a young person might organize a sports team of eager peers, thus demonstrating her capacity to collaborate and lead. But in a new professional setting, the same young person may be shy or disoriented; she may encounter coworkers who hold preconceived racialized or gender assumptions that she will not have what Arlie Hochschild calls "a certain type of middle class sociability."[10] Thus, she may be perceived as someone who doesn't play well on a team.

No one should be expected to learn these skills as they are too often taught—in a one-shot workshop. As Eddinger and Kazis argue in chapter 2, the best way for students to learn these skills is by participating in internships, studying the jobs students already hold, and reading and discussing the literature about work. Two important factors for students to understand are that, first, appropriate skills for a particular workplace are generally defined by those who hold power in that business, occupation, or sector; and, second, decisions about who has or lacks the "right" skills are highly subjective. Discrimination based on race and gender is illegal, but as Mary Gatta and I argue, it is easy for employers to justify hiring decisions based on whether a candidate fits the preexisting culture. One apt cartoon depicts an HR manager saying, "We need to focus on diversity. I want you to hire more people who look different but think just like me." While job seekers would likely not question judgments made by potential employers, students should be armed with the analytic tools to understand how they might be judged as they apply for or take on a new job. And they should know that one can keep one's authentic self while learning to "perform" as needed in a workplace.

CONCLUSION

If there is one takeaway from this book that the authors wish readers will act on, it is that greater attention to career preparation and knowledge about work in our colleges is critical if students are to have a chance at upward economic mobility. In sum, low-income students face barriers and disadvantages entering the work world and moving up the career ladder. Students must recognize these barriers as they arise and be armed with strategies that minimize the structures of inequality that hold them back. While the US may never have been a meritocracy, today's unprecedented levels of wealth inequality enable the affluent to invest greater and greater sums in their children, ensuring they receive educations that provide entrée to professional communities, while those of the middle class and below, who love their children no less, are scrambling to pay for school supplies, clothing, and day care.

Demographer Fabian Pfeffer points out that growing wealth gaps in education "can have multiplicative effects," making the poor poorer.[11] He notes that the "rising costs of college attendance lead to greater costs of failure." That is, if a student leaves college without a degree and with debt, the results are more consequential than in the past because his debt will be greater, his job options fewer, and his pay lower in today's economy. The structure of work appears to be rapidly shifting toward workers becoming entrepreneurs who construct a living from varied and changing work roles. If that is the case, we may be looking to a future where whom you know, how you behave, and where you come from are even more significant gatekeepers to good jobs than they are today.

The ideas and resources in this book could make up a community college course about work, inform advising sessions, or serve as the theme of a learning community or other group learning setting. At best, the authors hope that this book can be a resource leading to action.

Beyond College Completion

WHY WORK BELONGS IN THE CURRICULUM

CHAPTER 1

Putting Work at the Center of Community College Completion Reform

The College Mobility Narrative in the United States

– MICHAEL LAWRENCE COLLINS –

Over the last two decades, I have had the privilege of being a part of the community college completion reform community. While progress has been made and lessons learned, there is still a considerable way to go to increase college completion and close gaps in attainment and earnings by race, ethnicity, and income. In this chapter, I argue that we can improve outcomes by illuminating and taking action on a more comprehensive set of factors that influence completion and earnings than are typically included in the college mobility narrative. A powerful way to begin to fill in gaps in the college completion narrative is to situate work more centrally in college completion reform efforts.

Positioning work at the center of community college reform holds promise for helping low-income students and students of color make the most of the investments in time and financial resources that they make to earn a college degree. Paying more attention to what needs to happen for students to successfully transition from college to work requires that the higher education community make a shift. The vast majority of college completion reform efforts have been focused on the supply side—improving outcomes at the college. We argue in this volume that it is now time to focus more attention and action to the demand side—improving employment and earnings outcomes. We believe that this can be accomplished by putting work at the center of learning.

There are no doubt many problems to solve and challenges to tackle, but the college completion and earnings outcomes data are clear: we need to update the college mobility narrative. A college degree is not a sure bet to land a job that leads to careers and upward mobility. It is a high-stakes investment with potential for high yield, but it is not without risks. The community college completion reform agenda can help students of color and students from low- to moderate-income families optimize their investments in higher education by increasing transparency on the factors associated with the probability of degree completion and high earnings. We can support this effort by actively helping students mitigate risks associated with their demographic profile, and by situating work more centrally in the college experience.

THE MOBILITY NARRATIVE

The national narrative of college as a strategy for upward economic mobility is deeply embedded in the cultural fabric of the United States. Much like mobility narratives of Horatio Alger, the nineteenth-century novelist whose protagonist rose from rags to riches by virtue of hard work and honesty, many Americans believe that a college degree is the key to the American Dream. Our association of college with upward economic mobility is influenced by the esteem in which our nation's elite institutions are held and by early investments the country made in higher education, such as the GI Bill of 1944, which expanded higher education to millions of Americans who previously had not had access. The establishment of the nation's great colleges and universities has attracted students from across the globe, and the historical investments that we have made in higher education have contributed to upward economic mobility for millions, driving the dramatic growth of America's middle class.

By the early 2000s, however, this college mobility narrative began to unravel. Despite our extraordinary investments and world-class colleges and universities, troubling developments began to emerge. Newly available data showed that postsecondary completion rates were shockingly low, especially for community college students, who were more likely to be low-income, students of color, older, and attending school part-time. The low success rates drove investment in community college reform and contributed to the development of a cadre of organizations leading community college completion reform efforts. These organizations focused on improving student completion rates. Yet, after more than a decade of reform, completion rates remain low, and there are gaps in completion rates when disaggregated by race, ethnicity, and income. But our belief in the college mobility narrative endures.

Our nation's continued faith in college as a strategy for upward economic mobility and the community college completion reform agenda are influenced by our memory of the great economic success of the GI Bill; earnings data on degree completion reflecting that, on average, a college degree will pay more than a high school diploma; and lofty rhetoric about the individual and societal benefits of higher education. But a closer examination of these elements reveals that the college mobility narrative is more complicated than we have imagined. While the GI Bill expanded higher education and grew the middle class, it did not benefit all Americans equally. Although a college degree generally pays more than a high school diploma, there is huge variation in earnings from one degree to another. And despite the rhetoric of the benefits of higher education, not all Americans experience those benefits equally. Earnings data show that factors such as socioeconomic status, race, ethnicity, gender, institutional selectivity, type of degree, and social capital influence who benefits from college completion.

To be clear, there are elements of truth in the college mobility narrative. There is strong evidence that college completion can contribute to upward economic mobility. For example, people who earn a bachelor's degree make $2.8 million in lifetime earnings, which is 74 percent more than what those with a high school diploma earn.[1] And earnings outcomes for graduates of our nation's most selective colleges can be stratospheric. There *are* small percentages of low-income students at Ivy League colleges who graduate and earn salaries not just in the top quintile, but in the top 1% of earners.[2] Examples like these understandably fuel the mobility narrative. However, important factors have been left out. The often-cited wage premium for a college degree usually reflects average earnings for a bachelor's degree, not every degree. And only 4 percent of students in the lowest income quintile attend our nation's most selective colleges.

When factors such as type of degree, institutional selectivity, and others are taken into account, the narrative requires an update to reflect what the data say about the relationship between college, earnings, and economic mobility.

In addition to describing the way a range of demographic and income-related factors influence college completion and earnings, this chapter explores the issue of the role of work in college completion, earnings, and economic mobility and argues that we can increase completion and earnings for low-income students and students of color by acknowledging that, rather than a guarantee of a certain future, college is a high-stakes investment. These students in particular will need to take careful steps to optimize their chances for completion, access to good jobs that lead to careers, and upward economic mobility.

Policy Underpinnings of the College Mobility Narrative in the United States

In the United States, our national aims for higher education have long included a focus on access to good jobs, upward mobility, and economic growth. We see this demonstrated in our public policies and rhetoric framing higher education as an engine for individual economic opportunity and advancement and collective economic growth and competitiveness. Early examples of the stock we have placed in higher education for gainful employment and economic mobility include the Serviceman's Readjustment Act of 1944 (GI Bill), the Presidents Commission on Higher Education 1947 (Truman Commission), and the Higher Education Act of 1965 (HEA). These foundational postsecondary policies contribute to the college mobility narrative in United States—that a college degree is the primary vehicle to access jobs that lead to careers and is a sure bet to upward mobility.

The GI Bill is perhaps the most dramatic example of the college mobility narrative. It reflected our belief as a nation that a college degree was a powerful ticket to the middle class. The legislation marked an inflection point in our national history: the United States Congress agreed it was a compelling national interest to educate a broader swath of the population beyond the wealthiest and most privileged in the country. The GI Bill provided not only financial aid for veterans to attend college, but also financial support for them to purchase homes and start businesses. The legislation was considered an economic success, helping millions of veterans earn college degrees that provided access to good jobs and careers that allowed millions of Americans to enter the middle class and achieve the American Dream.

The Truman Commission, though not legislation, was a dramatic public declaration of a vision to make higher education accessible to more Americans, including women, people of color, people from different cultural and religious backgrounds, and people from low-income backgrounds who did not have the financial resources to go to college. Importantly, the Truman Commission posited that close to half of the population could benefit from a two-year degree and recommended that the nation increase the number of community colleges to accommodate the increased enrollment.[3] The Commission argued that increasing the number of community colleges would enable a broader swath of the population to earn associate's degrees, which in turn would facilitate entry into vocations that added value to local communities. The Truman Commission framed the reform of the nation's postsecondary system to accommodate a more diverse population as an investment in the nation and recommended that the federal government provide funding to implement it.[4]

While not all of the Commission's recommendations were implemented, it was an important vision for what our nation's higher education system should do, and its influence is reflected in the postsecondary enterprise today. It is one thing to expand community college; it is another for people to have the resources to attend. While the Truman Commission's recommendation for federal funding did not happen initially, the Commission's vision for funding is largely reflected in Title IV of Higher Education Act of 1965.[5]

HEA is another example of anchor legislation that reflects our national interest in broad access to college as a strategy that provides access to skills, credentials, and upward economic mobility. It is the foundation of postsecondary policy in the United States. HEA was designed to strengthen the educational resources of colleges and universities in the United States and to provide financial aid for college students. The legislation provided federal funding in the form of grants and loans that were designed to eliminate finances as a barrier to attending college. As a result of the legislation, low-income students were eligible for subsidized loans as well as grants, today known as Pell Grants, which did not need to be repaid. At the act's peak in 1975–1976, the maximum Pell Grant covered more than three-quarters of the cost of attending the average four-year college, a significant investment from the federal government in higher education.[6] Apropos of the Truman Commission's recommendations, the funding provided by HEA reduced cost as a barrier to attending college and made college financially feasible for many for whom college was otherwise unaffordable.

The legislation and funding in support of higher education affirms the importance that the United States has placed on college as a strategy for individual upward economic mobility and national economic competitiveness. They contributed to a dramatic increase in enrollment in higher education and the growth of a solid middle class, and resulted in the United States leading the world in postsecondary attainment for several decades after World War II. These policy and funding developments have fueled the college mobility narrative in the United States and continue to contribute to many Americans' thinking that college is a guarantee to upward mobility.

CRACKS IN THE FOUNDATION OF THE COLLEGE MOBILITY NARRATIVE

The assumption that college functions as an accelerator to upward economic mobility was largely grounded in higher education's reputation. When Americans thought about college, they often pictured our nation's most elite campuses with red brick, ivy-covered buildings nestled in bucolic landscapes. The almost 100 percent graduation rates and the high earnings of elite college graduates perpetuated the association between a college degree and economic success—an association that persists today. Tom Bailey, Shanna Jaggars, and Davis Jenkins describe this generalization of outcomes from highly selective colleges to all colleges in their book, *Redesigning America's Community Colleges*, writing, "the entire postsecondary sector was bathed in their positive aura, and the quality or effectiveness of higher education more generally was rarely questioned."[7] As late as the early 2000s, there were little to no outcomes data to challenge these assumptions. The college mobility narrative was firmly ingrained into the nation's consciousness and, lacking evidence, few challenged it.

But by the early 2000s, when graduation rates were publicly available as a result of federal legislation, a new, less glowing picture of higher education began to emerge.[8] Fewer than 30 percent of twenty-five to twenty-nine-year-olds held a bachelor's degree, a figure that has moved only slightly in 2019.[9] In many community colleges, fewer than 20 percent of students earned an associate's degree within three years.[10] Outcomes for low-income students and students of color, the very populations community colleges were intended to help, were even lower. The dismal results did not dampen the allure of college as a sure bet to economic mobility, however. Instead of questioning the assumptions of the college mobility narrative, the poor outcomes spurred the college completion agenda to double down on college as the solution, particularly for students in community college.

Community Colleges as Engines for Employment and Economic Mobility

The low community college completion rates prompted investment in community college completion reform. Just prior to the Great Recession, in 2004, Lumina Foundation launched Achieving the Dream: Community Colleges Count, an initiative that was explicitly created to improve outcomes for students enrolled in community colleges. The initiative brought multiple organizations associated with college completion reform together to provide technical assistance supports to community colleges. The focus of the initiative was on helping community college students complete developmental education, gateway courses, and credentials and degrees. For policy makers, the college reform community, and community college leaders, the laser focus on completion was considered a marked shift from previous postsecondary reforms that focused on access to college.

At the federal level, in 2009 during the Great Recession, the Obama administration announced the American Graduation Initiative, which set a goal to add five million more community college graduates by 2020.[11] Announcing the initiative at Macomb Community College in Warren, Michigan, President Obama cited the importance of postsecondary credentials to global economic competitiveness and training for the jobs of the twenty-first century. Pledging $12 billion to the initiative, he stressed the importance of the unique role that community colleges play in increasing credential and degree attainment and argued that there was a direct connection between increased postsecondary attainment and American prosperity. In a political compromise, the funding was reduced to $2 billion, but support for community colleges and increased postsecondary attainment remained a top priority for the administration.[12]

The Community College Completion Agenda

Other education-related philanthropies, including the Bill & Melinda Gates Foundation, the Kresge Foundation, and other local and regional funders, joined Lumina Foundation in support of increasing degree attainment for community college students. They provided funding for a series of reform initiatives that focused on different aspects of increasing completion success in community colleges. For example, in 2009, the Gates Foundation launched the Developmental Education Initiative, which identified weak academic preparation as a major stumbling block to graduation for community college students.[13] The initiative focused on redesigning developmental education with the purpose of increasing students' preparation for success in college. In 2011 a subsequent Gates Foundation–funded initiative, Completion by Design, expanded the focus from developmental education to a comprehensive community college completion strategy. It featured a framework that supported community colleges to redesign each step of the credential pathway—connection, entry, progress, and completion—with a focus on increasing completion outcomes.[14]

In 2010, the Kresge Foundation began funding a new initiative that would become known as a Student Success Center, a statewide entity that coordinates the multiple community college completion efforts within a state.[15] By 2014 seven Student Success Centers had been established, and today, in 2019, with the support of the Bill & Melinda Gates Foundation, there are sixteen Student Success Centers collaborating in a network to support all of the community colleges in their respective states to improve success outcomes, including credential attainment, transfer to four-year institutions, and employment.

The most recent community college reform initiative, guided pathways, builds on and expands lessons from Achieving the Dream, the Developmental Education Initiative, Completion by Design, and the Student Success Center Network. In guided pathways, community college students are guided to choose among a carefully selected set of default credential pathways that lead to either an associate's degree with immediate value in the labor market or a degree aligned with transfer requirements that allow students to earn a bachelor's degree without losing credits.[16] Guided pathways draw on a core element from behavioral economics, *choice architecture* or *structured choice*. Instead of having to choose from thousands of courses, community college students are presented with a select number of default credential pathways that allow them to see their entire degree path to their chosen destination, be it an associate's degree or transfer to a four-year institution.

The community college completion reform work over the last decade is deeply influenced by the college mobility narrative, which is generally aligned with economists' projections that, by 2020, two-thirds of all jobs will require some form of postsecondary education. The primary goal of reform is to increase credential completion and to close attainment gaps by race and ethnicity, so that low-income students and students of color will secure jobs, earn a premium in wages, and climb the income ladder. Community college completion reform is steeped in an almost universal positive association between a college degree, employment, and upward economic mobility. Insufficient attention to sociodemographic factors that can have a major impact on completion, however, contributes to the mistaken belief that a college degree ensures mobility for low-income students and students of color.

Omissions from the College Mobility Narrative

College can contribute to upward economic mobility and the realization of the American Dream, but there are multiple factors—including socioeconomic status, race and ethnicity, and gender—that can impact whether or not completing a degree will pay off in the labor market. These are not yet given sufficient attention in the narrative that associates college completion and upward mobility. The omission of these critical factors leads many people to believe that if they go to college, they will be able to get a good job and climb the income ladder. This has contributed to counterexamples in the media—of college graduates who are unemployed or underemployed and have oppressive student loan debt—undermining the success narrative. But it has also stoked "exceptionalism"—the myriad stories of the impoverished person who beat the odds. Fine-grained evidence tells a more complicated story.

The college mobility narrative typically omits a number of factors. First, college degrees do not pay off equally for all degree earners—the socioeconomic status of the student makes a difference.[17] The payoff is greater for people from higher-income backgrounds. In addition to being more likely to have educated parents and high-quality schooling, students from higher-income families are more likely to have social capital upon which to draw to secure opportunities that lead to employment opportunities. Low-income students need access to resources and networks—for example, financial support and introductions to people in positions of power and authority who can open doors, provide paid internships, make job recommendations, and offer employment. In short, these students need the kind of social capital that affluent job seekers use to enter the labor market.

Second, while in the traditional college mobility narrative, a degree is a degree, in truth there is huge variation in earnings depending on college major. According to research findings from the Georgetown University Center on Education and the Workforce, there is a $3.4 million difference in earnings between the highest-paying degree (petroleum engineering) and the lowest (early childhood education).[18] Generally, STEM-related majors earn more than liberal arts and social science majors. Business and health-related majors earn more than the average college graduate, while social science, liberal arts, and teaching and serving majors earn less than the average college graduate. Students of color are underrepresented in high-wage occupations like STEM, health, and business.[19] Instead, they are highly concentrated in the helping professions, like social work and community-serving majors. Overrepresentation in majors that pay less well may be a result of student preferences, but also may reflect a lack of awareness of the wide variety of types of work and available earnings.

Third, race and ethnicity affect college choice. Students of color are more likely to attend open-access four-year institutions and community colleges, which have fewer resources and lower success rates in comparison to the more selective four-year institutions where high-income white students are concentrated.[20] So the very students who have the least experience with college-going culture and weakest preparation attend campuses that are less able to provide them with the supports they need, especially with internships, work-based learning opportunities, and other experiences that would prepare them for employment in in-demand and high-wage occupations. In addition, low college persistence rates at open-access colleges impact momentum toward graduation—if fewer than one-third of students complete, then dropping out can become the norm.

MODERNIZING THE COLLEGE MOBILITY NARRATIVE

It is easy to understand the pervasive belief in college as the ticket to economic opportunity and upward mobility in the United States. Our historical policy support, such as the GI Bill and the Higher Education Act, and our public commitment as reflected in the recommendations of the Truman Commission are seemingly proof of our enduring faith in college as a primary strategy to upward economic mobility. However, a cursory review of some of the foundational elements of the college mobility narrative reveals considerable gaps.

The economic success of the GI Bill, for example, did not benefit all Americans. Its primary beneficiaries were white men. African Americans were not able to leverage the college benefits or the low-cost mortgage supports that were a part of the legislation.[21] For example, of the first sixty-seven thousand mortgages secured by the GI Bill for returning veterans, fewer than one hundred were taken out by people of color.[22] Ninety-five percent of black veterans had no choice in their higher education but to attend segregated, all black institutions, which could not keep pace with student demand and were severely underresourced.[23] The Truman Commission's vision for greater access to a community college education assumed that people from economically, racially, and ethnically marginalized backgrounds would successfully complete two-year degrees without any institutional changes or supports aside from access. Community colleges expanded, following the Commission's recommendations. Enrollment increased, but completion rates remained low, especially for low-income students and students of color. Finally, the buying power of the Pell Grant has fallen to less than 30 percent of the cost of college today from nearly three-quarters of college cost in the mid-1970s.[24] If public funding once subsidized the majority of college costs, that is not the case today. These additional details dull some of the luster of the college mobility narrative.

For college to pay off, low-income students and students of color need to make smart investments with their limited resources. Because of the diminished purchasing power of Pell, the trend of divestment in public support for higher education at the state level, and the rising cost of college, students who enroll in postsecondary education will pay more of their own money for college than in the past, when the public shared more of the burden. Tuition and fees at public colleges have risen nineteen times faster than average family income over the last three decades.[25] The shift of the cost of college from taxpayer dollars that benefit society to students and their families creates the rhetoric that college is solely a personal investment, when in actuality it is a contribution to civil society as well. The reality is that the reduced public subsidy means that low-income students must pay for higher education with a greater share of their personal income. If students end up in low-wage jobs because they lack the networks, knowledge of the labor market, and appropriate skills, then both the student and society lose.

Optimizing Students' Investments in College by Connecting to Work

Community college students go to college to find good jobs that lead to careers. Colleges should acknowledge this goal, be transparent about the hurdles students are likely to face, and provide a critique of the college mobility narrative. Community college students do understand that some education beyond high school is required to make it in today's economy. The fact that over 80 percent of community college students say that they want to earn a bachelor's degree or higher suggests that they are not merely interested in getting a job.[26] They are interested in the premium in wages that is available to bachelor's degree holders and people with advanced degrees. In short, they are interested in doing well economically.

Surprisingly, for all of community college students' interest in good jobs, there is little to no consideration of work in the college experience. Most of the college experience is focused on navigating the institution and mastering the curricular content that is specific to the subject area in which a student is majoring. Ironically, while professors often refer to "the real world," or life after graduation, they rarely address the real world in their classrooms. As noted in chapter 3, if there is a focus on work and careers at all, it is usually at the end of the students' college experience or after a student has graduated.

The lack of transparency hurts student outcomes. For example, African American college graduates are more likely to be unemployed or underemployed relative to white college graduates.[27] In 2013, for example, African Americans who recently graduated from college were twice as likely to be unemployed in comparison to all college graduates.[28] Moreover, that same year, more than half of African American recent college graduates were employed in jobs that did not require a four-year degree.[29]

Optimizing students' investments in college also requires transparency about the barriers students will face in making a successful transition from college to the workplace. Multiple studies, using experimental research designs showing causality, have consistently found strong evidence of racial discrimination in hiring decisions.[30] In one frequently cited study, researchers found that résumés with names typically associated with whites generated a callback rate for interviews that was 50 percent higher than for names more likely to be associated with African Americans, even if the skills and credentials were the same.[31] But the college mobility narrative is largely silent on structural discrimination in the labor market.

CONCLUSION

Advocating for college completion as a strategy for increased earnings and upward mobility without acknowledging that socioeconomic status, race and ethnicity, and gender factor into people's chances for degree completion and entry into high-wage careers is to perpetuate an incomplete mobility narrative. To make college a viable approach to increased earnings and upward mobility for low-income students and students of color, we need to update the college mobility narrative and fill in the missing pieces. The observations in this chapter are *not* intended to serve as evidence that college is not valuable or worth the investment, or that the barriers are intractable. On the contrary, college is a good investment that can lead to upward mobility. But for low-income students and students of color in our nation's community colleges, who have enrolled in higher education to increase their chances of getting a good job and climbing the income ladder, college is just not a sure bet—it is a high-stakes investment.

Reimagining Experiential Learning and Internships for Community College Students

— PAM EDDINGER AND RICHARD KAZIS —

Internships and similar forms of experiential learning have long been the gold standard for college students wishing to explore the world of work. Deep learning occurs on multiple levels, from content knowledge specific to the work site, foundational skills, and interpersonal competencies to organizational dynamics and management. The successful intern emerges with a renewed commitment to her chosen field and a plan for advancement, or the realization that she is more suited to a different career. In the best of scenarios, she comes away with a job offer, or a new network of professional contacts to call on for career advice and direction.

Given that community colleges will educate a substantial portion of our future workforce, internships are becoming increasingly attractive, if not mandatory, in the two-year environment. These opportunities are particularly valuable for students who want to move into professional positions but lack the necessary social networks and connections. This is a fair description of many of the low-income students, first-generation college-goers, and students of color who look to community colleges for a viable path to career employment and economic mobility.[1]

Unfortunately, there is a huge gap between the value of internship experiences for community college students and the availability of those opportunities. Yes, nursing and allied health programs require clinical hours, and, across the country, some community colleges are partnering with employers to mount apprenticeships in career areas outside of the trades, but such programs touch very few students. In the state where we've done most of our work, Massachusetts, community college students are significantly underrepresented in publicly funded internship programs in high-demand sectors compared to students in four-year colleges and universities. Sought-after internship programs in the life sciences, biotech, and clean energy tend to go to four-year students in STEM programs (at a ratio of four-year to two-year college students that is close to 9:1). A $1 million annual state appropriation to support college internships is available only to four-year public universities, not to community colleges. This is to the detriment of community college students and to the state's economy. With their technical expertise and certifications, community college graduates are well prepared to fill the many middle-skill jobs open in our state. Internships can help more employers learn that community college graduates are generally quite mature, have work experience, and are highly motivated to succeed. There is some evidence that employers are beginning to abandon their use of the bachelor's degree as a screen for job openings that do not require a four-year degree. Expansion of internship placements could accelerate this positive trend.

Limited access to internships and work-based experiences for community college students is not unique to Massachusetts. A national research scan, conducted by coauthor Richard Kazis and a colleague for the Boston Foundation to assess the extent of state-level support for large-scale community college internship programs, found only a handful of promising programs in place around the country, despite significant interest among educators, employers, and state officials. Coauthor Pam Eddinger's experience as president of Bunker Hill Community College (BHCC) in Boston underscores the range of challenges to institutionalizing and scaling internship programs in the community college sector—as well as lessons to date from her college's implementation of several high-quality internship programs.

THE NATIONAL LANDSCAPE

In 2018, the Boston Foundation commissioned coauthor Kazis and his colleague Nancy Snyder to look for statewide and national exemplars of large-scale paid internship programs that place community college students in a range of work settings aligned with their program of study. In their report,

Uncovering Hidden Talent, Kazis and Snyder found significant interest in such efforts from college leaders, career services personnel, and faculty, as well as from employers concerned about growing their sources of qualified new hires. However, when they scanned the nation, they concluded that the typical internship program available to community college students is small, often involving one employer or a few employers in a single industry sector. They found few large-scale programs operating at a statewide or regional level across multiple institutions, employers, and sectors. Significant staff and resource capacity to manage and build out internship programs and to sustain them over time is rare. And the research revealed few instances where community colleges or state community college systems had taken systematic steps to define the capacity needed to engage multiple and diverse employers, serve their needs efficiently, match students across multiple disciplines with internship opportunities in their field, promote equitable access for those most in need of social connections, and ensure that learning is taking place at the work site.[2]

In their national scan of internship efforts, Kazis and Snyder identified six large-scale internship programs in various stages of development and implementation. Three of these—organized by Ohio's Department of Higher Education, the philanthropic Great Lakes Higher Education Corporation (now called Ascendium Education Group), and the Indiana Chamber of Commerce—served both two- and four-year students. A fourth, created by the Iowa legislature in 2007, is open to community college students as well as students at four-year colleges and universities, but only about 5 percent of participants have been from a community college.

In 2012, Ohio's then-Governor John Kasich invested $11.45 million of one-time lottery funds to support the development of six regional consortia across the state, which included both community colleges and four-year institutions and their employer partners. Internships require a 1:1 private sector match to encourage business investment. Through 2017, the project had served 5,700 students, engaged 1,000 businesses, and generated more than $22 million in wages for student interns. The Ohio Department of Higher Education allowed flexible use of the funds—for wage subsidies, student and faculty preparation, as well as housing and transportation that would make it possible for students to participate.

Between 2014 and 2018, Ascendium, the philanthropic arm of the Great Lakes Higher Education Corporation, a student loan guarantor, invested $17.9 million in a program to explore how four-year colleges should design and implement large-scale internship programs for college students in midwestern states. The intent of the funding was to explore issues of access, scale, and quality and to provide guidance for states and other entities interested in building out internships that meet both employer and student needs. The programs funded sixty-two four-year colleges in Iowa, Minnesota, Ohio, and Wisconsin to develop their own local initiatives. In 2017, based on the enthusiasm and lessons from the initial investment, the foundation created a smaller fund ($2.1 million) to support one thousand paid internships at sixteen community colleges in six midwestern states. This project surfaced many of the same design and operational issues that have been evident in the programs developed by Pam Eddinger and her staff at BHCC (as discussed shortly): student wages had to compete with what students were already earning in their "regular" jobs, transportation costs were prohibitive for some unless supplemented, and poorly resourced career advising systems made it difficult to recruit and prepare students for success at work. Ascendium hopes that the lessons learned about both design and implementation will encourage better planning by internship initiatives and incentives for colleges to create scalable programs that meet the needs of the local economy and enrolled students.

Finally, Indiana INTERNnet, an employer-student internship matching platform, is open to applications from all higher education students whether enrolled in a two- or four-year school. The project was launched by the Indianapolis Chamber of Commerce and was expanded statewide by the state chamber of commerce. Funded primarily by the Lilly Endowment with some additional state support, INTERNnet is now a separate nonprofit organization that conducts outreach to employers and students, updates the information about available internships (for students) and interested students (for employers), and provides state-funded wage subsidies for low-income students. Such matching platforms exist in a variety of formats, and none has solved the problems that Indiana is encountering: students may register, but it is hard to track whether they actually obtain and complete an internship. In addition, the platform alone does not get the job done; the INTERNnet requires substantial staff interaction to update the postings; keep colleges, employers, and the state's workforce personnel engaged; monitor activity and problem-solve; and raise funds.

CHALLENGES AND OPPORTUNITIES

From the community college vantage point, it is no surprise that few states support community college internships and that most efforts are very local, somewhat idiosyncratic, and difficult to scale. Inequities in finance and access that favor students in four-year schools is a significant factor, but so too are other obstacles facing two-year institutions and their students.

First and foremost, there are the realities of students' complicated lives: the majority already work and need to work, so an internship has to be more attractive than existing employment for many students to sign on. Employer bias plays a role, too. Although employers who take on community college interns are typically happily surprised by the quality and value they get for their investment, many employers have no experience with community colleges and their students. They may have uninformed views of community college quality and academic rigor. Many are worried about a college's ability to manage the internship program effectively and minimize logistical burdens for participating employers. Employers are frequently right to be cautious. Staff capacity at many colleges is inadequate for the labor-intensive work of managing employer relationships, preparing students for success on the job, and working with discipline-based faculty to identify interns appropriate for specific employers.

Given the hunger among businesses for prepared employees in a tight labor market, it may be a propitious time to take on the challenges documented in the Boston Foundation report and identified by coauthor Eddinger based on her own college's experience, detailed in the following section. There is significant room for growth in the availability of internships for community college students, in Massachusetts and nationally. This is particularly true in today's hot economy, with employers eager to tap new sources of qualified workers and ready to experiment with varied talent pipeline strategies. Now is a good time to engage state officials, employers, and college leaders to support new initiatives that are realistic about what a quality internship initiative demands of a college and its partners yet are built from the outset to operate effectively at larger scale, to be integrated into the routine functioning of community colleges, and to open wider the doors to opportunity for under-represented groups in the community.

Resources will be needed to strengthen the capacity of colleges and their partners to meet these goals. However, money alone is not the answer. To achieve desired outcomes for community college students, some of the assumptions upon which traditional internships are based will need to be modified, so that programs acknowledge and address the very real challenges that face students, employers, and colleges as they bring the worlds of college and work closer together to the benefit of the local economy and community.

BUNKER HILL COMMUNITY COLLEGE: LEARN AND EARN

Vibrant Urban Institution; Highly Diverse Student Profile

According to the American Association of Community Colleges (AACC), the 1,132 community colleges across the nation enroll just over 13 million students, almost half of all undergraduates in the United States. Bunker Hill Community College is a typical midsize urban community college. It is the largest of the fifteen community colleges in Massachusetts, educating some eighteen thousand students annually. Located in historic Charlestown, the college serves Boston and a half-dozen adjacent cities. Almost all students live within eight miles of the college and commute via local transit, getting on and off at the prominent Community College metro station. The majority of students remain in the local area after graduation and are an important part of the economic and workforce base of the city and region.

BHCC's student population is racially and ethnically diverse: a quarter white, a quarter black, a quarter Latinx, 15 percent Asian/Pacific Islander, and 10 percent having multiple identifications. (The college also hosts eight hundred international students, speaking seventy-five languages, from over one hundred countries.)

The vibrancy of cultures on campus, now enhanced by BHCC's new Center on Equity and Cultural Wealth and by the culturally inclusive learning environments, belies the economic challenges facing students of this urban institution. Seventy-seven percent of BHCC students fall into the lowest two income quintiles. Of the eighteen thousand students served annually, approximately eight thousand qualify for Pell Grants, and one thousand receive SNAP (Supplemental Nutrition Assistance Program) subsidies.

The academic attainment profile of entering students is quite varied. Over 90 percent of entering students test below college level in mathematics, and 45 percent test below level in English. Over half speak English as a second or third language; many are first in their family to attend college. While there are huge challenges in developing this talent pool—challenges that are ubiquitous at community colleges—there is also the potential to prepare a culturally competent, multilingual, highly skilled, and socially mobile workforce from among these students. At Bunker Hill, this means an institutional commitment to replace the outdated notion that students must be "college ready" with the view that the college must be "student ready" and meet learners where they are.

A particularly challenging aspect of BHCC's student body is its age profile. Unlike the popular image of the undergraduate coming right out of high school, engaging in full-time studies, supported by parents with resources and a family history of professional work, a growing number of community college students are working adults who live complex lives juggling school, work, and family responsibilities. At BHCC, which trends slightly older in demographics than the average community college described by the AACC, two-thirds of the students are adults: the average age is twenty-seven.[3] Two-thirds work, many full-time. Fifty percent are parents, and 60 percent of the parents are single mothers with primary responsibility for child-rearing and economic support. Work and family are at the center of most students' lives. They are serious about higher education, because they know the path to social and economic mobility is through a college degree. But their hold on education is fragile and tenuous. When small disasters strike, as they too often do, many students make the difficult choice of stopping out of their educational program in order to continue working and supporting their family.

That so many BHCC students already work and the majority are older are facts that must be taken into account by higher education institutional leaders and policy makers who want to expand the availability of internships for this population. Students are eager for connections and a chance to demonstrate their skills and motivation to employers in their field, but they are also constrained by their existing responsibilities. For most BHCC students, an internship would have to be paid; it would have to offer enough value, in earnings and exposure, for students to alter their existing patterns of making ends meet and juggling time commitments. Because they tend to have had some work experience, though often not in their field of study, a low-skill, low-learning internship is not likely to be sufficiently attractive for the sacrifices required.

Bunker Hill Community College has taken steps to create paid internship opportunities that respond to the realities of students' lives and financial situations. Launched in 2012, the Learn and Earn program serves about one hundred students each semester. Students work sixteen to forty hours a week over a period of five to seven months. They earn $15 an hour working for one of eighteen companies in the Boston area. These companies also provide a transportation stipend for interns to get to work and mentors for each. Learn and Earn interns earn three elective credits. To date, 525 students have been placed, and over 40 percent of interns have either had their placement extended or been hired by their internship provider. Many have gone on to transfer to four-year schools.

The Learn and Earn model points toward an approach that can overcome many of the obstacles that discourage working adults from even considering an internship. It reflects an important paradigm shift away from the prevailing internship, which is designed primarily for younger students at four-year colleges who are near the end of their studies and can often afford an unpaid work experience (packaged in a way that provides them college credit) as an investment in securing post-graduation employment.

The design of Learn and Earn has meant that a student like BHCC's Cilia Moran Cruz has been able to participate and to benefit. Cilia moved to the US from Ecuador and struggled for several years to support her family while doing her best to learn English. Encouraged by friends and family to complete the business degree she began in Ecuador, she enrolled in an accounting program at BHCC and juggled a heavy course load, a series of part-time jobs, and family responsibilities, making the Dean's List three different semesters. When the opportunity presented itself in 2016, Cilia applied to the Learn and Earn internship program. She was offered an internship in real estate finance at Liberty Mutual Insurance Company. Cilia was retained for two internship cycles and was then offered a full-time position at Liberty Mutual as a Lease

Administrator. Today, she is on track to complete her Bachelor of Science in the honor's program at Suffolk University in accounting and big data and business analytics.

The creation and evolution of Learn and Earn has provided Bunker Hill leaders with additional lessons about what it will take to design a high-quality internship program and range of work-based and work-related experiences for large numbers of students. These include lessons about:

- the kind and level of skills that students want and need;
- the critical importance of competitive wages and a focus on reducing barriers to equitable access to opportunity;
- the need to expand and diversify outreach to employers and to new industries; and
- the need for creative strategies to increase the social capital and understanding of work and career dynamics for students who may never be in a position to secure a formal internship.

As we note in the next sections, some of these design and strategic questions can be addressed by colleges and their partners. In the end, though, public policy makers with control of resources and incentives will need to become full partners in efforts to make internships and work-based leaning more broadly available to community college students.

Beyond Job Readiness Mechanics to Advanced Career-Related Skills

For adult students, internships cannot simply offer experiential learning related to the mechanics of attendance, workplace protocols, and professional behavior. Adults in community college programs have likely acquired these basic work literacies in their prior or current workplaces. These experienced workers benefit most if they can gain experience that is tightly focused on skills in their field of study and advances the potential for job placement. Equally important for this population—if not more important in the long run—is learning to reflect critically on organizational structure and dynamics at the workplace and developing a clear understanding of the next-level competencies required to chart their path for advancement. These advanced skills and capabilities will elevate them and set them apart, in contrast to placement in a low-skill job unrelated either to their field of study or to employers who hire graduates in that field.

Adult students are often attractive to employers and internship partners because their life experiences have added to their resiliency and maturity. They certainly have taken great risks in entering college: they are putting not only their own future on the line, but that of their family and their children as well. Their commitment is frequently visible in the seriousness with which they undertake their endeavors and responsibilities at work, in school, and at home.

Jennifer Sheehan, a liberal arts major in her forties, would have been an unlikely candidate for a traditional unpaid internship. Jennifer was a single mother of a twenty-year-old daughter and seven-year-old twin boys, living in public housing and working in the office of a printing company when she decided to return to school. She was dissatisfied; she wanted to do something more for herself and "to set an example" for her children. She secured a Learn and Earn internship at Fidelity Investments where she earned $15 an hour and a transportation stipend. She was given significant responsibilities that recognized her fundamental level of work and life experience. "They were willing for me to take on responsibilities and trust me with them," she said. For her final internship project, she was charged with helping to coordinate Fidelity Cares Day, an employee volunteer event for more than seven hundred associates.

Economic Barriers to Equitable Participation in Internships

As the profiles here suggest, when internships are paid and lead to careers they can be affirming and even life-changing, but given the economic fragility of community college students, unpaid internships are not a realistic learning option for many. No student will give up a paying job that supports the family to take on a temporary and short-term internship, no matter how attractive or aligned it is with long-term goals. This presents an equity issue: How can community college students, particularly those who already work, have access to workplace experiences that can connect them to better career options, increase their social capital, and deepen their readiness to perform at a high level in the workplace?

When Bunker Hill Community College was asked by one of its early business partners, the Massachusetts Competitive Partnership, to pilot the Learn and Earn program, the college and the collaborative of industry CEOs first considered an hourly wage of $10, but quickly came to the agreement that an entry-level professional hourly rate of $15 would be the minimum expectation for internship positions, so that wages lost to internship participation could be adequately replaced. In addition, a transportation stipend up to $500 was included in the package. Like their counterparts at urban, rural, and suburban community colleges around the nation (as documented by the General Accounting Office in 2018), many Bunker Hill students experience food and housing insecurity: half of BHCC students are food insecure, and 14 percent are homeless.[4] Program partners acknowledged that spending $20 a week on public transportation to and from the internship site would cut into student and family budgets for basic needs such as food or utilities and might keep many students from considering Learn and Earn.

In addition to financial barriers such as replacement earnings and travel costs, participation in internships for adult and first-generation college students is fraught with logistical and psychological barriers. Over time, BHCC's Learn and Earn Program Office director realized she had to probe more deeply when students declined potential work-based learning opportunities. The initial "no" is often a defensive, learned response to unfamiliar risks; the director's job is to help prospective interns minimize and navigate these obstacles and related fear or shame. Whether it is stocking a closet with donated professional suits, scheduling interview rehearsals, helping students manage childcare logistics, or communicating high and attainable expectations of success, an effective community college internship program must be structured so that it is not narrowly about matching a student with an opportunity. There is much more to creating a "mind-set of possible." Rather than insisting that students be "ready" to fit into a traditional internship, the college has to find achievable, practical ways to help students cross the bridge from their current situation to the demands and expectations of their preferred world of work.

Diversification of Placements

Crafting an internship program to support students where they are in order to prepare them for what employers expect on the job is critically important to a program's success. At the same time, it is not only the student who needs to be supported and brought along. Thinking more broadly about the pool of potential employers who can sponsor internships, and what it may take to engage a larger and more diverse set of employers, is equally important to long-term success.

In reframing the optimal environment for experiential learning for community college students, those developing and implementing the program cannot afford to perpetuate common assumptions and preconceptions among employers. They will have to encourage the local employer community to take more risks on students from community colleges, since many have never provided internships or have limited their involvement to providing opportunities for four-year students. Government incentives for this have helped at least some additional community colleges secure internships in Massachusetts.

Effective support of interns and their employers by college personnel can make it easier for firms in nontraditional fields to open up opportunities for first-generation students, students of color, and working adults. A fine example is Hack Diversity, an initiative of the New England Venture Capitalist Association, which places black and Latinx interns in Boston-area computer science and engineering companies, where people of color and women are underrepresented. The program provides training, coaching, and mentoring, with the goal of doubling black and Latinx participation in the high-tech workforce. In their final reflection on their experience, held at Microsoft Garage, the industry giant's talent development arm, Hack Diversity students unanimously declared that their newfound self-confidence was their most valuable takeaway. They said, "We didn't know we could!" The field experience was extraordinary for this group of first-generation college students—and it was groundbreaking for the employer partners to bring equity-supporting practices to the industry and to diversify their talent pool.

The local nonprofit, cultural, and small-business sectors have also proven to be an underutilized source of internships and work experience for community college interns seeking viable careers. While funding has historically been scarce in these fields, cost-sharing agreements with private foundations to support paid experiences are beginning to get some traction. In 2017, Bunker Hill Community College launched a partnership with Boston's South End Community Health Center that made available a number of internships in the Health Center's back-office operations. The goal was to engage students who live in the vicinity of the Center and provide them with a professional experience in their own neighborhood, serving their own community. Local philanthropic organizations such as the Jacobs Family Foundation and the Fish Family Foundation have funded internships in these health centers. The effort to grow beyond traditional internship sites in business and industry is now expanding to include museums, public libraries, agriculture-food operation, and other local-facing businesses.

In a tight economy, reaching out to a more diverse and underutilized set of industries and employers can pay off—for the employers, the college, and participating students. Because the majority of community college students remain in the local communities after graduation, internships that lead to jobs are wise investments in the local economy. In the past four years, eleven BHCC partner companies have hired seventy-four interns into full-time jobs.

COMPETITION FOR PLACEMENT AND THE DILEMMA OF THE INCUMBENT WORKER

The value of work-based learning is widely understood in the education community and, increasingly, among employers. Consequently, community colleges compete against both high schools and four-year postsecondary institutions for internship and work-based learning opportunities for their students. Four-year students tend to have an edge: they are typically in their third or fourth year of studies, closing in on baccalaureate completion. Their schools have resources that enable them to build strong, ongoing relationships with employers, who tend to feel surer of offering an internship to a program that has already earned their trust.

Because of this, the aspiration of placing every learner into an internship they would find attractive is remote, even impossible. But that does not mean that students cannot learn in a formal, structured way from the low-wage, part-time jobs they hold while in school, or dig deeply into how the professions operate. Dr. Mary Gatta, a sociologist at Guttman College in New York City, leads a work-focused learning alternative grounded in a two-semester course entitled Ethnographies of Work that converts students' employment barriers into opportunities for learning. In this social science course, students examine the culture of work through a critical social science lens. They learn to step back and think critically about dynamics at work, how workers advance and how they get stuck, and what it takes to succeed in twenty-first-century work settings.[5]

BHCC has adapted these outcomes into a group of learning community courses: students stay in their entry-level jobs and interrogate the environment of their organization and their workplace from an academic and sociological perspective. They use their deeper understanding of the organization to map paths for advancement, to engage a mentor, and to understand that work can be a developmental process that leads beyond their current position. Paired with the real-time experience of a current job, the course accomplishes some of the goals of a traditional internship, preserving the student's economic stability and alleviating some of the pressures of competition among various educational institutions for work-based internship placements. The course also provides students with analytical tools that are helpful in seeking entrance to new areas in the labor market.

CAPACITY BUILDING AND SUSTAINABILITY: PUBLIC POLICY, FUNDING, AND EMPLOYER HIRING PRACTICES

The enthusiasm for internships in community colleges is evident and growing. As community colleges get better at shaping the internship experience for first-generation and adult students, the demand will rise even higher. The final barrier, as with so many effective new practices in our underfunded community colleges, is the lack of resources to support the capacity needed to develop and sustain a high-quality program that students want and employers trust. In Massachusetts, like many states, public sector tuition and fees are mostly fixed, and state appropriations took a big hit during the Great Recession of 2008, from which the state's higher education institutions have not yet recovered. In this environment, it is all but impossible to scale up an internship program at a community college with existing resources. The operational support and liaison work with employers are labor-intensive. Many programs run on spit and shoestring, with occasional doses of life support from philanthropy.

The Boston Foundation's research on large-scale national and state internship efforts noted that resources were not that important for funding intern wages, since employers are generally willing to pay wages if the program is well run. More important to developing a systemic and effective program are funds that can be used to build the capacity of the college and its partners to manage stable regional support systems to "expedite" employer engagement and field placements. In Massachusetts, a State University Internship Incentive Program has been funded through an annual state budget appropriation of $1,000,000 since 2013. The nine state universities in the Commonwealth are responsible for a 1:1 match of privately raised funds for internships. The funding is used for student stipends and institutional staff capacity. It also supports a consortium of practitioners and coordinators who meet regularly to share information and professional development. Each campus's program is unique, tailored to local need. Similar policies and provisions in law would be highly advantageous in ensuring that the nascent efforts in the community colleges are sustained and scaled.

Employers interested in developing a talent pipeline from internships can also create more direct paths from college to career by modifying established hiring practices. State Street Bank in Massachusetts decided to replace certain hourly worker positions with paid interns from Bunker Hill Community College. At the program's height, over twenty BHCC students successfully completed internships at State Street each semester, some of whom were eventually offered permanent paid positions. The tight-knit support system enjoyed by these interns, from formal credit-course structure to faculty guidance, workplace mentoring, and Learn and Earn program check-ins, ensured that students got the support they needed to succeed—and State Street supervisors and human resource professionals got the assurance they needed that students would be ready and productive from day one through the end of the internship.

A CALL FOR COMMUNITY COLLEGE–FOCUSED RESEARCH

In the coming years, it should be a priority of policy makers and program designers to seed and encourage further careful research on internships in community colleges. The field is in need of a succinct conceptual framework, a credible and practical set of outcome measures that includes postgraduate placements and employment stability, and more systematic data collection within and across institutions to validate the efficacy of experiential learning in the community college context. The community college student faces particular challenges and presents particular opportunities: research on internship design and outcomes needs to address those particularities in order to promote promising practices and design choices that make sense in the community college context.

The intern and internship program successes at Bunker Hill Community College, as encouraging and transformative as they have been, remain anecdotal. BHCC institutional researchers have found that participants in the school's Learn and Earn program during the last five years performed better than the college average in almost all areas, including retention, persistence, completion, GPA, and transfer; however, the sample size is small and susceptible to student self-selection bias. BHCC's attempts to measure gains in intern self-understanding, social growth, and professional connections can also benefit from more focused inquiry and analysis. Rigorous and large-scale research across community colleges of varied size and geography would serve the sector well in establishing efficacy, and in advocating for policy and resources at federal, state, or municipal levels.

CONCLUSION

The interest in and power of internships for community college students is evident in school after school. So, too, is the difficulty of building out an internship program that is effective, operates at a large scale, connects the diversity of students to employment opportunities in their field, and is sustainable. The community college population—often older, already working, and juggling school, work, and family responsibilities—presents particular challenges in design, implementation, and resource needs. Community college leaders and personnel are beginning to act on the recognition that their students need both stronger connections to employers and work experience—and that their institutions must develop programs that are better tailored to their students' needs. The challenge of developing internships that meet the needs of working adults upends long-held assumptions about internships and prompts practitioners to identify the most important elements of an internship experience and reevaluate the social and economic barriers to scaling this high-impact learning tool. No other strategy holds such promise for working adults struggling for social and economic mobility. However, a new understanding of internship and experiential learning will require deep inquiry with a team approach, involving scholars, field practitioners, students, and employers to build on lessons to date and be bold in imagining and creating strong models of community college internships and work-based learning.

CHAPTER 3

Ethnographies of Work

A Transformative Framework for Career Learning

– MARY GATTA AND NIESHA ZIEHMKE –

Higher education institutions increasingly recognize the importance of career development and workplace experience as the best way for students to acquire the skills necessary to succeed in an ever-evolving workplace environment.[1] Yet learning about the working world often remains on the margins of the curriculum, in workshops on professional skills and résumé writing. As a result, students often graduate from college with little knowledge of the larger systems at play in the world of work, job searching, career pathways, or how their interests do (or do not) align with labor market needs. Too often students take advantage of college career centers just months before graduation or enter internships late in their college tenure with little background on the intricacies of the workplaces they will enter. They lack a concrete understanding of the day-to-day life in many careers they have interest in and have not learned the critical skills necessary to build up and use networks of family, friends, professors, and colleagues to connect with opportunity. The lack of attention to career preparation in many postsecondary institutions serves only to intensify the class and racial divide. The most privileged students, mostly white, are able to anticipate and prepare for professional careers like those of their parents. Meanwhile, students from low-income families continue to think of work mainly as a way to survive and are often left disappointed when, even with a degree completed, few new doors open to them.

In this chapter we problematize the ways that colleges traditionally deliver career education—often at the margins of the college experience. We advocate instead for building on existing models of education where careers are embedded within the academic curriculum, providing the opportunity for students to not only learn about careers but also investigate the ways workplace culture, systems of inequality, and other structures create constraints and impact opportunities in the labor market. In this chapter we also share original research on a career preparation alternative—Ethnographies of Work (EOW), created by Guttman Community College of the City University (CUNY) of New York.

The instructional model implemented at Guttman Community College has become a beacon of innovation and knowledge creation in higher education since the College welcomed its inaugural class in August 2012 as the first CUNY community college to open in over forty years. Research-based, high-impact, best practices in curriculum design—active, project-based, student-centered, and experiential learning—are combined with critical support structures beyond the classroom, as in proven models like CUNY's Accelerated Study in Associate Programs (ASAP).[2] By remaining on the forefront of innovation and best practices in higher education, Guttman has maintained three-year completion rates of 43 to 49 percent, hovering around twice the national average of 22 percent for community colleges.

EOW is a required first-year course that integrates individualized reflection on the character of work into the academic curriculum, rather than keeping work-centered learning as a separate endeavor. EOW is a required social science course that gives students both a theoretical and applied context by putting the subject of work at the center of learning. The course helps students identify and begin to build a pathway toward a "vocation," meaning an occupation to which a person is particularly drawn. The theory of change that underlies EOW is as follows: students who understand the meaning of work in human lives and who have a critical understanding of work experience will have greater agency in entering and navigating the labor market than those who believe they need only a credential. EOW students are asked to reflect on their own workplace and community experiences with a social science lens, gaining new insights into their work lives. This chapter explores how this theory of change is evidenced in the experiences of the course and helps to reshape the way we deliver career education with a social justice framework.

TRADITIONAL WAYS TO PREPARE STUDENTS FOR CAREERS[3]

Many colleges tend to address careers and career preparation in the margins of the academic curriculum. Career centers exist outside of the academic affairs offices with little or no connection to the academic experience. The offices often employ staff who deliver a variety of cocurricular career programs and services to students, such as career counseling and assessments, experiential career opportunities (e.g., internships and cooperative education), educational and career information, job-hunting assistance, and employment information. In this common structure for career development and support, the career center can serve only a small percentage of students due to modest staffing, the fact that students visit career centers very late in their college career, and the disconnect between center staff and the classroom experience.

One way colleges have tried to address these challenges is to require students to take an academic success class. Such courses orient students to college life and include self-management skills, such as how to use time effectively, find and use academic support services, and ask for help.[4] Not surprisingly, research shows that while such courses have a short-term positive impact, that impact fades over time.[5] Such courses do not deal centrally with careers, although they may recommend that students take part in short-term workshops that teach a set of skills and competencies often called *soft skills*—how to write a résumé, dress for success, write an application, present oneself both in an interview and in a work setting, and collaborate on a team, to name a few. Many job training programs teach a similar set of skills, which have the benefit of alerting students to a set of expectations employers are likely to have. Although the topics are useful, such training does not ensure that students internalize the skills or can deploy them in demanding work settings. (The exception is the health professions and a few other career areas for which clinical hours are required as part of the degree and to qualify the student to sit for a licensing exam.) Nor does the training help students to critically approach their own career pathways, either by opening up career options to them or by providing the space to explore possible careers. And finally, it does not provide an intellectual context for the role of work in human lives; how labor markets operate; why social networks are important; or how race, class, and gender impact experience in the workplace.

Certain groups of young people are particularly disadvantaged entering working life. They are ill-informed about the labor market and how careers are developed, and they are not linked to the networks that might help them on their way.[6] In the traditional ways of career access in colleges, students do not often probe such big questions as the role of work in human lives or, more practically, how the labor market operates. While social science courses may address race, class, and gender barriers to employment, few help students figure out how to navigate such barriers, let alone help young people understand that even with a degree they will need to activate informal social networks that will help them find a first job. Relatively few schools collaborate at any scale with employers to help students get in the door for internships, summer jobs, or even job shadowing. In his recent book, *Our Kids*, political scientist Robert Putnam decries the disappearance of vocational education from most American high schools, and advocates for more programs that offer "a curriculum that mixes academic coursework with hands-on technical courses designed to build work skills."[7] He contrasts the situation of low-income youth entering the job market with only a high school diploma and no job skills with that of affluent young people whose parents set them up for the future by spending on "music lessons, summer camp, travel, school supplies, books, computers, extracurricular activities, recreation, and leisure," all of which introduce youth to the adult world, including the world of careers.[8]

In the US and most other wealthy countries, elites (and the organizations they sponsor) work hard to ensure that their children develop social capital, often through their own social networks, which ultimately yield economic benefit. For example, professional parents take care to have their children meet other young people of similar background, their parents, and colleagues. In the US such parents invest in their children's cultural capital by enrolling their children in afterschool enrichment activities, such as music and language programs, and summer internship or academic programs where they interact with professionals in fields of interest.[9] Such parents reach out to "helping professionals" when they see signs of anxiety, stress, and other maladies impeding their children's well-being and achievement. They take care that their children meet the social norms of their reference groups. Mutually reinforced at school and at home, carefully constructed social and cultural experiences produce young people who know how to ask for help from adults, make appropriate small talk, and recognize peers, as well as how to interact with those outside their social circles.

Annette Lareau has documented what many sense intuitively—that privilege increases privilege, or, as she asserts, the transmission of differential advantages takes place among middle-class families. In *Unequal Childhoods: Class, Race, and Family Life*, she studied what she called "the cultural logic" of parenting styles as they impact home, afterschool, and school lives of working-class and middle-class youth. She carefully documented the reasons for the higher achievement and success rates of more privileged young people, describing the "concerted cultivation" of children.[10] Middle-class parents work to "develop" children in ways that fit the standards of mainstream institutions and that benefit their children later in the working world. Such families may not know the term *cultural capital*, but they are adept at cultivating it. In contrast, Lareau characterizes the working-class parenting style as privileging "natural growth," with the result that children have long periods of unstructured time, clear boundaries exist between children and adults, and play is child-initiated without the mediating parental proviso that it be a learning experience as well.

Reconnecting in 2011 with the children she studied earlier, Lareau shows that the "intensity of middle-class and upper middle-class parents in building their children's social capital only increases as children grow into young adults. Middle-class parents continued the process of gathering information and intervening in their children's lives . . . even when the children had moved hundreds of miles from home."[11] As young adults repeatedly turned to their parents for guidance, the parents treated them, in key ways, as children. In working-class and poor families, the parents saw the young adults as "grown," which was a view shared by the young adults themselves. Nonetheless, when the kids ran into problems in school or other institutions, the middle-class parents were heavily involved in managing situations to maximize opportunities. For the working-class families, it was harder to comply with the demands of professionals. Thus, trajectories that began when the children were ten continued to unfold over time. The middle-class kids generally achieved much more educational success than the working-class and poor kids. Since education is the foundation for shaping labor market chances, the career prospects of the middle-class young adults are much brighter than those of their less privileged counterparts.

Understanding the role of social capital is critical for college students. In their research on first-generation college students, Kevin Tate and his colleagues found that, overwhelmingly, first-generation college students, "while not having a significant network in place, believed that having one was important to their success beyond graduation."[12] These students further reported that university staff and faculty members made assumptions about their access to networks, which then led to ineffective advising and career support. These disparities highlight the importance of identifying and deploying new ways to prepare students for careers.

ETHNOGRAPHIES OF WORK: LEARNING ABOUT CAREERS, DIFFERENTLY

Guttman Community College has developed a career-preparation alternative in EOW, a required first-year course that provides the opportunity to dynamically improve student engagement in career-focused learning and offer traditionally underserved students—low-income, first-generation, and students of color—the opportunity to gain agency as they explore their work futures. The EOW model integrates individualized reflection on the character of work into the academic curriculum. Since EOW is a social science course, students interact with workplaces in distinctive, theoretically informed ways. Rather than entering workplaces as interns, they enter as researchers, able to spend significant time uncovering the dynamics that will help inform their career decisions and future work experiences. For example, students read an academic ethnographic text about a particular workplace dynamic; topics include hierarchical leadership structures, racialized norms in the workplace, and cultural matching in hiring practices. They then visit selected workplaces to replicate the ethnographic study. In doing so, they are able to use theory and observational methods to gain critical cultural knowledge while learning firsthand about specific workplaces they may one day enter as employees.

EOW is a two-part, yearlong college course and set of experiences that gives students tools for understanding and addressing the challenges and opportunities they face in the labor market; it does so in both a theoretical and applied context by putting the subject of work at the center of learning. While enrolled in EOW, students complete a paired corequisite advisement-centered course, Learning About Being a Successful Student (LaBSS), which explores academic majors and develops some of the soft skills necessary to enter the workplace setting successfully during their EOW projects, as well as in the future for internships or other work-based learning experiences. To return to our earlier point, EOW links the intellectual, liberal arts learning about work with the more skills-oriented lab rather than presenting them as two decontextualized and separate endeavors.

In EOW I, the students master ethnographic methods: research design, observation, workplace mapping, and interviewing. The signature course assignment is a semester-long ethnographic investigation of a career/workplace that the student has an interest in pursuing. In EOW II, having mastered the research methodology and gained comfort as researchers in workplaces, students focus on applying ethnographic methods to address a workplace problem. This approach provides students the opportunity to build ethnographic skills (e.g., interviewing, observation) that are necessary for success in both education and employment.

EOW students are asked to reflect on their own workplace and community experiences with a social science lens, gaining new insights on their work lives. Most students in this majority-minority student body have experience with discrimination based on class and race/ethnicity, but a powerful aspect of the class is to put these often painful anecdotes in the context of institutional and structural racism. Their yearlong exploration directly engages students with working people as informants and equips them with deep knowledge about employer expectations and behaviors. They can become better job seekers, able to cast an informed and critical eye on potential workplaces as they make sense of their career options. EOW also introduces students to the reality that social networks and connections—forms of social capital—matter in the labor market, and helps students see and understand their own networks and work intentionally to engage new ones. Armed with this knowledge, students who understand how networks operate will enter the job market more successfully, with their eyes wide open about what they may experience as people of color and how they might engage authentically when equity is in question. Several chapters in this book delve more deeply into these issues.

As mentioned earlier, the EOW framework informs career learning beyond the first year in early internships and career-based experiential learning. In three out of five of the majors available at Guttman, internships are required, and its Center for Career Preparation and Partnerships works to build relationships with employers. Often the employers see themselves as coeducators. In the Urban Studies and Liberal Arts–Social Science and Humanities majors, employer partners are invited into courses to work with student groups to do real-world projects, conduct relevant research, and offer recommendations. In the Liberal Arts–Science track, there are multiple opportunities for in-class and one-on-one undergraduate research supported through the CUNY Research Scholars Program and the National Science Foundation's Louis Stokes Alliance for Minority Participation. Guttman's commitment to early internships and career-based experiential learning aims to offer students the kinds of career learning and professional networks necessary to build more social and economic mobility.

The EOW framework is designed to enhance the social capital of students. Episodes of employer engagement are often viewed within research literature as developing forms of social and cultural capital, commonly because students are accessing new sources of information that influence changes in thinking about their prospective future selves. Such analysis draws heavily on Stanford University sociologist Mark Granovetter's conception of the strength of weak ties.[13] Within the EOW course, students are able to expand their social networks, gaining access to new and useful people and information that can raise, broaden, and challenge occupational aspirations. This opportunity to develop new connections is particularly important for CUNY students, as many of them are first-generation college students without expansive social networks offering access to economic mobility. Through the EOW work, students interact as researchers with employers in professional settings. This is a low-key way for employers to meet a set of young people whose backgrounds may not be familiar and about whom they may have preconceived notions.

Over the years, these observations have led to trusted social relationships of demonstrable value to both student and employer, as witnessed in internship placements and even job opportunities.

As noted earlier, in contrast with the common ways postsecondary students learn about careers, students in EOW spend a significant part of the semester in workplaces as ethnographers and thinking about careers. This is a perhaps the most distinctive piece of the course. Students enter workplaces prepared to make social science observations, conduct interviews, and take detailed field notes. In addition to written field notes, students take pictures and videos in the field. In some classes, students share those photos and videos in real time with their professor and peers via an online platform. When they come to class, they analyze their field notes and experiences within the context of sociological and anthropological studies of work. In addition, being in a workplace as a researcher gives them a new experience—employees are often curious about their presence and the students must take responsibility for explaining what they are studying and why.

ETHNOGRAPHIES OF WORK EXPERIENCES[14]

A series of focus groups we conducted with students highlighted some of the ways EOW not only informs their career choices but also provides the opportunities to explore sociological aspects of work. One of the goals and learning outcomes of EOW is for students to use ethnographic methods to investigate a career they are interested in (EOW I), and to address a workplace problem/research question using ethnography (EOW II). The use of ethnography to directly and indirectly help inform students' career opportunities is unique in academic classes. One of the central challenges is that faculty must ensure that the students' career exploration occurs within the academic disciplines of sociology and anthropology. This challenge is what differentiates the course from a more straightforward career exploration activity. It is not just exposure to careers and career pathways that is critical to a successful course and to student learning, but also putting work in a theoretical and evidence-based context. Through our focus groups we learned that the impact of this framing on students includes not only a more informed and wide range of career options, but also a deeper understanding of how workplace and societal structures provide both opportunities and constraints on individuals' work and career lives.

Career Field Work

Several themes emerged in our focus groups relative to students' career ideas. First, EOW provided students with opportunities to explore careers and workplaces that they may not have had access to in the past, as one student explained:

> Visiting the workplace exploration seems really cool to me. I had a friend in class who got to go to the office of a major technology company here in New York City; he showed me pictures and it looked really cool. But, at the same time, it was interesting to see this whole different world. I just feel so foreign right now, because we are in school; we are not in the corporate world. And to explore how that relates to our life.

Second, students began to better understand not just what type of work they were interested in, but also what type of work environment or workplace practices were important to them. One student noted: "I feel that helps me consider the core aspects of a job. You are able to go to the interview or job tour and notice the environment, what type of people are there, how they interact. You notice a lot of the more important [aspects of the job] than the pay, or just getting the job. It's also the environment."

Another student built on this comment, noting: "It's a magnifying glass onto your environment. It helps you recognize what is good and bad for you. And recognize yourself because when you reevaluate what you can tolerate on the job, you'll reevaluate like what you . . . would avoid. It's kinda like knowing yourself more."

Students also began to see how specific workplace practices and experiences may be different from what they previously thought. This helped to dispel myths about careers, many of which were developed from TV and movies. Students could let go of conceptions not developed from direct knowledge of people who work in the fields of interest. For example, this student came to understand more about types of law firms:

When I thought [about] just observing people in the workplace, I thought it would be pretty boring [to] observe someone doing their office job. But for my final project, my first year, I had to go to a law firm and see how that workplace was like and I thought it was cool because it exposed me to, like, what an actual courtroom looked like and how things function. It just taught me a lot, like a law firm in general. I didn't know people could just own their own law firm and just only have two people within the law firm. I thought it was like on TV, where it's a big building with several divisions.

As students explored careers with in-depth ethnographic methods, one theme that emerged relatively frequently was that, once students conducted their research in the workplaces, they began to wonder if the career originally of interest was actually a fit for them:

But I remember going to a site—it was a public school—at that time I wanted to be a principal. I remember going into that setting and actually observing a principal's office and observing what the principal does and writing a report about that and my reflections on that. So, that assignment stood out to me because it helped me figure out, kind of, what direction I wanted to go in, and I realized that maybe being a principal isn't really what I want to do. So, that helped me in terms of navigating, like, do I want a more hands-on approach, do I want to be interacting with students more, rather than being in an office and kind of overseeing things or controlling things or whatever? It helped me in that aspect and I can still reflect on that to this day.

By delving deep into an occupation, students were able to gain a sense of the education and career pathway for that profession, thereby informing their own career development. The next quote, however, raises concerns for the student: for instance, is she lowering her aspirations because she doesn't see a way to keep on her original career path? "The class helped me be realistic and we looked at income, we looked at the amount of years that it was going to be to actually accomplish that goal. So, we broke it down and I was able to be realistic of myself. 'Okay, I don't want to be, you know, doing this many years of work before I actually delve into this.' So, it helped me navigate through that process."

Such reflections from students provide an opportunity for faculty and advisors to help the student not only understand the demands of a job, but also determine how they align with the student's life experiences.

Structures of Work

While ethnography is a key focus of the course, so is the sociological/anthropological analysis of work. In EOW I and EOW II, through ethnographic investigation and study of research literature, students learn about the structures of work: nuances of workplaces, implicit and explicit culture and norms, and power relations and inequality dynamics. One interesting finding through our focus groups was that students took this perspective beyond classroom assignments into their everyday worlds; they applied the lens and the sociological concepts to the different workplaces they interacted with in their daily lives. For instance, students entered many of the service-sector establishments around New York City to order food and drinks. As a result of EOW, in these service establishments they now paid new attention to the work structures around them: "So, usually, if I go to Starbucks or McDonald's, I just order something and leave. But sometimes when I go to these businesses, I'm not looking at just myself in the business, but looking at it as workers and how they integrate with each other and how it's structured."

Another student recounted observing "sometimes the energy of the workplace or the language that workers use with each other or just the way they, like, their body language—the way they look at each other—to see if it's more teamwork or more like 'do this or do that.'"

Student also saw structures of inequality—such as gender, race, and class—in a new light. This helped them better understand their interview data within the larger sociological context: "When it came into the second part of EOW, I was also learning how to interview with people. So, I had to interview people . . . and [I] looked at people who worked in [terms of] gender. I look at an organization, [and ask] 'how do you feel, like, you're being a woman working this [job?].' She was just explaining how, like, she had a man who was here for a year before her, and he got promoted and stuff like that."

Students also began to identify how certain people in an organization can open doors—in the next quote, the student calls such people "gatekeepers" and recognizes that they can influence access to jobs: "I felt it the most when

I'd go to the workplace because you get to know all the gatekeepers. Like, boom, I got attached with the vice president, so now I'm in Albany doing this and doing that. So . . . I think about that every time . . . whether at work and just in life in general." Although the student doesn't use the term "social capital," she has recognized the value of building relationships beyond her usual circle with those who have positional authority and power.

Another student explained his understanding of social capital, and how his college experiences fit into that understanding: "I had two internships in high school—one in a defense attorney's office and a DA office. I worked with data. I sat in on cases. I got to assist in hand-picking a jury—it was really cool. I have recommendation letters so when I'm ready to go to law school, I can use them."

That same student commented directly on race issues in the workplace, observing that:

> there are not enough black lawyers in the DA's office. It's a prestigious place to work. You have to have certain grades and connections to work there. If you don't get connections, you don't get the job. You have to start from bottom and work your way up. My supervisor's last name sounded black, so she had to work as a paralegal for two years to work up. She said it would be different if she had a white last name.

One interesting common theme is that students began to see the complexity of career choice in relation to identity, social status, racial/ethnic identity, and family values. In many ways, students began to see their careers differently than before the class. The next quote is from an alumna, now in graduate school, who has gained insight from EOW and her subsequent experiences:

> One of the things that I learned was that our careers are kind of created and built. It's not just something that you just—you get your degree, you learn a set of skills, and you just get a job and you apply it; it's not given to you that way. So, I learned more of like career dynamics and how we're always learning and navigating through different stages. It's not as clear-cut as, you know, learning how to do one thing and then there's a clear definition and task description for a specific thing that you'll do.

Another student struggled with the degree to which a person's value should be related to the status of their job, and she was puzzling it out as a result of class discussion and readings:

I believe the way I look at work has changed. I grew up being taught that my value would be based on my job—that in society, I won't have a say to make decisions and that I won't be respected if I have a low-skill job. And I learned two things. In part what I was taught is partly true that, that is a reality in this society that I work, but also that it doesn't have to be that way—that I don't have to see my value or my identity in my choice of career. So, I try to see my work as important, like anyone else's is important and it's a component or something that needs to be fulfilled and I am that piece of that larger system. So, that's something that I see now. But it's also created some like agency in me needing to do well in school because I'm realizing that, if I'm going to impact people and policies in places, that it's going to have to be based on whatever number or title is on that degree.

An additional way the students' perspective may have shifted during the course of the EOW experience is that they acknowledged agency over their careers. Students became metacognitive about the choices they had before them, to the extent of understanding that a first career may not be the last career, and that they can give themselves permission to choose a pathway that may be at odds with their family's expectations:

I'm afraid of investing myself into something knowing that my likes always change, and what that will mean for me in the future, when maybe I'm older and don't have, like, the help to learn something new or start new careers? What does that mean when you're changing at a different pace than what life is taking you to?

I think [that] this class, EOW, definitely made me want to pursue what I like a little bit more, whereas my mom does not agree with that necessarily. She wants me to have a safe job or something that's going to make me money because that's what she does. I think the class has helped me open my mind a little more.

GUTTMAN'S CAREER FRAMEWORK: EQUITY AND ETHNOGRAPHY

Guttman's approach to career education is grounded in this understanding of the inequities of society, schools, and the workforce. It therefore builds from the EOW course to an EOW framework, which is carried out beyond the first year through a deep commitment to early internships and career-based experiential learning aimed at offering students access to new professional networks and professional experience.[15]

As EOW continues to evolve, we are learning about students' experiences in the class, but also more broadly about the challenges in teaching the class. Guttman leadership, faculty, and staff are aware of the complex dynamic of teaching from a social justice perspective, often directly discussing societal inequities. This has led the campus to comprehensively embrace culturally responsive practices and racial literacy in its professional development and approaches to curriculum, pedagogy, and support delivery. Pioneered by educators concerned with the negative socioeconomic and psychological effects of ostracizing experiences of black and Latinx youth in traditional educational settings, *culturally responsive teaching* can be defined as using the cultural knowledge, prior experiences, frames of reference, and performance styles of ethnically diverse students to make learning encounters more relevant to and effective for them. It teaches *to and through* the strengths of these students. Culturally responsive teaching comprises the behavioral expressions of knowledge, beliefs, and values that recognize the importance of racial and cultural diversity in learning.[16]

Guttman's initial trial of incorporating strengths-based culturally responsive practices has been manifested through the Culturally Responsive Leadership (CRL) Series it has initiated in partnership with Dr. Yolanda Sealey-Ruiz of the Teachers College at Columbia University. An eminent scholar of inclusive and equitable educational practices and their impact on students of color, Dr. Sealey-Ruiz is also the facilitator of the professional development series Developing Racial Literacy: A Foundation to Sustaining Culturally Responsive Pedagogy. These professional development series explore *racial literacy*, a term Dr. Sealey-Ruiz utilizes to describe the "skill and practice," the ability "to probe the existence of racism and examine the effects of race and institutionalized systems on [one's] experiences and representation in US society," and "to discuss the implications of race and American racism in constructive ways."[17] Using a culturally responsive pedagogical strategy, Guttman has worked to improve its EOW curriculum to equip its majority black and Latinx students with even more of the tools they will need to face, overcome, and dismantle structures that oppress by race, ethnicity, and/or nationality in the workplace.

CONCLUSION

Guttman's EOW framework offers a paradigmatic shift in career learning in higher education, centering career learning in the curriculum in a way that faces the societal inequities in the labor market head-on in hopes of making positive societal change. This model of career learning puts students in the driver seat to become the researchers and agents of change. It is our hope that this model of career education empowers our students and those in other institutions now adapting EOW for their student populations to enter the labor market well informed and ready to take on the challenges that arise as the workforce diversifies.

Good Jobs,
Good Careers

CHAPTER 4

When Can a Job Launch a Career?

*What Students Need to Know About the Real Economic
Opportunities of Middle-Skill Work*

– SARA LAMBACK AND CHARLOTTE CAHILL –

Challenges in matching the speed at which the world of work is changing with the offerings of our education systems are likely to intensify in the
coming years. Technological innovations, such as analytics, big data, and artificial intelligence, have made it possible to automate many routine tasks
once performed by human workers. Research demonstrates that this trend is
likely to accelerate and intensify in the coming years.[1] As jobs shift to include
less routinized work, workers with the ability to perform complex cognitive
tasks that are difficult or impossible to automate are valued ever more highly
by employers. Hiring managers seek job candidates with skills such as critical thinking, strategic reasoning, troubleshooting, management, verbal and
written communication expertise, and an array of social skills.[2] The curricular pathways now available at many colleges do not always fully reflect these
changing skill requirements. For example, colleges often emphasize career
pathways focused on STEM and technical skills as the best bet, a focus well
aligned with available labor market information in most regions of the country.[3] However, research indicates that, while STEM skills are of high value to
job seekers in the short term, they depreciate more rapidly than the critical,
analytical, and social skills needed for the jobs of the future.[4]

Effective career planning requires students and educators to find answers
to complex questions and to use data and resources that, while readily available, are infrequently made accessible to those who need them most. What
do students need to know in order to successfully navigate a shifting, complex
labor market? What is the difference between a job and a career? Which jobs

have the potential to lead to fulfilling careers, and which may lead to dead ends? If students hope to be competitive job applicants, what skills should they acquire and what educational credentials should they earn? How does a student know what sectors of the economy offer the best options in her region or what kind of job to look for in a specific field? With the aim of answering these questions and providing educators with tools to support student career planning, this chapter highlights a framework that categorizes jobs according to the type of opportunity they offer. It also provides an overview of key labor market information, resources, and strategies to prepare students for both current workforce opportunities and the rapidly evolving demands of the future of work. The following chapter, a companion to this one, provides a complementary framework that takes on the question of whether a job meets both basic and higher human needs.

THE OPPORTUNITY FRAMEWORK[5]

Résumé data, a relatively new data source, can offer valuable insights into the relationship between jobs and careers by illuminating the progressions of job seekers over time, enabling college faculty and career advisors to gain a more nuanced understanding of which career choices and pathways offer the strongest opportunities for students as they make career decisions. A recent analysis of approximately four million résumés of middle-skill workers across the country conducted by Jobs for the Future (JFF) and Burning Glass Technologies examined the potential of middle-skill jobs in health care, IT, business, and manufacturing to promote career advancement and income growth based upon four metrics (defined in box 4.1): job stability, career stability, advancement, and pay.[6]

The analysis found stark differences in opportunity between one middle-skill job and another and identified a new method of conceptualizing middle-skill jobs, known as the *Opportunity Framework*, in three distinct job categories:

- *Lifetime jobs.* Lifetime jobs *are* careers. They pay well and offer a high level of stability. For many workers, they are the final step on a career path. Some people do get promoted to different jobs, with greater responsibility and pay, but many don't. However, the entry-level jobs in

BOX 4.1	METRICS FOR ANALYZING POTENTIAL CAREER ADVANCEMENT AND INCOME GROWTH

- **Job stability.** The likelihood that a job seeker would be employed in the same occupation five years after entering the position. This does not include when an individual changes employers but maintains a similar title and duties.
- **Career stability.** The likelihood that a job seeker will be employed in an occupation within the same career area (i.e., manufacturing, business, IT, health care) within five years.
- **Advancement.** Progression from a starting occupation to a different occupation within the same career area, with a median salary that is at least 10 percent higher than the starting occupation salary, within five years.
- **Pay.** Workers in each occupation are assumed to earn the median wage for that occupation based upon the US Bureau of Labor Statistics, Occupational Employment Statistics.

this category tend to be well paid relative to other middle-skill jobs, offer high job security, and bring modest—but consistent—wage increases over time. Middle-skill lifetime jobs are most often found in health care and in advanced manufacturing.

Example: A licensed practical nurse (LPN) who has recently earned an associate's degree starts a hospital job that pays $21 per hour. After five years, the nurse is in the same position, earning slightly more ($24 per hour); however, the position offers a high level of both job and career stability and includes a modest raise each year. While advancement to a registered nurse position is possible (often with a bachelor's degree), the high demand for LPNs coupled with the solid earnings and stability make this job a strong option for middle-skill workers. Dental hygienist and welder are also examples of lifetime jobs.

- *Springboard jobs.* Springboard jobs *lead to* careers. They offer high potential for advancement within their career areas. Some of these entry-level jobs offer relatively low entry-level pay ($18 per hour for a bookkeeper, for example), but they serve as gateways or springboards to better positions. Because people in these jobs move up quickly within the same field, their low-to-moderate job stability is

an advantage, not a challenge. High turnover results in many openings as people advance to higher-level jobs. Springboard jobs are typically found in business and IT. Often, industry certifications—such
as the Cisco Certified Network Associate or Microsoft Certified Solutions Expert—enable job seekers to build in-demand skills on the job
and to advance within their careers.

Example: A human resources (HR) assistant who is just starting out
typically earns around $18 per hour. With at least one year of experi-
ence in field, the HR assistant can begin coursework to earn the Professional in Human Resources (PHR) certification, a credential associated
with advancement in the field. After completing the PHR certification,
the HR assistant is promoted to an HR specialist, a position that offers
around $28 per hour and both strong job and career stability. This ad-
vancement pattern is not uncommon, as evidenced by the fact that 50
percent of PHR certification holders advance within five years.[7] Similar
patterns of progression were also seen among computer support specialists and bookkeepers, which are also springboard jobs.

• *Static jobs.* Static jobs typically do not become careers and rarely lead
to higher-paying jobs. They are just jobs. They are characterized by low
pay, low stability, and low advancement potential from the entry level.
Many who start in static jobs move into other occupations in entirely
different fields, such as retail clerk or customer service representative.
Often, departing employees leave by choice in search of better pay, stability, and/or advancement opportunities in another field.

Example: A machine operator at a heavy manufacturing plant lands
a job with a high school vocational certificate and begins earning
around $16 per hour. However, because of the volatility in the industry,
the company shifts to a contract workforce. The machine operator is
laid off and finds a temporary job as a delivery driver while looking for
better work.[8] Strikingly, only 1 percent of manufacturing workers ana-
lyzed in the study by JFF and Burning Glass Technologies advanced to
a higher-paying occupation in the field—the lowest advancement rate
across all career areas. The résumé data analysis surfaced similar patterns
in several health-care support occupations (e.g., medical assistants,
pharmacy technicians), which are also classified as static jobs.

The Opportunity Framework suggests a new approach to understand the potential of middle-skill jobs to offer long-term career opportunities. College faculty and advisors are encouraged to utilize this framework—and career outcomes data more generally—to help inform their approaches to career planning, curricula, and programmatic decisions. With these resources and an understanding of how to use labor market data (the subject of the following section), community colleges have an opportunity to equip students not just for an entry-level job, but for long-term career success.

LABOR MARKET INFORMATION STRATEGIES AND RESOURCES

Labor market information encompasses data that details both supply and demand for labor in a particular location, including industries, occupations, wages, demographics, projections, and job postings. Together, these data can provide deep insights into local economic conditions—and offer an important foundation for college faculty and staff to help create stronger linkages between educational programs and jobs. Labor market data can support planning by answering questions such as: Which manufacturing jobs are likely to grow in the next ten years? What is the average salary for a licensed nurse practitioner in a particular region? What credentials are most in demand for IT support specialists? While labor market information is complex, a number of robust tools are publicly accessible and can provide details on local employment and workforce dynamics related to both supply and demand. Methodologically, a distinction is often made between two key types of labor market data:

- *Traditional.* Drawn from federal or state surveys conducted by public agencies (e.g., the US Bureau of Labor Statistics), traditional labor market data—such as employment and industry data, occupational projections, and demographics—are robust and reliable, available free of charge, and can be accessed via federal websites or through a state labor market agency. In addition, many colleges have subscriptions to tools such as Emsi or the JobsEQ service from Chmura Economics and Analytics, both of which aggregate a range of federal, state, and local sources and facilitate customized searches and analysis. In some cases, there may be significant lag time between data collection and publication, since traditional labor market data is released only at set intervals.

- *Real time.* In recent years, vendors such as Burning Glass Technologies and Monster.com have developed tools that allow for the real-time aggregation and analysis of online job postings that detail the skills, credentials, and other characteristics that are in demand among employers in a particular geography. While these data are continuously updated and can offer insight into new and emerging trends in demand, they generally require a paid subscription. Another caveat is that jobs in certain industries (e.g., manufacturing, construction) are often underrepresented in real-time data because employers in those industries do not rely heavily on online job postings to hire.

As college faculty and staff work to build alignment between their programming and regional labor market needs, it is important to draw upon a range of sources—including both traditional and real-time data—and to analyze both the local labor market demand and supply. The following steps can serve as a guide for collecting and analyzing these data:

1. Define a geography that accurately reflects your labor shed.[9] Colleges that serve rural regions may want to conduct an analysis that encompasses a large geographic area, especially if students commonly relocate as they pursue jobs or drive long distances for work.
   - The US Census Bureau's OnTheMap tool provides insights into commuting patterns in a particular region, along with useful visualizations of worker movement.[10]

2. Identify the high-demand, high-wage industries and occupations in your area. It is important to distinguish between *industries*, which are used to classify business establishments based upon the type of goods or services they produce, and *occupations*, which are used to classify jobs.[11] Since frameworks for classifying both businesses (NAICS) and occupations (SOC) are tiered, a multilevel analysis can provide insight into the broad trends in industry sectors (e.g., manufacturing) as well as more granular shifts within detailed industries (e.g., aircraft engine

and parts manufacturing) in a region. A similar approach can be used to analyze occupations. In reviewing wage data, it is often informative to compare entry-level and median wages for a target occupation to the living wage needed in the region. Useful resources include:

- The US Bureau of Labor Statistics, which provides a list of fastest-growing occupations and industry projections.[12] More detailed local and state data is available through a state labor market agency.[13]
- O*Net OnLine, which provides occupational profiles, including a list of fast-growing occupations, needed skills and competencies, wages, and lists of related occupations.[14]
- MIT Living Wage Calculator, which identifies the living wage for US states, countries, and metropolitan statistical areas by family configuration.[15]

3. Compare local demand with supply to identify emerging needs and opportunities. First, estimate future demand by combining the projected job growth with the number of replacement hires to understand the total number of anticipated openings. Second, gauge supply by considering the number of workers who could potentially fill a position. This can be done by analyzing the number of completions in relevant programs of study, via a crosswalk, as well as those in the public workforce system seeking jobs in a particular field or occupation. For additional information, see:

- The US Department of Labor created a CIP-to-SOC crosswalk, which links the Classification of Instructional Programs (CIP) codes to relevant occupational codes.[16]

4. Analyze the skills and credentials associated with target occupations using resources such as:

- Real-time job posting data, which can offer detailed insights into the demand among employers in a particular area, including the specific technical and baseline skills, credentials, educational qualifications, and other characteristics they seek by industry and occupation.
- O*Net OnLine, which can be used in conjunction with JFF's toolkit "From Placement to Partners," which details how to identify the various skills needed for target occupations.[17]

5. Vet findings from the labor market analysis with industry partners and identify implications. An industry advisory board or other employer partners can provide valuable feedback on the data, context on local conditions, and suggestions on how these findings can inform programs and curricula. In addition, employers can often offer insights into long-term industry trends or shifts that are underway that have implications for the local labor market.

Developing insights on a particular labor market requires not just data, but also analysis that can help build a deeper understanding of local conditions and needs. A comprehensive labor market analysis that includes steps 1 through 5 is recommended for the development of career pathways programs, to help ensure that they are aligned with the local economy and workforce needs. More broadly, this approach enables a "deep and regular engagement with employers and others in their communities [which] is essential to understanding how to match student education with job needs."[18]

BEYOND LABOR MARKET INFORMATION

Labor market information is a powerful tool for identifying promising job and career options and the skills and credentials needed to stand out and succeed in a competitive labor market, but the data are complex and often not readily accessible. Colleges and universities can address this challenge by fully integrating labor market information into the design of their programs of study and encouraging data-driven decision-making by faculty, staff, and students. Real-time labor market information is a snapshot of the labor market at a particular moment. Traditional labor market information is based on historical data; while this type of data does offer projections intended to provide a picture of the labor market in the future, forecasts based on past trends may not fully account for rapid changes and new developments in the employment landscape. Thus, it falls on institutions of higher education to help students navigate these changes by providing career-focused curricular pathways that integrate technical and academic learning; supporting students in developing the analytical, communication, and social skills sought by employers; and expanding access to paid work-based learning.

Career-Focused Curricular Pathways

In recent years, a growing number of colleges have implemented curricular pathways designed to support student persistence and completion and, in some cases, to help students plan for careers. Pathways are a necessary response to the increasing complexity of the higher education and employment landscapes. As a recent report on pathways by Georgetown University's Center on Education and the Workforce notes, the number of colleges and universities in the US more than doubled between 1950 and 2014. Growth in the number of available postsecondary programs has been even more explosive, with a fivefold increase—from 410 to 2,260 programs—in the three decades from 1985 to 2014. This growth was paralleled by a dramatic increase in the number of occupations, which more than tripled between 1950 and 2010.[19] This proliferation of higher education and career options requires thoughtful strategies to support student navigation.

As of 2018, more than 250 community colleges across the country had committed to guided pathways reforms aligned with state, national, and regional efforts, with additional colleges developing guided pathways on an individual basis.[20] Guided pathways reforms are intended to increase completion rates and to support students in planning for further education and careers. Students develop academic plans based on clearly mapped programs and course sequences, milestones, and learning outcomes; these pathways are designed to support academic and career exploration, as well as students' decision-making. Student support strategies, including academic advising, are also a key component of guided pathways.[21]

While guided pathways reforms have most often focused on the academic side of community colleges, workforce programs within colleges have frequently adopted career pathways models. Like guided pathways, career pathways use strategies such as program mapping, course sequencing, and advising to help students navigate the complexities of higher education and develop clear educational plans. Career pathways initiatives also seek to align postsecondary programs with labor market demand. Key career pathways strategies include the use of labor market information to drive decision-making; "reverse mapping" programs of study from the labor market; soliciting employer input on program design and curriculum; and career advising for students.[22]

Despite the career pathways movement's national momentum, it has proven difficult for many colleges to design and implement programs quickly enough to keep up with the changing world of work. A recent study of the 115 institutions in the California community college system found that, while colleges did increase the number of certificates and degrees offered in in-demand occupations, they did so at only half the rate at which those occupations grew. In addition, colleges were not always successful in matching the credentials offered to labor market demand. In instances where colleges did expand programs to better align with labor market demand, they often did so in response to student interest.[23] Although career pathways initiatives are intended to help students better understand labor markets, in this instance students seem to have been a step ahead of colleges in connecting education and employment.

Support for Analytical, Communication, and Social Skills Development

Students who pursue programs of study that include technical as well as academic coursework can build both sets of skills, setting themselves up for both short- and long-term job and career success. Nearly all liberal arts and humanities courses provide students with opportunities to develop and refine at least some of the analytical, communication, and social skills prized by employers who are looking to the future of the work.[24] Indeed, the possibilities for career preparation already embedded in liberal arts skills have been acclaimed by some American business leaders who have called for a renewed focus on and appreciation for liberal arts and humanities education.[25] Student interest in such courses persists, with the number and share of humanities and liberal arts degrees awarded annually by community colleges having increased since 2000.[26] However, liberal arts and humanities courses do not generally enjoy a good reputation for preparing students for careers. Too often, liberal arts and humanities courses and departments do not make explicit connections between academic learning and careers, nor do they have strategies in place to help students understand how skills gained in these courses could be usefully articulated to prospective employers.[27]

Liberal arts graduates are far more likely to change careers than graduates in other majors. While over 60 percent of new graduates in information technology remain in one of two fields over the course of their careers, 70 percent of liberal arts graduates change jobs from their first to their second careers.[28]

This tendency suggests that liberal arts graduates would benefit from additional career information and advising, since changing careers can affect seniority and, ultimately, lifetime earnings, putting liberal arts graduates who change careers at a disadvantage in terms of their overall career outcomes. A survey of humanities departments at four-year institutions found that few have integrated career-focused learning into the curriculum. A majority of departments offered some career-focused programming in the form of presentations by employers or alumni, but fewer than half offered career-focused coursework or workshops.[29]

Work-Based Learning

Work-based learning—wherein students complete meaningful job tasks in a workplace—is another proven strategy for providing students with opportunities to learn about career options and build professional networks while developing their technical and employability skills, knowledge, and readiness for work. Work-based learning encompasses a wide array of learning experiences, from exposing high school students to careers through activities like job shadowing to providing incumbent workers with specialized training. Research has demonstrated that participation in work-based learning improves academic and employment outcomes.[30] The core purposes of work-based learning are to expose participants to the world of work and to career fields, to strengthen and practice academic learning, to enhance professional and/or career-track skills, and to provide a temporary or permanent job.[31] Work-based learning is also a critically important equity strategy that provides participants with opportunities to build professional networks and gain paid experience in a career field of interest. That is why Pam Eddinger and Richard Kazis argue in chapter 2 that, challenging as it may be for working adult students to take on internships, community colleges and employers together must find a way to integrate paid work experiences into community college offerings.

CONCLUSION

With the rapid evolution of occupations and shifts in the skills required for success in the labor market, colleges and universities have a critical role to play in helping students interpret labor market data and apply it as they make educational choices. Faculty and staff can use labor market data to advise students and to drive decisions about which programs of study to offer and how to structure them in a way that sets students up for long-term career success. To do so effectively, educators should support the development of career planning infrastructure—accessible to faculty, staff, and students—within their institutions.

We hope that this chapter spurs readers to think through how a career planning infrastructure might be designed through which students can access critical information about jobs and careers and their relationship to postsecondary education. There are three key areas colleges might consider in order to set students up for success in careers: supports and resources for faculty and staff, curriculum and program design, and student supports. Each of these needs to be developed to respond to the needs of specific institutions and to reflect the opportunities in the region's labor market. Most important is that more students graduate from college prepared for jobs and careers—and that students know the difference between the two. Careful attention to career planning using all the resources available will improve the employment outcomes of college graduates and help postsecondary institutions fulfill their missions. A strong career planning infrastructure equips students to find good jobs and pursue careers that support meaningful economic advancement.

CHAPTER 5

What Makes a Good Job?

– KATIE BACH AND SARAH KALLOCH –

Work is a central part of our lives. It takes up nearly a third of our waking hours. We rely on our jobs to put food on the table, pay rent, save for retirement, and access health care. For those with good jobs, work can also provide meaning and purpose, learning and growth, and friendship and support.

Unfortunately, it is not always easy to find a good job. Millions of jobs in America don't provide a living wage. The two most numerous job titles in the US are retail sales worker and food and beverage server, comprising over 15 million people. The median wages for these roles are \$11.33 and \$10.33, respectively.[1] The fastest-growing major job titles are home health aide and personal care aide, which have a median wage of \$11.57 per hour.[2]

Many workers do not get good—or any—benefits. For example, one study found more than 90 percent of low-wage workers had no access to paid family leave.[3] Thirty-five percent of workers don't have access to retirement accounts through their employer.[4] Workers often face unpredictable schedules that don't align with the demands of their lives, with last-minute changes and hours that shift week-to-week. Many jobs make no provision for career growth and are structured in ways that disrespect workers: their time is wasted, their input is ignored, and they're treated as easily replaceable cogs.

Nonetheless, many good jobs exist. For anyone whose job it is to train and place students, and for students themselves, it is critical to understand how to determine if a job will be a good one. This chapter provides guiding questions for students—and those who work with them—for assessing the quality of a potential job. We note up-to-date sources of information for workforce development and community college professionals as well as job seekers to use in searching for a good job and good employer. Like the sources cited in many of the chapters in this book, the information is public but rarely put to the service of learners. For example, how would you learn about living wages in your region? How would you find out what it's like to work at a particular company? And most important, what are the human needs that you would want your job to meet? Understanding good jobs also means learning how to balance job needs throughout one's career, and how employees can make the most of a job once they are hired.

WHAT IS A GOOD JOB?

People often use "good job" to mean "good compensation." They're not wrong: a good job provides take-home pay sufficient to cover the basic costs of living, with some left over for savings. But a good job is more than that. It also offers a schedule that fits workers' lives, a path to more responsibility and earnings, and the conditions for learning, engagement, and productivity.

The mission of the Good Jobs Institute (GJI) is to help companies thrive by creating good jobs—that is, jobs that help workers both make a living and build a career. GJI President and MIT Sloan School of Management Professor Zeynep Ton created an employee pyramid to capture the various elements that constitute a good job, including both "basic" and "higher" needs (see figure 5.1).[5] These nine factors are rooted in the academic literature on human motivation and work design, including Maslow's Hierarchy of Needs; Herzberg's Motivator-Hygiene Theory; Hackman and Oldman's Job Characteristics Model; and more recent work by Teresa Amabile, Dan Ariely, Francesca Gino, and Adam Grant.

Basic Needs

PAY AND BENEFITS Good jobs pay people enough to cover their basic expenses—rent, food, transportation, health insurance, childcare, and basic necessities (clothes, personal care items, etc.)—with enough left over for saving. Your cost of living will depend on where you live and how many people you're providing for. Tools like the MIT Living Wage Calculator and the Economic Policy Institute Family Budget Calculator provide realistic monthly living costs for every US county and a range of family sizes.[6]

FIGURE 5.1 The elements of a good job

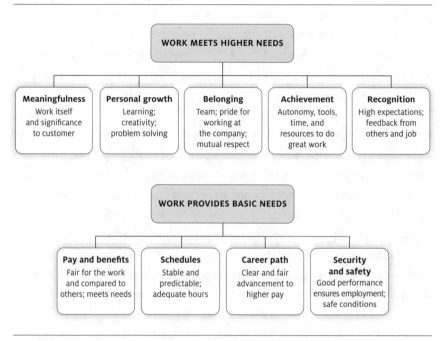

Good jobs also provide good benefits. While some Americans have access to Medicare, Medicaid, or health insurance exchanges, many rely on their employers for health insurance coverage. It is important that employers provide options with affordable premiums and deductibles to ensure that workers are able to seek and obtain care. Good jobs also provide access to retirement savings accounts—ideally with some form of match or stock share. The Economic Policy Institute has found that nearly half of American families have nothing saved for retirement.[7] The right job can help a worker avoid that situation.

SCHEDULES Wages are important to meeting basic employee needs, but so are hours. First, hours must be adequate. It's your take-home pay that matters, so if you make a living hourly wage but have inadequate hours, you will struggle to make ends meet.[8] Second, it's important to have control over your hours. Many workers are juggling a primary job, a secondary job or school, a family, and other commitments. This requires a lot of planning, and it's important to be able to set the hours when you can and cannot work. Finally, workers need schedule predictability if they are to plan their lives (childcare, school commitments, and so forth). Several cities, including Seattle, San Francisco, and New York City, have implemented scheduling laws to provide more protections for workers.

CAREER PATH Not every job is a "forever job," but companies should have clear career paths with increasing levels of responsibility and pay. This gives workers the opportunity to grow and advance without having to go through another job search. Many companies have career paths to supervisor or manager roles. Some even commit to promoting almost 100 percent from within, providing clear opportunities for upward mobility. In addition, some companies offer technical career paths, which can be a good option for someone who does not want to be a people manager. For instance, at Quest Diagnostics, you can become a supervisor or a technical call rep.

SECURITY AND SAFETY The final basic need is security and safety. This includes freedom from fear, discrimination, and harassment—a good job is one in which such conduct is dealt with swiftly and clearly. It also includes freedom from fear of layoffs. Layoffs cause immediate financial stress for workers but can also harm their career and earning potential over time. Studies show it can be harder to get a job if you don't have one, and the longer you are out of work, the harder it can be to get a job.[9]

A good job also protects workers from accidents, to the extent that it can. In 2016, 5,190 workers died in workplace accidents, and an additional 1.5 million nonfatal accidents or incidents of illness caused workers to miss days of work or be transferred, which can undermine already fragile household economies.[10]

Higher Needs

Jobs must meet basic needs, but they should also spur motivation, productivity, learning, and contribution. These five higher needs are central to giving workers the opportunity to build a career and grow as people and professionals.

BELONGING Good jobs foster strong teamwork, respect for workers, and pride in working for a particular company. Manager strength and relationships are key: Gallup has found 70 percent of employee engagement is tied to manager quality, which can help drive or undermine belonging (and frankly, all of these higher needs).[11]

ACHIEVEMENT Employees are motivated when they have the autonomy, tools, and time to do great work. Workers want to do a good job, and employers need to set them up for success. Companies that design work to respect how workers use their time and enable them to succeed create outsized value for their customers and investors.[12]

RECOGNITION Recognition is key to motivation. This doesn't just mean employee-of-the-month awards or occasional pizza parties. Recognition is about companies setting high expectations for their employees, providing positive and constructive feedback, and acknowledging good work. Companies that do this well have clear *key performance indicators* (KPIs) and task allocation, provide frequent feedback, and don't tolerate poor performance.

MEANINGFULNESS Jobs are meaningful when workers can understand how their particular tasks drive impact—for example, customer happiness or company success. Many academics have focused on job meaningfulness as a key to good work. Hackman and Oldham look at both task significance—whether the work has an impact on other people—and the work itself: does the work allow someone to complete a task top to bottom and use a variety of skills?[13] Jobs that do that tend to be more meaningful.

PERSONAL GROWTH Workers do best in roles where they can learn, grow, and problem-solve. Workers' personal growth can also drive company improvement. Many companies that offer good jobs set up systems to gather feedback and input from frontline workers. This provides workers opportunities to problem-solve, and improves standards, policies, and procedures for improving company-wide operations.

We've focused here on what a good job looks like from the perspective of the workers, and how it can benefit them. However, good jobs can also be beneficial for companies. To give just three examples of findings:

- Professor Ton, in her 2014 book *The Good Jobs Strategy*, describes how four retailers were able to deliver market-beating financial and operational results by investing more in their workers and structuring operations to maximize worker productivity, motivation, and contribution.
- Professors Carrie Leana and Jirs Meuris of the University of Pittsburgh demonstrated that financial insecurity imposes a cognitive tax on employees that can be costly to employers. In particular, they showed that financially insecure truck drivers have more accidents, and financially insecure Certified Nursing Assistants (CNAs) see worse patient outcomes.[14] A recent MetLife report stated that employees' financial stress can cost a company of ten thousand more than $28,000 in lost productivity each week.[15]
- A recent study by The Gap, Inc., and academics from the University of California, San Francisco, the University of Chicago, and the University of North Carolina at Chapel Hill found that stabler schedules decreased employee turnover (a major cost for retailers) and increased sales by 7 percent in select Gap stores.[16]

MEASURING GOOD JOBS

How does one determine if a job meets these criteria? In this section we discuss several ways of evaluating whether a prospective job is a good one.

Company Data

If you have access to a company's data, you can directly measure the quality of jobs the company offers. The GJI Good Jobs Scorecard provides categories, qualitative questions, and quantitative metrics that anyone with access to company data can answer (see box 5.1).[17] But most workforce development organizations, community colleges, and job seekers don't have that level of

BOX 5.1	**GOOD JOBS INSTITUTE EMPLOYEE METRICS SCORECARD**

Pay and Benefits
- % of employees making a living hourly wage
- % of full-time employees whose monthly compensation meets a living wage
- % of employees whose annual pay is <$10K, $10–$20K, $20–$30K, >$30K
- % of full-time employees on federal assistance
- % of temporary and/or contract workers
- Average wage compared to industry average
- Equality of pay among people doing equal work
- Benefits offered and cost to employees (health/dental/vision, paid time off, retirement, life insurance, etc.)
- Benefit eligibility requirement (usually # hours/week)
- Benefits uptake %

Schedules
- # of days/weeks' notice for schedules
- Deviation between actual and planned hours/employee/week
- % of employees working (per week): <10 hours, 10–20 hours, 20–30 hours, 30–40 hours, >40 hours
- % full-time employees
- Minimum guaranteed hours for part-time employees

Career Path
- Clear career path shared with employees early in their time with company
- % of frontline managers promoted from within
- % of field leaders promoted from within (e.g., regional and district managers)

Safety and Security
- # of safety incidents (both employee and customer)
- # of layoffs in last five years

Higher Needs
Companies may assess higher needs through employee surveys, exit interviews and stay interviews, feedback sessions, and more. If you have access to these data sources, you can use the guiding questions in the GJI scorecard to map answers to the five higher needs.

data access. Nonetheless, it is possible to assess what kind of jobs a company provides based on publicly available information and, if possible, employer interviews.

If you do have access to company data, we recommend an in-depth assessment of basic needs. This can be illuminating for employees and for companies. When we assessed average number of hours worked per week, one company partner was surprised by how many of its employees worked fewer than fifteen hours a week. Offering to help companies analyze these metrics may give community colleges and workforce organizations a path to better information on job quality.

External Sources

Institutions and applicants looking to evaluate job quality can look to several external sources for more information on both basic and higher needs met by different employers.

GLASSDOOR AND INDEED Glassdoor and Indeed crowdsource company job reviews from companies' current and former employees. While any crowdsourced platform is susceptible to bias, Glassdoor has put systems in place to reduce it.[18] Investors have begun using these sources as well. For example, Blackrock "scrapes" Glassdoor for employee sentiment, and hedge funds are also analyzing Glassdoor and other alternative data for investment insights.[19]

Both Glassdoor and Indeed show easy-to-understand overall ratings for each company, as well as the percentage of employees who would recommend the job to a friend, and the percentage who approve of the CEO. They also crowdsource wage rates, though we recommend always talking to hiring managers about pay, as the Glassdoor numbers may deviate from what a job applicant can expect.[20]

These numerical rankings are important and can give some insight into job quality. But the qualitative measure on Glassdoor can provide even more insight, especially into the harder-to-measure higher needs. Good Jobs Institute analyzes recent Glassdoor reviews of any company partner to understand what workers like and dislike about their jobs. Examples of themes GJI has seen include bad management, poor work-life balance, unsafe stores, lack of training, and bad communication, as well as pros like strong teams, good pay, stable schedules, and career growth.

Looking at reviews of job interviews on these sites can also be illuminating: you can see what kinds of questions a company asks, how formal the process is, and how applicants' time is respected—or disrespected. This can help applicants not only prepare for interviews, but also determine if the company respects workers and sets high expectations from the very beginning.

We recommend that workforce organizations, colleges, and applicants do their own analysis on Glassdoor. Reading through one or two hundred recent reviews can give you a good idea of whether a company offers good jobs or not, and what some tradeoffs may be in taking a job there. But artificial intelligence can also lend a hand. In partnership with Glassdoor and MIT Sloan Management Review, MIT senior lecturer Donald Sull and CultureX cofounder Charlie Sull have launched the Culture 500 project, which ranks major companies, based on over one million Glassdoor reviews, on nine key dimensions of corporate culture: agility, collaboration, customer centricity, diversity, execution, innovation, integrity, performance, and respect.[21] On their website, you can see rankings by dimension, company, or industry and see how companies score across these key measures.[22] Culture 500 has found companies that respect their workers score higher on overall culture—something GJI has identified as key for good jobs.

JUST CAPITAL JUST Capital ranks the one thousand largest, publicly traded US companies across a crowdsourced set of categories, including environment, community contribution, and workforce. It looks at whether a company provides benefits (including paid time off, access to health insurance, paid parental leave, and retirement support), a living wage, a safe workplace without discrimination, and other measures. Its data are publicly available.

B CORPS B Lab has certified more than 2,900 companies in 64 countries as "benefit corporations" (B Corps), which must meet high standards of social and environmental performance, transparency, and good governance. B Corps exist in every state and include everything from startups to long-established companies. For example, Ben and Jerry's, Patagonia, Cabot, Eileen Fisher, and New Belgium Brewing are all B Corps. To qualify, companies must fill out an assessment, which includes an extensive section on workers. Questions include data about:

- **Pay:** lowest paid wage, percentage of employees making a living wage, percentage getting a bonus
- **Benefits:** percentage of workers participating in health-care plan, eligibility by hours worked, number of paid days off, retirement plan offered
- **Schedules:** number of full-time, part-time, and temporary workers

In keeping with B Lab's commitment to transparency, these assessments are public for all Certified B Corporations.

CEO/WORKER PAY COMPARISON As part of 2010's Dodd–Frank Wall Street Reform and Consumer Protection Act, publicly traded companies are required to disclose their CEO pay and median worker pay. More than one thousand companies shared this data in 2019, though without full access to their data sets it can be hard to understand median worker pay.[23] For instance, Abercrombie & Fitch reported an average employee wage of $2,991 versus Macy's $21,855, but without the full data set, it is hard to know what this means about wage levels (e.g., it may reflect a very high number of seasonal or part-time workers at Abercrombie). That said, these median-wage rates can indicate whether a company has a lot of workers who work few hours. You can see data by industry and compare company mean wages to see who may offer higher wages and more hours.

Customer Satisfaction

Employees' experience with the company is not the only marker of a good job. Customer satisfaction scores are another potential indicator of good (or bad) jobs. If customers are unhappy, it is often the case that employees are too.

CROWDSOURCED REVIEWS Yelp and other crowdsourced platforms can provide a different snapshot into job experience through the customer lens. Workplaces that are dirty and unsafe, with employees who aren't well trained and/

or don't provide great service, likely do not offer great jobs—all things customers pick up on and describe in reviews.

RANKINGS There are many customer service rankings and reports available to the public, often by industry. ACSI, *Consumer Reports*, Temkin index, NPS, and others may all give insights into customer satisfaction, which can (but doesn't always) translate to better employee experiences.

Interviews and Informal Conversations

If you're considering joining a company, we recommend talking with the people in your network (e.g., friends of friends) who work for the company to get their perspectives. A job interview is also a good time to ask questions about the job. For organizations and agencies that place workers, setting up a system to vet potential employers can help ensure you are putting students into good jobs. The following questions, organized by category, can be a good starting point for workforce development organizations, community colleges, and job seekers to ask people from different companies.

PAY AND BENEFITS

- What is the starting pay?
- How often do workers get pay increases? By how much does pay increase at those times? (Make sure you're asking for the role you're considering.)
- Are there any incentive programs in place (including bonuses)? How do they work? On average, what percentage of workers get that incentive?
- What benefits are available to full- and part-time workers—and what counts as full time? When do the benefits go into effect (i.e., is there a waiting period)?
- For benefits that workers have to buy into (e.g., health care): How much do they cost? (For example, for health care: What is the premium? How high are the deductibles under each plan?)
- For 401(k) or retirement accounts: Does the employer provide a match?

SCHEDULES If an hourly/shift-based job:

- How much control do workers have over the hours they work (total number, and when they work)?
- How many hours can a worker expect to get per week/per month?
- How far in advance do workers get their schedule? How often are there last-minute changes?
- Can workers swap shifts with other workers if they need to? How?
- How do workers access their schedule (e.g., online, in-person only)?
- Are workers expected to work weekends/holidays? Do they get extra pay for any holidays?
- What is the employer's percentage of full-time versus part-time workers?

If a salaried/nonshift job:

- How many hours would someone [in the relevant role] be expected to work each week? (Here, it's possible you'll hear something different from an informal chat versus an interview. It's important to go in with your eyes open—some jobs that claim to be forty hours per week demand much more in actuality.)
- How often does that include weekend work? How often do people have to stay late?
- How much flexibility is there in the role? (For example, is it possible to work from home ever? To come in late or leave early if you need to?)

CAREER PATH
- What is the career path for an employee [in the relevant role]?
- What percentage of people who start in this role are promoted? How long does it usually take?
- What percentage of supervisors or managers are promoted from within?
- How much training will a new employee [in the relevant role] receive? How much when they first join, and how much later? How does the training work? (For example: In your first few weeks, will you have a mentor to help you? Whom do you go to if you have questions?)

- How is performance evaluated? For example: What performance indicators matter most for this role? Do employees get formal reviews? How frequently do employees get informal feedback from managers and coworkers?

SAFETY AND SECURITY
- When was your last round of layoffs?
- How many safety incidents have you had in the past year? What are you doing to make workers more safe?
- Do you have an anti-harassment policy? If there is harassment, whom does the employee tell?

HIGHER NEEDS
- How would you describe the work environment? What about the company culture? (For example, you may want to ask if it's warm, supportive, hierarchical, strict, etc.)
- What are the company values? (And, in informal chats, ask if the company lives those values.)
- Are employees set up to succeed? How?
- Are employees empowered to solve problems, come up with new ideas, and manage their own work?
- Does the job allow employees to use personal initiative? Judgment? Creativity?
- Are there opportunities for teamwork? How often?
- What is your turnover rate? Why do people leave? Why do people stay?

MAKING ANY JOB A BETTER JOB

Career Tradeoffs: Now Jobs Versus Careers

Not every job has to be a forever job. Even jobs that don't meet every one of our "good jobs" criteria can help build experience, skill sets, and careers:

- *Job experience builders.* Some jobs, which Aspen Institute refers to as "now" jobs, can serve as a stepping-stone for workers to gain experience and build a résumé.[24] For young workers with limited experience, they may need a first job that provides income, proves they have mastered the basics of employment, and gives them a professional network/ reference. These jobs may not offer great pay, benefits, or career paths, but they can help young workers get the experience they need to get a good job.

- *Skill set builders.* If there is a particular skill set a worker wants to build, he may want to take a job for a period of time that does not meet all the good jobs criteria. This may be particularly relevant if he's trying to make a career change. For example, a newly trained nurse may decide to work in a hospital for a year or two even though the schedule isn't a great fit because there is a hospital skill set that can't be acquired elsewhere. Then, he can switch to a job with better hours.
- *Career builders.* For companies that offer clear (and reasonably quick) career paths, it may make sense for workers to take a lower-paying or lower-responsibility job and work their way up. One Costco employee we interviewed was offered two jobs during his job search: one running a butchery at a grocery store chain and one as a meat cutter as Costco. Even though it was a lower-paying and lower-status job, he took the Costco job because he knew the company offered good jobs and strong career paths. Making a short-term sacrifice made sense for him: he quickly worked his way up to meat manager, and now helps launch butcheries in new stores around the country.

On-the-Job Improvements

Ideally, all workers would be able to find jobs that are already good jobs. In reality, even decent jobs won't be perfect. Once a worker is on the job, she can take steps to get the most out of the experience, build skills, build her network, and identify opportunities for advancement.

1. *Understand career and mobility paths.* Be proactive in asking about career paths, skills needed to move up, and other opportunities for advancement or growth. These may include lateral moves to other locations or business units.
2. *Ask for feedback.* Ask your managers for feedback on your performance—and, if you can, link it to what you know about what it takes

to move up in the organization. For example, a good question to ask is, "What should I be working on if I want to move up to the next level?" This helps your managers target their feedback, and it flags that you're looking to move up. If possible, work with them to set a performance development plan—formal or informal—which can help outline what skills and experiences you want to build and how they can support you.

3. *Ask for additional responsibilities.* If you want to build skills or grow in your job, ask for more responsibilities. Offer to learn a new technology or support a team on a project. This can expand your network, give you more skills, and highlight your talent to managers.

4. *Network at work.* Get to know other employees and managers. Learn about their career paths and what has made a difference to them. Ask about their best job and what they liked about it. This can build a network to answer your questions, provide ideas on how to succeed, and possibly lead to opportunities to work in a different department or help out with new projects outside your team.

5. *Identify and build transferable skills.* To maximize growth and career flexibility, find opportunities to develop "transferrable" skills—those that can be used across a range of work environments. For example, these might include communication skills (presenting, using Power-Point, writing), analytical skills (using Excel, conducting any sort of quantitative analysis), problem solving, or specific technical skills (for example, knowing how to program in a specific computer language).

6. *Find a mentor.* A mentor could be a supervisor in another department or an experienced employee with a great skill set. A mentor may also be outside your workplace—a former manager or teacher, for example. Mentors can help people sharpen their professional goals, outline transferable skills, network, and reach new career goals. To make the relationship work for both of you, make sure to be respectful of your mentor's time, and try to support your mentor wherever possible.

7. *Keep in touch with your wider network.* Just because you've landed a job doesn't mean you will be there forever. Keep in touch with professors, former colleagues, classmates, and community contacts. Share with them what you are learning and what your goals are for your career.

Ask about their career paths and why they made the choices they did. And when it comes time to find a new job, ask them to connect you to contacts they may have.

8. *Start a job search.* If a job is not the right fit, do all of the above—and start a job search. It is easier to find a job when you have a job, so engage your networks and find the next opportunity to build your career.

CONCLUSION

Good jobs can provide workers a living as well as meaning, dignity, growth, and community. Having clear criteria for which jobs may meet basic and higher employee needs is critical for job seekers, educators, and job placement agencies. Asking the right questions and accessing key publicly available information can provide the data needed to make more informed decisions and help workers build stronger career paths and a firm financial future.

Theory and Evidence

IMPLICATIONS FOR PRACTICE

CHAPTER 6

The Psychology of Working Theory

A Theory of Change for Personal and Systemic Intervention

– DAVID L. BLUSTEIN AND MAUREEN E. KENNY[1] –

I never was one of those kids that say, "I'm just going to do that one thing." I wanted to do everything! But in thinking about it, I knew that . . . God, resources were constrained. And thinking about how do you get there . . . I mean, I saw it: it would be exciting to be that person, or do that thing, but how do you get there? So, I think one of the challenges and obstacles was the in-between stuff. And it's hard to quantify what that looks like. It's just like: OK, I need to get to college to get to the next step. All right, so how do I get to college? I need to submit an application and so forth. . . . Well, my parents never went through that process, so. . . . Navigating it wasn't something that was intuitive. It wasn't hard necessarily, but it was just something that others that have had relatives or others that went through that, it was easier for them to navigate. So I think just navigating the challenges, and really . . . gaining understanding as you go from one challenge to the next, how fortunate. . . . You know, you think, "Wow! It's really interesting not having. . . . If I only had this particular resource; it would be easy to move to the next step."

The quote that starts this chapter is part of the Boston College Working Project, which has sought to explore the nature of work in the US.[2] This participant, Benny, a thirty-eight-year-old African American career development practitioner/administrator at a major university in a northeastern city, conveys a story that he shared about his adolescence, growing up on the South Side of Chicago in a working-class family. His discussion of trying to navigate the "in-between stuff" captures an important aspect of this chapter, and indeed, this book. How can educators, public policy leaders, and workforce/ career professionals provide culturally relevant, authentic, and effective interventions to help students like Benny move from being a young man with dreams to a purposeful professional who is making a difference in the lives of so many?

Throughout the twentieth century, theories and practices in education and counseling were developed to help young people navigate the maze of work-based options that became more prevalent with the advent of the Industrial Revolution and ongoing technological innovations.[3] For the most part, these theories focused on helping people make decisions that optimally reflected their values, interests, and abilities. By the end of the twentieth century, the field of career development (which includes career counseling, vocational psychology, and career development education) had established a firm foundation of evidence-based theories to promote adaptive interventions for adolescents and adults. Some of these theories focused on enhancing the fit between individual characteristics and the demands of a given work setting, while others focused more on promoting adaptive decision-making across the life span.[4] However, many of these theories were not sufficiently inclusive, resulting in marginalizing students and adults who most needed help in navigating their educational and work contexts. In this chapter, we present a new and innovative theory to describe how people navigate the world of work: *psychology of working theory* (PWT).[5] We argue that PWT is perfectly suited to describe how Benny—with help from his community, schools, teachers, mentors, family, and his own psychological resources—navigated the many barriers in his life to not just land on his feet, but to attain a level of meaning and fulfillment in his career that is one of the great gifts of life.

OVERVIEW OF PSYCHOLOGY OF WORKING THEORY

Although the world of career counseling and vocational psychology (the research arm of career development) seemed robust in the late twentieth century, something was amiss. Vast pockets of American society were struggling to gain a foothold in the promise of an upwardly mobile society. By the end of the century, most career choice and development theories focused on individuals with relative volition in their lives. In effect, the career development world morphed into a field focusing on the lives of those with career choice privilege—the capacity to create and implement a career based on one's interests, values, and aspirations. Throughout the latter part of the twentieth century, however, many advocates and practitioners critiqued this circumscribed approach, highlighting the struggles that women, people of color, immigrants, and the working class/poor faced in gaining access to the American Dream.[6] As an alternative to the traditional focus on career choice and development, PWT sought to be a game-changer in the career development and workforce development world.[7] This conceptual movement complemented a shift in the labor market as relatively decent jobs in manufacturing were lost due to globalization and technology, thereby reducing one of the most viable ways for working-class youth to move into the middle class. With the advent of increasingly precarious work (i.e., short-term contract work, gig economy jobs, and jobs that are inherently unstable) and the awareness of the implicit limitations of traditional career counseling and education, it was time to rethink the career development enterprise, which is what PWT represents—a significant turn toward greater inclusion and broader impact.[8]

PWT sought to unpack the implicit and explicit assumptions of career development by arguing that access to education and work is in fact more constrained, and the sources of the barriers are more often located in contextual factors and not necessarily within individuals. The barriers identified included poverty, racism, sexism, heterosexism, classism, and other forms of social oppression that regrettably plague societies around the world. In addition, PWT sought to develop an interdisciplinary perspective, embracing psychology, education, sociology, and economics. A recent summary of PWT identified the following assumptions underlying this framework:

- work functions as a major context for individual well-being and the welfare of communities;
- work shares psychological space with many other salient life domains with mutual and recursive impact;
- access to work is constrained by powerful social, economic, and political forces;

- working includes both efforts in the marketplace and in caregiving contexts; and
- psychological and systemic interventions need to include all of those who work and who want to work.[9]

These assumptions capture a broad and critical set of guideposts for the development of a formal theoretical statement of PWT. PWT represents a specific interdisciplinary model that encompasses relationships between macro-level contextual factors and psychological factors that shape access to work.[10] At the center of PWT is *decent work*, a concept that was developed by the International Labor Organization (ILO), which is a long-standing affiliate of the UN.[11] The advent of the Decent Work Agenda by the ILO represented a major initiative to create better work conditions for people across the globe. The ILO advanced this concept to create a consensus about the fundamental aspects of work that should be available to all who work and who want to work. These attributes include the following characteristics: "(a) physical and interpersonally safe working conditions (e.g., absent of physical, mental, or emotional abuse), (b) hours that allow for free time and adequate rest, (c) organizational values that complement family and social values, (d) adequate compensation, and (e) access to adequate health care."[12] Decent work would not necessarily include a career that has intrinsic meaning for individuals; rather, the ILO views it as a set of globally agreed-upon attributes that should guide the development of working conditions that are fair and humane. Despite the consensus about decent work across the globe and among relevant constituencies (governments, labor unions, employers), the reality is that decent work is not available for all who work and who want to work.[13]

Predictors in PWT

PWT proposes that two sets of macro-level factors provide a powerful shaping influence on access to decent work: economic constraints and marginalization, which have often been viewed as secondary influences in many career development theories. *Economic constraints* capture such issues as poverty and lack of access to the needed resources that can provide the social capital needed for an adaptive transition to decent work (e.g., health care, housing, good schools). *Marginalization* refers to the pervasive impact of racism, sexism, heterosexism, and other forms of social barriers that serve to constrain opportunities for so many people.

Both economic constraints and marginalization shape two particularly important psychological attributes—work volition and career adaptability, which are central in PWT. *Work volition* reflects one's perception of the capacity to actually implement decisions and choices in one's work life. Although work volition is clearly shaped by real barriers in life, it is also a psychological variable that may be amenable to change and intervention.[14] For example, developing skills to overcome barriers might enhance one's work volition, which could enhance opportunities and options. Considerable research has identified the important role that work volition plays in career decision-making, meaning at work, and job and life satisfaction.[15] *Career adaptability* refers to "an individual's readiness and resources for coping with current and anticipated tasks of vocational development."[16] Career adaptability for high school and community college students would be reflected by the capacity to explore one's options, plan ahead for the future, and feel confident and agentic about the career development process.

Moderators in PWT

As in our lived experiences, various external and internal factors have the capacity to moderate or influence our lives. In PWT, four specific moderators are identified.[17] The first three moderators reflect internal psychological factors and the last reflects a macro-level condition. The first moderator is *proactive personality*, which taps into individuals' disposition or tendency to take action and engage in mastering the challenges in their own lives. The second moderator is *critical consciousness*, which refers to the capacity to understand the overt and covert contributions of systemic factors in the allocation of societal resources and human outcomes and to respond to this awareness in a purposeful manner. This construct is discussed in depth in the second part of this chapter given that it has significant implications for practice and policy. The third moderator is *social support*, which has a clear role in the work-related context; people with access to supportive family, friends, teachers, mentors, and work supervisors benefit from the relational connections and instrumental assistance of others in their work lives.[18] These three moderators, when considered collectively, reflect the importance of individual and interpersonal factors in providing a way of attenuating aversive life circumstances and in enhancing the resources that individuals can enlist to support their hopes and dreams for a better future.

The fourth moderator is *economic conditions*, which represents the influence of such factors as the unemployment rate in a given community, access to decent work and jobs, and the availability of living wages for workers.[19] Economic conditions capture the broad and complex impact of national, regional, and local work-related factors that clearly influence one's aspirations, volition, and adaptability as well as the attainment of the rewards of working, which are reviewed next.

Outcomes in PWT

Locating a job that includes the attributes of decent work is certainly a valuable goal; however, PWT views work, when it is going well, as having the potential to meet an array of psychological needs, optimally leading to feeling fulfillment at work and overall well-being.[20] In articulating outcomes beyond decent work, PWT shares underlying goals of traditional career choice and development theories—work, at its best, can provide people with lives of meaning and purpose as well as well-being.[21] The needs taxonomy that PWT has developed is based on an integration of previous needs frameworks, including the work of Abraham Maslow and others.[22]

The first of the needs included in PWT is the need for *survival and power*. At its most fundamental level, work has been embedded in human history to provide people with a means of ensuring that they can survive and even thrive in the world. The power aspect reflects the need for people to attain a capacity to exert power and influence in their lives. The second set of needs is *social and relational* in nature. Working provides people with one of the key social locations in their adult lives. Thus, working can fulfill our natural needs for affiliation and connection; at the same time, it can provide people with a sense of contributing to the overall welfare of the world, which also reflects a natural striving for meaning and connection to others. The third set of needs taps into our striving for *self-determination*—a life wherein people can experience a sense of authentic engagement in activities that are intrinsically meaningful and that fulfill our extrinsic needs.

The ultimate outcomes of an optimal satisfying and dignified work life would include work fulfillment and well-being. *Work fulfillment* reflects the ideal hope that one's work life will yield activities that are meaningful and optimally satisfying. *Well-being* refers to one's evaluation of life; this evaluation encompasses both emotional and cognitive dimensions, reflecting an internal sense of how well an individual feels about life, including but not limited to work.[23]

As reflected in this summary of PWT, this new theoretical approach has the capacity to explain and inform the work lives of a wide range of students and working people across regions and communities. Using constructs from psychology, economics, and sociology provides the framework for a theory that replicates life—we are influenced by our contexts, writ large, and we also shape our contexts. In the section that follows, we summarize how PWT has informed career development practice and workforce development efforts.

APPLICATIONS OF PWT TO CAREER DEVELOPMENT AND WORKFORCE DEVELOPMENT

In offering a revised understanding of the role of work in human lives and the factors that limit access to the psychological and economic benefits of work for so many people, PWT can transform how we prepare individuals for work and can be applied to shape societal institutions to more inclusively meet the needs of workers. As a growing body of research is supporting the central premises set forth by PWT, the Boston College Working Project has also articulated the practical implications of the model for educational and vocational intervention.[24] The practice implications of PWT largely focus on enhancing PWT outcomes by intervening to shape the array of predictor and moderator factors. Following from the central role afforded to social and economic factors as facilitators and constraints in shaping access to need fulfillment in the contemporary workplace, PWT offers a framework for research and intervention at the personal and systemic levels. In this regard, PWT is "a theory of change for a new era," one that can powerfully reshape career and educational services across high schools, higher education, and the workplace by aligning educational and vocational practice with a social justice agenda.[25]

Although much attention has been given to the need for prospective employees to gain advanced educational and technological skills in order to be competitive in the rapidly changing workplace, this perspective overlooks the powerful role of systemic barriers in limiting access and advancement in work and life more broadly.[26] In recognition of the power of social and economic factors, PWT directs attention to an array of individual factors that can equip individuals to better navigate, negotiate, and transform the barriers they are likely to encounter. PWT also recognizes the importance for those who are in privileged positions and those who have been marginalized to strive to reduce systemic barriers and to increase the availability of stable work that fulfills the economic, social, and psychological needs of employees. We will discuss individual and systemic interventions separately, while also recognizing how critical reflection and action, proactive engagement, and social support and community engagement are integral in propelling agentic action and effective intervention at both levels.[27]

Following from PWT and supported by empirical research in career and related fields, we put forth a model of individual intervention and systemic change to guide practice and policy work in diverse settings.[28] The first of the three clusters outlined is *critical reflection and action*, which is aligned with the construct of critical consciousness, defined earlier in the chapter. Critical consciousness, which includes critical reflection and action, has been described as an antidote for oppression based on the premise that by gaining critical awareness of the systemic roots of social ills, individuals can dispel negative stereotypes and gain a sense of agency to effect personal and social change.[29] In support of this premise, a growing body of research has documented positive associations between the presence of critical consciousness and the academic and work attainment of youth who have faced numerous economic constraints and marginalization.[30] *Proactive engagement* addresses the role of agency in responding to, managing, and altering environmental factors, and is aligned with the constructs of work volition, career adaptability, and proactive personality in the PWT model. *Social support and community engagement* are also aligned with the recognition of relational support in the PWT model and are based on the large body of research that attests to the importance of social support, as well as collaboration and community organizing, in managing stressors and mobilizing for social change.[31]

Individual Interventions

By building critical reflection and action, proactive engagement, and social support, PWT can be effectively infused across individual and group career and personal counseling interventions, career development education, and broader education initiatives. In building critical consciousness, students who have experienced economic barriers and marginalization can learn to recognize and resist the negative impact of societal barriers, without unduly blaming themselves or others who have been disempowered or disadvantaged by political, social, and economic factors.[32] At the same time, interventions that foster critical reflection and action can guide students who have not personally experienced marginalization in increasing awareness of societal barriers and gaining the motivation and agency to join with others in reducing barriers and expanding access to decent work.

Critical reflection and action have been effectively integrated in educational courses in the social sciences, sciences, and literary arts and in service-learning activities at the high school and higher education levels.[33] We maintain that critical reflection and action are increasingly central to career development interventions that seek to reduce barriers and increase access to decent work among young people who have been traditionally marginalized. Some examples of this are evident in current practice. For example, critical consciousness has become an integral component of some programs designed to increase interest and entry of underrepresented groups into the sciences by helping students to critically assess social problems and to identify how they can use science to provide solutions to social ills experienced in their community.[34] With regard to work preparation, Mary Gatta developed a required social science course at Guttman Community College, Ethnographies of Work, that fosters critical reflection. Students complete analytical readings and enter the workplace as researchers who observe and reflect on the nature of work in ways that develop critical awareness of systemic factors and cultural knowledge of the workplace.[35] At the high school level, Leigh Patel developed a critical consciousness internship program for recently immigrated youth, which included a professional-level internship in the workplace along with a space outside of the internship where critical conversations about power, status, and society were facilitated along with reflections on their personal and workplace experiences.[36] Critical reflections can help students think about the skills that are needed and rewarded in the workplace; how to identify and navigate obstacles; how changes in the global economy are changing the work opportunities and requirements; and the nature of decent work, who enjoys it, and how individuals can more effectively access these opportunities.

Theory and research in critical consciousness maintain that critical awareness is not enough, as awareness of systemic oppression by itself can be discouraging and lead to hopelessness.[37] Many interventions do not move beyond critical reflection to foster social action.[38] Proactive engagement and social support are crucial additions in moving from critical reflection to individual action and social change. Proactive engagement in the contemporary workplace refers to developing the capacities to adapt to ongoing change and to maintain effort in working toward one's goals despite constraints. Developing an action plan or strategy to address barriers and work toward a more just society is also integral for social change. Eliciting social support, building collaborations, and community engagement are vital not only for meeting the omnipresent need for human relationship, but also in offering supports needed to cope with inevitable challenges. Collective effort also strengthens the power and capacity for effective social action. Given the inequities and challenges of contemporary society and the working world, educational efforts that seek to prepare young people and adults for accessing and advancing in decent work would do well to incorporate critical reflection and action, proactive engagement and social support, collaboration, and community engagement. Some programs that have employed participatory action research in guiding young people in analyzing a social problem, and then moving forward in a plan for collective social action, offer examples of how this might be facilitated.[39]

System-Level Intervention

As a theory of change, PWT also emphasizes the critical need for system-level change in order to realize equitable access to decent work for all. In this way, PWT goes beyond the traditional focus of work preparation and career intervention on helping individuals to adapt to existing systems to a focus on actually mitigating oppressive structures. System-level change can be implemented proximally at the school, university, community, or workplace levels, and on a macro level by focusing on structural or policy change at the state, national, and international levels. The processes of critical reflection and action, proactive engagement, and social support remain integral to system-level intervention. A careful needs assessment represents a first step in analyzing how system-level factors are contributing overtly and covertly to marginalization, inequity, and economic constraints along the pathway to decent work. Critical consciousness offers the lens for the needs assessment, which serves to identify the public policies, economic structures, and labor practice that become the focus for proactive engagement and critical action. Gaining community support and building coalitions are particularly important as one seeks to effect systemic change and to bolster oneself from the pushback that often accompanies efforts to challenge established systems of power.

System-level intervention begins with the development of critical awareness among individuals and groups to identify the systemic forces that maintain the status quo, rather than to blame individuals for their disadvantage. While students can be empowered to effect systemic change through social action, system-level intervention needs to be a focus of adults in community organizations, educational institutions, employment settings, and government entities. Those who hold power to effect change by themselves, or in alliance with students or other groups experiencing marginalization, have the capacity to enact substantive changes in systems that can have a real impact in the lives of students seeking a place in a work life of decency and dignity. Critical awareness can be developed through participation in group seminars, attending lectures, and individual reading and reflection, among other strategies. For individuals and groups, challenging the system may entail activities such as supporting and working for political candidates with agendas that affirm human rights and decent work, joining existing organizations that are working for systemic change, and pushing professional organizations to advocate for equity and decent work.[40] Scholars can conduct research on vital work and educational issues, author editorials and blogs, and publish their research findings in forums that bring critical awareness and reflection on issues of decent work to a broader audience. Presenting relevant research to legislative groups at the local, state, and national levels can be another important strategy in systemic intervention.

At the school and higher education level, critical reflection and proactive engagement can be applied by developing and implementing admissions and hiring policies to decrease inequity and marginalization. Other applications include designing curriculum structures, policies, and courses that promote success for all students. Particularly relevant to the focus of this volume is developing internships and courses on work that challenge the status quo, as well as creating school policies and structures that ensure the success of such courses. Employers similarly need to examine personnel policies and work structures that perpetuate marginalization in hiring and advancement and threaten employee well-being in their workplaces. Challenge to oppressive systemic structures can be exerted by leaders and other employees with critical awareness within organizations, or by groups outside of the organization, who can join with oppressed groups to present their needs assessment and press for change through collaborative action.

CONCLUSION

We believe that PWT provides a critically needed lens that can inform interventions and education designed to promote adaptive and creative strategies that support individuals as they navigate an increasingly uncertain world. As reflected in the vignette from Benny at the outset of this chapter, the "in-between stuff" often is where the obstacles—inadequate schools, inconsistent relational support, racism, classism, poverty, ineffective social institutions—are the most pernicious. PWT seeks to highlight the complexity of this in-between stuff, which is made up of contextual and individual factors, and which looks different across communities, cultures, and time periods. We hope that this chapter helps to set the stage for these important efforts and that it also draws more educators, policy experts, and workforce development professionals to the challenging task of ensuring that all of our citizens can attain a life of decency and dignity at work.

Work-Related Barriers Experienced by Low-Income People of Color and Indigenous Individuals

– GLORIA MCGILLEN, LISA FLORES, AND GREGORY SEATON –

Oppression and marginalization within the US are long-standing and deeply ingrained across all institutions in our society. Enduring social disparities in academic achievement and educational attainment result in and are promoted by socioeconomic stratification and occupational segregation, and this has had adverse effects on both individuals from these marginalized racial/ethnic groups and society as a whole. When a society does not fully utilize the human capital among its people, talents that can advance society are lost.

Across the life span, people spend a considerable amount of time in school and work settings, and people from socially marginalized groups in the US (most notably, people of color, indigenous individuals, and people from poor and working-class backgrounds) experience institutional barriers within these settings that prevent them from realizing their potential and achieving their educational and occupational goals. This is manifested in several ways, such as persistent racial/ethnic and social class disparities in academic performance and achievement at secondary and postsecondary levels; disproportionate unemployment and underemployment rates among diverse racial/ethnic groups; underrepresentation of diverse racial/ethnic individuals in high-paying, professional jobs; and the lack of diversity in leadership positions within business and other professional sectors. Today, people of color, indigenous individuals, and people from poor and working-class backgrounds continue to struggle to gain access to quality education and decent work, and these disparities persist at a time when the representation of people of color as a portion of the total population is growing in the US. These struggles are enhanced among individuals who belong to multiple marginalized groups, such as poor people of color or women of color. Consequently, professionals who work with people of color, indigenous people, and people from low-income backgrounds need to carefully understand their experiences with barriers in both academic and work contexts to better serve their needs, to assist them in reaching their work-related goals, and to find ways to reduce institutional barriers within the systems where they study and work.

Barriers are different than obstacles. *Obstacles* include any challenge that impedes or delays progress toward one's goals, whereas *barriers* refer to structural challenges that are more difficult to overcome, prevent access to fulfilling one's goals, or shape one's path in such ways that individuals may avoid or abandon some work opportunities altogether. Everyone experiences obstacles in life; however, experiences with barriers and lack of access to the resources to overcome real or perceived barriers vary across individuals. So, too, will individuals' awareness of anticipated barriers and their ability to accurately identify barriers as they occur. Thus, it is important to consider ways to educate students about the barriers they may face in the process of pursuing education or searching for a job or in the work setting. It is equally important to help students label barriers that are rooted within institutions, to prevent them from internalizing or attributing their academic and work challenges to personal or group limitations.

An awareness of the work barriers encountered by people of color, indigenous individuals, and people from poor and working-class backgrounds is important because these barriers can have both direct and indirect effects on work opportunities and outcomes. In fact, research indicates that people of color do not differ from whites in their educational and work aspirations.[1] However, they anticipate more academic and work barriers and report greater difficulty in overcoming anticipated barriers than whites.[2] These differences are further exacerbated among immigrant high school students of color without documentation, who report additional barriers to postsecondary education.[3] Latinas and older students with documentation challenges were less likely to report plans to attend college than their male and younger student counterparts.[4] The anticipation of barriers to achieving their academic and work aspirations may in part explain why people of color report fewer perceived career options and lower expectations for reaching their work goals when compared to their white peers.[5]

Perceived barriers may also impact work and work options in other adverse ways. For example, high perceived barriers were related to career indecision, low-prestige occupational choices and occupational choices dominated by one's gender group, and low career aspirations.[6] Others have noted that the effects of barriers are related to those factors that influence occupational choices, such as vocational identity, interests, self-efficacy beliefs, and outcome expectations.[7] Recent meta-analysis studies found that barriers also were negatively related to grade point average, engagement, and persistence.[8] Clearly, barriers have a significant influence on job choices, and can alter the effect of other variables that have been shown to positively influence academic and career decisions.

First-generation college students and prospective first-generation college students, or students whose parents did not complete a bachelor's degree, are more likely to come from poor and working-class backgrounds.[9] These students report high academic aspirations, but more barriers than their peers with parents who completed college.[10] These experiences with barriers slow their progression in college or prevent their completion of a bachelor's degree altogether.[11] Indeed, research indicates that among prospective first-generation college students, perceived barriers were related to self-efficacy beliefs, an important predictor of a range of occupational outcomes.[12] This has important occupational implications, given that in today's labor market, college education is a necessary pathway for a broad range of jobs, particularly those that are stable and provide financial security. Considering the challenges that first-generation and other economically disadvantaged college students encounter in their academic pursuits, more attention is needed to support their educational goals and especially their transition into the world of work following college.[13]

This chapter will cover common barriers that are experienced by people of color and indigenous individuals from low-income backgrounds in academic and work settings and will offer a strengths-based perspective on how professionals can empower students from such backgrounds to address the barriers they encounter. After a brief discussion of the origins of academic and workplace barriers in the first section, we highlight general structural or institutional barriers that people of color and indigenous individuals experience in their career development. We also address internal barriers that can develop as a result of the persistent, pernicious systemic barriers faced by people of color, indigenous individuals, and low-income people. In the second half of the chapter, we review strategies for dealing with work barriers at both the individual and systemic levels. Our hope is that professionals who work with students of color and indigenous students from low-income backgrounds can help these students become aware of the barriers that they might face and equip them with the skills for dealing with them effectively. More importantly, we offer suggestions for how professionals can advocate for students of color and indigenous students to reduce barriers and increase relevant supports within the academic settings and other systems that may affect the work options and workplace experiences of these students.

ORIGINS OF ACADEMIC AND WORK-RELATED BARRIERS

Since its founding, the US has been marked by steep hierarchies in institutional access to power, resources, and educational and economic opportunities according to racial/ethnic group and social class position. Low-income people of color and indigenous individuals have persistently faced special hardships at the intersection of racial/ethnic and class marginalization and oppression, while groups of European working-class and poor migrants who joined in the settler project, in contrast, became steadily incorporated into notions of a white, self-governing "American" people to whom the nation properly belonged.[14] This culture of white supremacy existing across the class spectrum created deep, persistent fissures in the US working class.[15] These divisions became more numerous after the passage of the 1965 Immigration Act enabled greater immigration to the US from Asia, South and Central America, and Africa.[16] Privilege attached to white racial status continues to contribute to significant intraclass racial disparities among the US working class and poor today in areas including neighborhood resources, schooling, and employment, with implication for youths' academic and career development.[17] In the following section, we provide an overview of both structural and internal barriers that low-income people of color encounter in their academic and work pursuits. We take a developmental approach to address how these barriers are manifested at different stages of the career development process for low-income people of color.

STRUCTURAL AND INSTITUTIONAL BARRIERS

People of color and indigenous people from poor and working-class backgrounds routinely face the most challenging economic and social conditions of all individuals and the most structural barriers to upward social mobility.[18] The implications of these conditions for their academic and career development are numerous. They can be organized developmentally, beginning with childhood development and K–12 and higher education, and then transitioning to labor market and workplace experiences and their interaction with individuals' family lives. While many of these conditions have existed for generations, others emerged during the Great Recession of 2008 and have since persisted.[19] We pay special attention to these recent concerns to offer a picture of the evolving and, in many respects, increasingly difficult educational and vocational landscape that people of color and indigenous people from low-income backgrounds in the US must navigate.

Childhood Development and K–12 Education

The pervasive nature of racism and colonialism, and the manner in which they are compounded by class disadvantage for many families of color and indigenous families, impacts children from the beginning of development. Children of color and indigenous children from low-income families are 3 to 12 percent more likely than low-income white children to live in poverty.[20] Low-income black children are also roughly 10 percent more likely than low-income white children to experience "deep poverty" (i.e., to live in a household that falls below half of the federal poverty line), and Native American children are also impacted at higher rates.[21] Exposure to poverty is associated with outcomes that harm children academically, including poorer mental and behavioral health, more difficulties in forming relationships, and delays in cognitive development.[22] During the Great Recession and in the first years of the post-recession recovery, black and Latinx families experienced 9 percent and 6.3 percent growth in child poverty, respectively, in contrast with white families, who saw an increase of only 3 percent.[23]

Most youth in the US attend public schools or public charter schools that receive much of their funding from local taxes.[24] The prevalence and concentration of poverty in settings where families of color and indigenous families reside have important implications for their children's likelihood of attending an underresourced school. Concentrated poverty is more prevalent in public schools serving neighborhoods where a majority of residents are people of color rather than white.[25] This pattern is influenced by decades of racial "redlining" and residential segregation, government and business disinvestment, and other institutional practices that have deprived communities of color of tools to build neighborhood wealth and school equity.[26] High-risk home loans targeted at people of color in the run-up to the Great Recession stripped families of billions of dollars in financial equity during the foreclosure crisis.[27] By 2008 alone, approximately 504,600 Latinx children and 281,200 black children are estimated to have been impacted by a home foreclosure, placing them at higher risk of homelessness, school disruption, and attending an underresourced school.[28]

In addition to poverty and predatory financial practices impacting their early development and access to well-resourced schools, low-income youth of color also face systemic racial and class biases in K–12 education systems that pose barriers to their learning and development of a sense of academic belonging. Youth of color and low-income youth are less likely than white and higher-income youth to be viewed by their teachers as academically talented and motivated.[29] Additionally, teachers report more discomfort interacting with parents of color and low-income parents and less routine contact with them, promoting the erroneous view that these parents are educationally disengaged.[30] Racially and class-biased perceptions of low-income youth and families of color among educators and other school personnel promote reduced educational expectations for these students, use of less effective instructional practices, less engagement in mentoring and socialization of these students to postgraduate opportunities, and more routine and punitive forms of discipline.[31]

Cumulatively, these conditions create an educational service gap for low-income youth of color and indigenous youth that underlies the more frequently cited racial and class achievement gaps seen in K–12 settings.[32] They contribute to lower rates of high school graduation among black and Latinx youth than white youth across all states and the District of Columbia.[33] Youth who graduate from high school enroll in two- and four-year colleges at lower rates and are often less academically prepared for postsecondary education than white and higher-income youth.[34] These conditions reduce low-income youth of color and indigenous youth's access to educational grants and scholarships, and, coupled with family economic constraints, increase their need to rely on borrowing to finance postsecondary education, which may serve as a deterrent to postsecondary enrollment.[35]

Higher Education

The US higher education system is among the most robust in the world, but it is also marked by stratification between and within institutions that disadvantages low-income youth, youth of color, and indigenous youth in their academic and career development.[36] Conditions were not always as stark as they are today. After a long period of legally sanctioned racial segregation was forced to an end through the civil rights movement and other social movements of the 1950s and 1960s, US public universities began to diversify and become more equitable, aided in many states by low-cost or free tuition policies that created access for low-income youth of color and indigenous youth.[37] Reductions in state funding for higher education in recent decades, however, which increased considerably during the Great Recession and in some states have not returned to prerecession levels, have steadily returned these costs to students and families.[38]

This "great cost shift" has disproportionately impacted families of color and low-income families, particularly those of undocumented immigrant youth denied residential tuition rates in most communities.[39] Today, educational debt forms a significant and growing portion of the racial wealth gap between black and Latinx households and white households.[40] For individual students, increased educational costs lead to reduced college enrollment following initial acceptance, persistence to graduation, academic performance due to part- or full-time employment during the academic year, and sense of freedom in career choice.[41]

In addition to financial barriers to college entry, low-income youth of color and indigenous youth, once established in higher education settings, continue to face systemic biases similar to those seen at the K–12 level.[42] White, middle-class cultural norms predominate on most college campuses, and students from marginalized groups commonly report that they must adapt to thrive, a process that can induce stress, alienation, and reduced self-esteem and academic self-confidence.[43] Many members of the majority-white professoriate in the US demonstrate a lack of competence in addressing racism in the college environment as well as intersecting forms of marginalization such as classism.[44] This places the burden upon low-income students of color and indigenous students to develop support networks to understand, cope with, and in some cases contest these marginalizing forces as they impact their postsecondary learning and career development.[45]

Additional barriers salient for low-income students of color and indigenous students include the proliferation of unpaid internships, a widespread and important outlet for career networking and vocational socialization during the college years.[46] (See chapter 2 on the importance of paid internships for low-income students.) Racially and class-exclusionary features of campus social life, such as fraternity and sorority systems that are historically white and have become increasingly financially inaccessible to the average family as college environments have become more privatized, also pose distinct challenges.[47] These barriers may provoke a sense of isolation and cultural "otherness" among low-income students of color and indigenous students.[48] They also threaten students' career development potential given the powerful influence of personal social networks in career advancement in the US.[49] Indeed, differences in the social networks of white and black college graduates have been found to explain disparities in movement into managerial positions across multiple sectors of the workforce.[50]

Labor Markets, Workplaces, and Family Roles

Similar to and informed by the unequal structures of K–12 schooling and higher education, US labor markets and workplaces are stratified by race and class, features that impact all stages of working life.[51] Many factors underlie labor stratification and occupational segregation, including transportation systems and the geography of jobs relative to low-income communities and communities of color, the effects of structural and interpersonal forms of discrimination on development of social networks, and the influence of racial and class biases on hiring decisions.[52] Together, these forces lead to higher rates of unemployment and underemployment for black, Latinx, and Native American individuals with college degrees than for white degree-holders.[53] They also promote their concentration into lower-paying industries and workplace roles than those accessed by whites.[54]

Within the workplace, employees of color, indigenous employees, and employees from low-income backgrounds encounter complex, intersecting forms of stereotyping, stigma, and discrimination, including harassment, that shape the workplace climate.[55] Effective diversity policies and culturally competent management and supervision can help mitigate the impact of these problems and reduce their occurrence.[56] Despite considerable evidence that employing individuals from marginalized racial-ethnic groups in leadership roles promotes the implementation of effective diversity policies and positive workplace climates, they remain significantly underrepresented in these roles relative to whites.[57] This is particularly the case when access to a managerial position would grant them decision-making power over white subordinates.[58]

The challenges faced by workers of color and indigenous workers from low-income backgrounds do not end at the workplace, but also extend to the interface of work and family life. The US ranks the lowest among highly developed nations in social benefits available to families and policies that promote work-family balance.[59] While these conditions affect all households, those without private and community resources to compensate suffer disproportionately. The economic and social barriers linked to racial and class membership detailed in this section promote vulnerability to these gaps among workers of color and indigenous workers and subsequent experiences of work-family conflict, particularly among women of color and indigenous women.[60]

INTERNAL BARRIERS

Structural barriers manifest and impact academic and career development not only through restricted opportunity and increased episodes of hardship, but also through their effects on youth and young adults' self-perceptions, knowledge, feelings, and attitudes relevant to their working lives. In this section, we explore the occurrence of these internal barriers to academic and career development and their relationship to the environments in which low-income youth of color and indigenous youth are educated and employed.

Career Knowledge and Experience

Information about the world of work and opportunities to develop relevant vocational skills are important resources that promote effective career decision-making and long-term vocational development.[61] From a young age, low-income youth of color and indigenous youth's encounters with barriers linked to race and class reduce their access to these resources relative to class-advantaged and white peers. As adolescents, they demonstrate more circumscribed knowledge of available career paths than nonmarginalized peers, as well as less intention to pursue a wide range of careers.[62]

Restricted exposure to a range of types of work in family and community settings, particularly jobs requiring a college degree, as well as the prevalence of stereotyped images of the working lives of members of marginalized racial-ethnic and social class groups in the media, are key proximal influences on these outcomes.[63] In the absence of these examples, and when faced with challenges such as greater levels of familial and community unemployment and awareness of discrimination in the workplace, youth of color and low-income youth report less hope related to their future working lives as well as a diminished sense of purpose relative to peers who do not face such barriers.[64]

Social Identity and Self-Esteem

Social identity formation, including the establishment of a positive self- and group-concept underlying self-esteem, is a complex developmental process that begins in the earliest years of childhood.[65] It is central to academic and vocational identity development and is influenced by school and workplace experiences.[66] Emerging research further documents the important influence of historical knowledge of the social groups to which one belongs, including their accomplishments in the world of work.[67]

Low-income youth of color and indigenous youth face numerous challenges in securing positive social identities and reliable feelings of self-esteem due to the systemic, intersecting racial, colonial, and class barriers they face during development, as well as challenging life events linked to these forces.[68] Such challenges manifest in higher rates of mental health conditions (e.g., anxiety and depression) within these groups, as well as concerns such as relational difficulties and reduced attachment to social institutions (e.g., schools and community organizations), which may limit their academic and vocational development.[69] Youth who perceive and internalize discriminatory attitudes about their racial-ethnic and social class groups are at particular risk for impairments in academic and vocational functioning despite their equal ability.[70]

ADDRESSING STRUCTURAL AND INTERNAL BARRIERS

We believe that work-related supports should be directly aligned with work-related barriers. That is, work-related supports (internal and external) should be framed, understood, and administered across multiple contexts from a strengths, or nondeficit, perspective. In this section, we discuss types of supports that leaders situated in education, business, and community-based organizations may deploy to facilitate the successful transition of low-income people of color and indigenous individuals into the labor market. Moreover, we highlight potential skills and strategies that youth and emerging adults can develop to effectively overcome these barriers. Practical examples or models are provided for each strategy.

Supports are the resources that either lessen the initial stress encountered (perceived or actual) or improve the likelihood that responses to barriers lead to long-term positive outcomes.[71] Any interventions to address barriers should focus on both the organizational and individual levels.[72] At the organizational level, the goal is to minimize or eliminate the institutional barriers that low-income people of color and indigenous individuals encounter in academic and work settings. This may take the form of making places of employment more accessible to marginalized communities by developing comprehensive diversity, equity, and inclusion (DEI) policies and making career access and growth opportunities more accessible to low-income people of color. At the individual level, the goal is to help low-income youth of color to identify barriers and to prevent them from internalizing these challenges. Here, we aim to improve the capacity of low-income people of color and indigenous individuals to manage the structural barriers that limit career exploration and commitment in middle- to high-wage job sectors. We describe interventions that target individual-level characteristics such as skill building, social network capacity and access, and critical consciousness.

Eliminating Structural Barriers

DIVERSITY, EQUITY, AND INCLUSION As noted previously, structural work barriers for low-income people of color and indigenous individuals often manifest in the form of discrimination and/or asymmetric distribution of resources. Here we will focus on research-based principles that can guide the efforts of leaders across business, education, and nonprofit organizations as they work to minimize or eliminate structural barriers. We begin by highlighting the need to have a robust DEI program among a wide variety of employers across different job sectors. Next, we discuss ways to increase access and opportunity for work exposure, exploration, and commitment.

People of color are much more likely to experience structural racism and interpersonal racism in the workplace.[73] Further, low-income people of color are less likely to have the supports or resources at their disposal to overcome or cope with work-related barriers. For members of marginalized communities, barriers tend to be more pronounced and sources of support are more scarce than for their peers from privileged backgrounds. Low-income youth of color often feel confident in their ability to excel in a career field.[74] However, while marginalized youth are appraising their ability to be effective in a career, they are also appraising their ability to overcome barriers (racism, microaggressions, and isolation) associated with their desired career.[75] If the psychological and economic cost of coping with work-related barriers is deemed too high, youth may opt out of the career choice altogether. According to diversity and inclusion expert Jennifer Brown, "workforce composition will only change when you do two things: proactively hire more diverse talent on the front end *and* maintain a long-term, consistent commitment to creating an inclusive workplace where all kinds of talent are attracted to your company and want to build their career there."[76]

We see these two items—hiring more diverse talent, and committing to an inclusive workplace—as inextricably linked and critical in decreasing both the perceived and actual harm that many low-income people of color and indigenous individuals appraise as an unavoidable cost of participation in the labor force. A strong focus on DEI is not just the morally or legally appropriate course of action to improve the work experiences of marginalized communities, it is also the profitable course of action. Research indicates a direct positive relationship between a corporation's ethnic and racial diversity and profitability.[77] Given the demographic shift toward a majority nonwhite population in the US, the relationship between corporate diversity and profitability will likely strengthen.

DEI is particularly important for sectors that have high growth projections in the new economy, such as IT, health care, and advanced manufacturing, as employee supply in these sectors rarely keeps up with demand. There is an opportunity to strategically link corporate DEI efforts with the career exploration and training of low-income people of color and indigenous individuals. While we strongly encourage the continuation of and leveraging of existing DEI work to diversify the pool of potential employees, we also strongly suggest that efforts are not the exclusive responsibility of DEI departments or committees. Otherwise, equality becomes the sole responsibility of one department or group of individuals rather than a shared collective responsibility.

ACCESS AND OPPORTUNITY Due to the pervasive, systemic barriers that low-income youth of color and indigenous youth encounter throughout their lives, targeted career exploration experiences and career counseling supports must begin in earlier grades. In many school systems, low-income students of color have limited access to comprehensive career resources that provide opportunities for career exposure, exploration, and commitment. Further, when students do receive access to career-oriented educational pathways and counseling, it is not until their high school years. A longitudinal study of youth's career aspirations indicated that eighth-grade career aspirations were highly correlated with twelfth-grade career aspirations, suggesting that career aspirations that are formed by eighth grade endure to early adulthood.[78] Youth are making decisions about their future careers in the absence of comprehensive exposure to the vast array of options and corresponding educational requirements.[79] These students may opt out of critical foundational courses that provide the pathway to advanced courses and, subsequently, opportunities in certain job sectors such as STEM fields.

This is in part due to both the changing roles of school counselors and the shortage of school counselors. At one time, career counseling was a high school counselor's primary task.[80] Today, according to the American School Counselor Association (ASCA), the role also includes a responsibility to "help students focus on academic, career and social/emotional development so they achieve success in school and are prepared to lead fulfilling lives as responsible members of society."[81] School counselors are expected to act as college, career, and mental health experts, while also maintaining administrative duties. According to Mary E. M. McKillip, Anita Rawls, and Carol Barry, varying expectations for high school counselors have resulted in substantial role confusion.[82] Not only are counselors unsure where to focus their energy, but overwhelming caseloads make it next to impossible for them to achieve any one of these stated responsibilities.[83] As a result, tacking career development onto the job description of a high school guidance counselor has done little to provide adequate career services to young people. Further, the recommended student-to-counselor ratio is 1 to 250, but in reality, across all schools, the ratio is 1:464 and 1:311.[84] According to the same ASCA report, those that need counseling support the most—low-income youth of color—have the least access to school counselors.

It is highly unlikely that schools will hire enough counselors to meet the overwhelming student need in the foreseeable future. This shortage is further exacerbated as youth—particularly low-income youth of color and indigenous youth—are experiencing more traumatic events and greater mental health supports are needed. Professional school counselors are an essential piece of the puzzle; however, a new approach that aligns services, utilizes all educators in college and career planning, and engages parents is needed to address the broad needs of low-income students of color.

One strategy is for schools, nonprofit organizations, and government services to join efforts to identify and provide social-emotional health programs at local schools and organizations and refer students to wraparound services to address their stress levels and the adverse childhood experiences that can impact academic and life outcomes. This interorganizational collaboration can be further driven by philanthropic giving. That is, philanthropy can make these types of supports and collaboration a requirement for funding.

Individual Level

Individual-level barriers can be either internal or external. Marginalized youth have limited input on the types of structures and opportunities they encounter as they explore vocational possibilities. At the same time, youth have some degree of power and agency regarding how they perceive, leverage, and respond to vocational opportunities and stressors. Next, we identify support opportunities and describe how practitioners may be able to offer targeted supports or competency-building experiences that promote positive career outcomes for marginalized youth. The list is not exhaustive. However, it represents the psychological contextual dimensions that are high-leverage opportunities.

EFFICACY-BUILDING SKILLS The effects of self-efficacy on career outcomes, such as interests, goals, and work performance, is well established.[85] Furthermore, efficacy beliefs are an important intervening mechanism that accounts for the effects of perceived barriers on career outcomes.[86] Thus, low-income students of color can benefit from activities, interventions, and programs that aim to build efficacy beliefs.

Theory suggests that self-efficacy beliefs are developed from four primary sources of information: prior success at performing the tasks, verbal persuasion (receiving encouragement from others), vicarious learning (watching others perform the task), and low affective arousal while performing the task.[87] Prior research supports the effects of these sources on self-efficacy, with performance accomplishments having an especially strong influence.[88] Interventions designed around the four sources that feed into self-efficacy beliefs can increase their confidence in work-related activities, such as the job search, job decision-making, and coping with work barriers. Learning activities designed such that students experience success on work-related tasks can be especially impactful for students of color, while also attending to opportunities to connect them to successful people in the workplace who can serve as role models (a type of vicarious learning experience), linking them with mentors who can actively encourage their progress (a type of social persuasion experience), and teaching them skills that they can utilize to manage stressors in the workplace (a type of physiological arousal experience).

COPING SKILLS To understand the labor market experiences of low-income people of color, it may be useful to explore how individuals respond to or cope with these experiences. Coping involves one's strategy to deal with stress or threat, and represents the course of behavior after the appraisals. Coping involves the connections between appraisals (perceptions and evaluation), stress (e.g., institutional racism), and behavior (responses to the stressors; e.g., work-related decisions). As individuals from low-income marginalized communities evaluate job options, they also evaluate and anticipate the barriers and corresponding levels of stress (e.g., rejection, isolation, racism) that are associated with jobs and in-work settings.[89] Thus, coping is the sum of two psychological assessments: the appraisal of contextual stressors and the appraisal of possible responses to the stress.

It is important to help students of color develop strategies for coping with workplace stressors, as coping strategies are important mediators of the relationship between work stressors and work and personal outcomes. For example, a meta-analysis study reported that coping was related to work performance, job attitudes, and both physical and psychological well-being.[90] At the same time, it is important to underscore that the work-related stressors that people of color experience, such as discrimination, are structural in nature. Therefore, it is critical that we work to address inequitable workplace structures and policies that result in an uneven playing field and that overburden workers of color and indigenous workers, instead of just helping them adjust to these workplace harms. We can do so by advocating on behalf of people of color and indigenous individuals in the workplace, and by educating companies about the challenges that low-income students of color experience in the transition from college to work and the supports that they need in the workplace. We can also work with students of color to help them advocate for themselves in the workplace and understand the importance of identifying coworker allies with whom they can tackle these issues in a company.

COUNSELING SUPPORTS Educators and counselors can play a critical role in helping youth explore not only career options, but also their underlying assumptions regarding vocational possibilities and their ability to make work-related decisions. Steven D. Brown and Nancy Ryan Krane identified five critical ingredients for career counseling: written exercises, individual feedback, information about the world of work, modeling, and building support.[91] A recent study found that support, values clarification, and psychoeducational interventions had the strongest effects on career counseling outcomes, with writing activities, self-report assessments, individual feedback, and world of work information serving as additional activities that produced effective outcomes.[92] Although these studies focused on career counseling where career choice was the outcome, these activities can be incorporated into interventions with low-income college students of color and indigenous students that aim to prepare them for success in the workplace.

RAISING CRITICAL CONSCIOUSNESS Critical consciousness, or increasing the awareness of sociological factors that influence the work experiences of people of color and indigenous individuals, is an important goal for community college students and the personnel who interact with them. Prior work has linked critical consciousness among youth of color to career outcomes.[93] One such intervention that can be conducted in a group or classroom setting is the Career Path Tournament, which aims to raise awareness of contextual barriers to work, to increase attentiveness to one's emotional reactions to prior discrimination experiences, to increase understanding of the career development process, and to identify strategies for dealing with discrimination.[94] Another example is Ethnographies of Work at Guttman Community College of New York, the subject of chapter 3. Using ethnographic research methods, students in the course document and make meaning of work culture, differences among workplaces, and power dynamics among employees.

BUILDING A PROFESSIONAL NETWORK Low-income people of color identify a limited professional or career network as a barrier to work.[95] This can be a problem for students who are unable to access a professional network through family and friends, thus lacking common routes for job referrals. Thus, it is important to help students develop relational supports and to connect them to people and programs that can help them to establish a professional network, including student organizations (particularly those that are associated with the profession that they want to enter), national professional organizations, and mentoring programs. It is also important to ensure that students understand the high value of work experiences such as work study and internships during college. These experiences not only provide students with relevant work skills, but also represent opportunities to establish professional relationships with coworkers and supervisors who can help to build their professional networks.

One workshop intervention that included activities to learn about jobs in students' areas of interest, explore beliefs about the value of education to work, and expand sources of support for urban minority youth was effective in increasing sources of support to facilitate school, work, and life goals.[96] This intervention was also effective in increasing students' knowledge of supports for seeking job information and contacting role models in their areas of interest. Such workshops, which constructively challenge work beliefs and provide information about accessing supports, may be beneficial for low-income students of color and indigenous students in college.

SOFT SKILLS Increasing attention has been paid to the role of soft skills for youth in general and for low-income people of color and indigenous individuals specifically. Soft skills include the ability to problem-solve and communicate in service of a shared goal. Communication, responsibility, interpersonal skills, professionalism, and positive attitude, respectively, have been ranked as the top six most desirable soft skills. While we agree that there is value in making sure that the workforce is proficient in these skills, we also know that there is a strong chance that people of color will be evaluated with a cultural metric that is not their own. Historically, this has resulted in people of color being viewed as deficient. In some respects, soft skills can be viewed as a metric of cultural assimilation rather than career competency. This has the potential to be at odds with what Jennifer Brown describes as the "work of inclusion." Brown writes, "Part of the work of inclusion is helping those already in the workforce to feel safe bringing more of themselves to work, versus what they have done historically, such as downplaying parts of themselves for the purpose of assimilation."[97] We contend that there needs to be both meaningful discussion and input from diverse communities around what is meant by "soft skills" and how those skills are taught in low-income communities of color and indigenous communities.

CONCLUSION

In this chapter, we provided an overview of the normative challenges and barriers that low-income people of color and indigenous individuals experience in academic and work settings. More specifically, we addressed a variety of general structural, or institutional, barriers and how these external barriers can result in the development of internal barriers. We focused on how these barriers are manifested across developmental stages, including childhood, in postsecondary education, during the transition from school to work, and within work settings. We highlighted how the experience or anticipation of academic and work barriers impacts the individual's vocational development and work-related outcomes. The academic and work barriers that low-income youth of color and indigenous youth face are deep-rooted and long-standing within US institutions. It is important to take an ecological or systems perspective in tackling these barriers, and it will take individuals who are committed for the long term to *changing the educational and work systems*, especially those within their immediate work contexts, to reduce and eliminate the structures and policies that enable and sustain these barriers. We concluded with a discussion on how professionals can intervene at the institutional level to reduce these barriers for students and provide tangible recommendations for working with students to manage the effects of these barriers.

CHAPTER 8

"Implicit" Skills

Meeting the Challenge of the Twenty-First-Century Workforce

– BRENT ORRELL, WITH CALEB SEIBERT –

AN UNCONVENTIONAL ARGUMENT

In an era of science- and technology-focused, sector-based training strategies, this chapter will make an unconventional argument: based on employer feedback, the biggest challenge in the US labor force is unrelated to technical skills. While they value and seek to develop the technical skills of their workforces, employers routinely list nontechnical, or what I will call *implicit* skills, as the main deficit in the US workforce.

Explicit skills are related to specific business or mechanical processes (e.g., how to use tools on a factory floor, build code for a software product, or design and populate a complex spreadsheet), while implicit skills—also known as *noncognitive* or *soft skills*—are overarching "master" skills that form the capacity for learning, on-the-job training, and professional advancement as well as managing relationships with managers, coworkers, and customers. Explicit skills are a function of formal educational processes, while implicit skills are typically developed through social trial and error over time. Explicit skills are visible, formal, and more easily measurable. Implicit skills are the "hidden half" of the skill puzzle and arise in the social domain—informal, invisible, and more difficult to quantify, measure, and teach.

This chapter will trace some of the possible sources of the implicit-skills gap and its relationship to labor market demands. It will also argue that, paradoxically, such skills are growing in importance as technologies like artificial intelligence and robotics spread within the workforce, a fact recognized even by the major high-tech firms who increasingly prioritize implicit skills over explicit skills in their hiring and promotion policies and practices. Finally, the chapter will discuss strategies for increasing the stock of implicit skills in the American workforce and better positioning workers for an economy that prizes such capacities as automated processes take over an increasing share of the routine cognitive and physical work of business and industry.

A Word on Definitions

One of the main challenges in addressing this topic is arriving at terminology that satisfactorily captures its scope and meaning. Depending on the domain of study, the implicit skills I am addressing are called *soft skills* or *professional/ workplace skills* (workforce development), *noncognitive skills* (psychology and economics), or *social-emotional skills* (education). Each of these terms is descriptively useful and each has limitations. For instance, since all human thought and behavior is "cognitive" at its source—that is, it arises in the brain—why would we describe our social behavior as "noncognitive"? "Soft skills," while it expresses the fuzzy edges of the concept well, can lead readers to believe that these abilities are somehow secondary to "hard skills," when labor market data suggest that both are crucial to worker success and employer satisfaction and are increasingly in demand.

My basis for settling on the terms *implicit* and *explicit* to express the differences between nontechnical and technical skills arises from some recent neuroscience research reflections by British psychiatrist Iain McGilchrist. McGilchrist argues that much of what we have been trained to believe about the hemispheres of the human brain—that the left hemisphere handles logic, language, and math, while the right manages art, emotion, and relationships— has largely been discredited. It turns out, according to McGilchrist, that both sides of the brain are engaged in all of these activities. The main question we should be asking, he says, is not "What do brain hemispheres do?" but rather "What are they like?"[1] In the animal kingdom, which includes human beings, the left hemisphere provides narrow, sharply focused attention, while the right looks outward, scanning the environment for the new and atypical. This permits, say, a bird, to focus narrowly on separating seeds from gravel while simultaneously remaining alert to predators.

Human brain hemispheres operate in a similar way. The right takes in experience from the wider world, while the left "encodes" that experience in mental maps that can be accessed for later use. The left hemisphere breaks information down; the right puts it back together and carries it back into the world. The use of tools provides an interesting and, for our purposes, apt example. The mechanics of using a screwdriver (right to tighten, left to loosen) is encoded in the left hemisphere irrespective of whether the person using it is left- or right-handed. But for the person to use that screwdriver effectively, the right hemisphere must identify and assess the nature of the problem, consider possible solutions, persuade a coworker to assist in the task of repairing a machine, or explain the solution and its cost to a customer.

The explicit component of screwdriver use can be frozen, broken into steps, and easily turned into part of a classroom curriculum. The implicit component is the social content of learning how to use a screwdriver (coming to class, paying attention to the instructor, cooperating with other students in practicing) and the on-the-job requirements involved in deciding when and how to use the screwdriver. Implicit skills go well beyond the technical, entering the domain of human relationships and interpersonal communication, but are nonetheless critical to operationalizing explicit skills. Implicit skills, because they operate in a broad sphere of interpersonal behaviors that includes social-emotional perception, executive functioning, and communications and leadership, are typically much more difficult to quantify and develop through formalized instruction. They arise and are developed in long-term, up-close exchanges, first within immediate and/or extended family and then with peers; they are the products of millions of micro-interactions that shape our understanding of the social world.

THE GROWING NEED FOR IMPLICIT SKILLS

The use of *implicit* and *explicit* helps define skill domains without offering characterization of importance and priority. The two things go together and are both essential to a smoothly operating and productive workplace. In light of this interdependence, I have long puzzled over the asynchrony between what employers say they want and what our educational and training systems produce. Beginning with the 1957 Sputnik crisis and continuing up to today, government and educational systems at all levels have prioritized the acquisition of explicit skills and especially knowledge, degrees, and credentials in science, technology, engineering, and math (STEM) fields as the indispensable keys to individual and national economic success. Yet in survey after survey—as well as in innumerable conversations with business owners and human resources executives—employers complain first about how workers lack implicit skills like character, persistence, integrity, professionalism, teamwork, communication, and dependability.[2] Frustration about this problem runs deep among employers because, in increasingly networked, team-based working environments, the absence of implicit skills is a drag on productivity and a human resources headache.

Table 8.1 outlines the responses from the most recent survey by the National Association of Colleges and Employers. Of the top ten attributes employers looked for in a potential candidate, eight out of the ten, including the top four, refer to implicit rather than explicit skills. Surveys for college and MBA graduates have found a similar emphasis on oral and written communication, adaptability, and presentation rather than quantitative skills.[3] A 2018 LinkedIn survey of over four thousand talent development managers,

TABLE 8.1 Attributes employers seek on a candidate's résumé

ATTRIBUTE	% OF RESPONDENTS
Communication skills (written)	82%
Problem-solving skills	81%
Ability to work in a team	79%
Initiative	74%
Analytical/quantitative skills	72%
Strong work ethic	71%
Communication skills (verbal)	67%
Leadership	67%
Detail-oriented	60%
Technical skills	60%

Source: Reproduced from NACE Staff, "Employers Want to See These Attributes on Students' Resumes," National Association of Colleges and Employers, December 12, 2018, https://bit.ly/2Vor2mb.

line managers, and executives found strong majorities favoring implicit skills such as leadership, communication, and collaboration over role-specific skills, while a 2015 *Wall Street Journal* survey found that 92 percent of executives valued soft (implicit) skills as much or more than technical skills—but 89 percent said they had difficulty finding someone with those skills.[4]

Recent trends suggest that employer demand for implicit skills will continue to grow as the economy changes. In 2015, David Deming, professor at the Harvard Graduate School of Education, published a study outlining the increasing importance of social and noncognitive skills in today's labor market.[5] According to Deming, from 1980 to 2012, wage growth for occupations that require both cognitive and social skills consistently increased, while occupations that require only cognitive skills did not. Moreover, Deming found that social (implicit) skills are more predictive of employment and wages today than in the 1990s or 1980s, whereas "the importance of cognitive skills has declined modestly." Building on these findings, a 2016 Brookings report tracks the dramatic growth in social and service job tasks relative to math and routine tasks within jobs over the last three decades, while also highlighting a significant jump in economic returns for noncognitive (implicit) skills during the same time period.[6]

One explanation for this phenomenon is that many roles that once occupied people are on the path to automation, and basic cognitive tasks are often easier to automate than more implicit tasks. A study by David Autor emphasizes this trend, noting that rote tasks—especially in manufacturing, clerical, and administrative positions—are increasingly prone to automation and may be a driver of the well-publicized hollowing out of middle-class jobs.[7]

According to the *Future of Jobs Report* in 2018, roles that are expected to grow in the future are those that "leverage distinctly 'human' skills."[8] In the report's top-ten list of skills with the highest increase in demand from employers, eight of them were implicit skills (a familiar trend), while demand for skills such as technology use, monitoring, and control is in decline. A report recently released by the Strada Institute echoes this sentiment, estimating that, by the year 2020, there will be 24 million new types of positions created, emphasizing skills such as "active listening, leadership, communication, analytics and management."[9] Another recent study by the McKinsey Global Institute looks at the tasks associated with a given job and projects that demand for social-emotional skills will grow at double-digit rates until 2030.[10] Using data from a survey of over three thousand international business leaders, the report also examines how important a given skill is perceived to be today and the expected demand for that skill in the future. Notably, the findings suggest that implicit skills like leadership, communication, and empathy, as well as explicit skills like advanced IT and technology design, are both "important and growing." Interestingly, the demand for implicit skills is even (and perhaps, particularly) invading STEM occupations. A recent Burning Glass report analyzing over 150 million distinct job postings found that "transportable skills" like problem solving, critical thinking, communication, and collaboration are now in higher demand among STEM-related job postings than in other occupations.[11] Google conducted a study in 2013 analyzing employee data to identify hiring and promotion potential. The researchers found that, even among highly technical positions, an employee's implicit skills were fundamental to success at the company.[12] STEM skills and knowledge were ranked as some of the least important factors, whereas skills such as communication and empathy toward others were more highly valued.

Findings like these are echoed in a forthcoming analysis of interviews with current and former STEM workers conducted by AEI and Reuters-Ipsos. Preliminary review of this data shows that worker characteristics such as interpersonal communication, leadership, and management are critical to career success. When asked about the relative importance of interpersonal skills and high-level math and analytical skills, 84 percent of STEM workers said interpersonal skills were "extremely" or "very" important, compared to 61 percent who said the same for math and analytical skills and 24 percent who applied the description to operation and repair of machinery. The AEI-Ipsos survey shows that worker emphasis on the importance of interpersonal skills also grows substantially as income rises, suggesting a connection between implicit skills and economic mobility.

HOW DID WE GET HERE?

A glance back at US economic and workforce history is useful for shedding light on the implicit-skill deficit. According to Claudia Goldin and Lawrence

Katz, the long period of rapid economic growth that began in the late nineteenth century and continued into the second half of the twentieth century was tightly correlated with the introduction of universal high school. During this period, marked by rising literacy, numeracy, and skills acquisition, the US stock of workforce skills was precisely balanced with the demands created by emerging technology and industrialization, an economic partnership that drove growth and rising incomes. Beginning in the 1970s, this partnership began to fray, creating a gap between the economy's needs and the available pool of human capital. After assessing the possible causes, Katz and Goldin concluded the problem was not that skill demands had suddenly accelerated but that American educational attainment had stalled.[13]

What changed in the makeup of American society that could account for this deterioration in literacy, numeracy, and skill acquisition among American workers, especially when automation and changing technology is increasing the demand for them? Public policy has tended to focus on improving schools to boost math and reading, yet scores remain flat and dropout rates high, especially among disadvantaged and minority populations. If we accept the premise that implicit skill development is informal and continuous and that these skills form the basis for the capacity to learn, it makes sense to look beyond the formal education system toward the institution that is chiefly responsible for implicit-skill development—namely, the family.

Family data from past decades are clear: at about the time educational attainment began to lag, America was experiencing a rapid acceleration of divorce, and unmarried births spiked.[14] As has been well documented, children born to unmarried parents, and to a lesser degree those who experience family fracture through divorce or separation, face challenges in a range of educational, social, and economic outcomes that extend into adulthood.[15] In the past, it has been common to think of this as mainly a problem affecting African Americans and other minority groups. Today's reality is quite different. While rates of such births are highest among African Americans (71 percent), they are growing the fastest among whites, having nearly tripled, rising from just under 10 percent to almost 30 percent.[16] It is important to note that the sources of deterioration in family formation are many and varied, and this chapter is not intended to explore such factors in depth. A brief list of the contributing factors might include eroding social constraints on single parenthood; addiction to opioids and other drugs; declining middle-skill, middle-wage work opportunities for men that reduce their "marriageability"; and the legacies of racism, discrimination, and trauma. Moreover, as documented in notable recent work by writers such as J. D. Vance (*Hillbilly Elegy*), Tim Carney (*Alienated America*), and Chris Arnade (*Dignity: Seeking Respect in Back Row America*), the impact of these factors is in no way restricted to any one race but is increasingly present in all.

Whatever the causes, the broad-based declines in family stability help explain the deficit we see in implicit skills, which evolve over time and are heavily affected by parental support and life experience. The development of implicit skills depends largely on the degree to which children form and maintain stable attachments to caring adults (e.g., parents, extended family) who help children navigate developmental challenges and "buffer" against trauma.[17] Emotional self-regulation, a key to establishing and maintaining interpersonal and professional relationships, is developed in early stages of infancy and is highly correlated to parental involvement and family functioning in the face of adversity.[18]

For instance, research has found that children with depressed parents are more likely to have deficits in emotional regulatory competencies. A mother's self-reported social level is linked to a child's ability to self-regulate as he or she grows older.[19] Neuroscientists have suggested a child's executive function ability—essential for self-regulation and school readiness—is disadvantaged at early ages because of high levels of prolonged stress and trauma.[20] Left unaddressed, such deficits in self-regulation and executive function hurt childhood, adolescent, and adult social and economic outcomes and inhibit effective workforce attachment and participation.

HOW DO WE MOVE FORWARD?

To shore up the implicit skills in the workforce, thoughtful leaders will take a life-cycle approach to human capital development. As my American Enterprise Institute colleague Katharine Stevens points out, the foundation of social-emotional or implicit skills is laid early—very early.[21] If we want to effectively develop these skills in the workforce of tomorrow, we need to focus our attention on family formation, parenting, and early care while helping to build implicit skills among adolescents and young adults who are already in or preparing to enter the workforce. While the audience for this book will likely be working with older adolescents and adult students, these interventions should be understood in the context of a continuum of strengthening opportunities from early childhood to adulthood. The programs described in this section, and others like them, may effectively develop implicit skills.

Family Formation and Early Childhood Development

HEALTHY MARRIAGE INITIATIVES As noted previously, the main source of implicit-skill deficits is frequently the challenges associated with family dissolution and single parenting. It follows, therefore, that one of the most important strategies for preventing these deficits is to invest in family formation, divorce prevention, and the strengthening of parenting behaviors.

The US Department of Health and Human Services Office of the Administration for Children and Families (ACF) invests $150 million annually in programs that support family formation, marital stability, and parenting skills through the Healthy Marriage & Responsible Fatherhood (HMRF) program.[22] These funds support educational programming, public education activities, and online informational clearinghouses that educate low-income individuals, couples, and fathers about the importance of marriage and parenting for them and their children. A recent evaluation of healthy marriage initiatives found that couples taking part in relationship education programs were less likely to break up (63 percent were still together at the one-year follow-up compared to 59 percent of the control group), felt higher levels of commitment to their spouse, and reported improved coparenting behaviors and higher levels of affection.

Importantly, these programs also reduced levels of destructive behavior, including domestic violence. Reported levels of domestic violence were one-third lower in the treatment group versus those in the control group.[23] Earlier evaluations of HMRF programs also showed important positive impacts on relationship quality, coparenting, child well-being, levels of anxiety and depression, and family stability.[24] Although they have received two decades of less-than-glorifying press, research suggests these types of programs are an important "upstream" antipoverty strategy designed to interrupt intergenerational cycles of family dissolution and strengthen the transmission of implicit skills. As Brigham Young professor Alan Hawkins concludes in a recent analysis:

> A careful examination of the ongoing, developing, and full work on ACF's [Healthy Marriage & Relationship Education (HMRE)] policy initiative contradicts the death sentence that many prematurely pronounced. Instead, it reveals large and serious rigorous evaluation work that shows promising successes, disappointing failures, and nuanced findings. Certainly, compared to other social policy initiatives with greater public funding and much less early evaluation, ACF's HMRE policy meets the standard of showing potential and promise.[25]

Healthy Marriage strategies and approaches that have been successful should be expanded and replicated as a key implicit skill development priority.

NURSE HOME VISITS One of the best-known noncognitive interventions is the Nurse-Family Partnership (NFP) program, developed by David Olds.[26] NFP is an evidence-based service that pairs low-income women who are pregnant with their first child with a registered nurse for periodic at-home visits.[27] Nurses check on the expecting mothers to offer guidance on pregnancy and child development from birth to age two. Several randomized controlled trials show the program's ability to improve child school readiness, family economic self-sufficiency, maternal health, and positive parenting.[28]

Starting interventions early in a child's development allows for significant improvements in a child's development and a parent's nurturing skills, maximizing returns on investment during an impressionable and malleable time for an expecting mother and her child.[29] A recent evaluation found that NFP improved children's cognitive skills, parenting attitudes, and mental health for mothers.[30] A RAND study also found that every $1 invested in NFP could yield up to $5.70 in public savings attributable to reduced criminal justice system involvement and increased wages, employment, and education among NFP-served children.[31]

EARLY CHILDHOOD EDUCATION One of the more prominent early childhood interventions is the Perry Preschool program. The program targeted African American children with low IQ and socioeconomic status for a two-year preschool program focused on executive functioning, self-control, and interpersonal relationships. Program evaluations in follow-ups at ages nineteen, twenty-seven, and forty showed children who participated in the Perry program had improved life outcomes in education, marriage, crime, and earnings.[32] Researchers found that substantial improvements in two key personality skills—lower externalizing behavior (measure of aggressive, antisocial behavior) and higher academic motivation—were responsible for improving adult outcomes. The effects of the Perry program are visible into adulthood, suggesting noncognitive skill interventions in early childhood are beneficial to long-term life outcomes.[33]

Like the Perry Preschool program, Head Start has shown similar positive long-term outcomes. A paper by the aforementioned Harvard scholar David Deming comparing siblings who attended Head Start to those who did not found that Head Start participants were more likely to graduate from high school, have higher wages, attend college, be less idle, and be in better health.[34] More recent research on Head Start has found positive correlations of Head Start participation to self-control and self-esteem compared to siblings who did not attend preschool.[35] Consistent with other research on early childhood education, the Deming findings suggest that since Head Start's cognitive impacts on math and reading fade by third grade, higher levels of positive adult outcomes among Head Start participants are likely related to noncognitive skill development.

FRIENDS OF THE CHILDREN Another instance of a successful program aimed at supplementing parental support comes from Portland, Oregon's Friends of the Children (FOTC; http://friendspdx.org/). FOTC pairs paid, professional college-educated mentors with the highest-risk kindergarten-age children and maintains the mentoring relationships through high school graduation. FOTC mentors and mentees meet with each other sixteen hours a month, with a strong focus on developing implicit skills. FOTC, which now serves nine sites in the US and UK, has shown positive program outcomes related to educational attainment, employment, crime, and early parenting. An ongoing randomized controlled trial has shown positive impacts in reducing the negative externalizing behavior that is a leading indicator of school dropout, drug use, juvenile crime, and early parenting.[36]

Interventions for Adolescents and Young Adults

Many young adults enter the labor market from backgrounds in which family distress, incarceration, poverty, and the implicit-skill deficits that frequently accompany them are common occurrences. Evaluations of work-based interventions that incorporate the development of implicit skills alongside skill-based learning have successfully improved employment and earnings outcomes.[37] Apprenticeship programs have shown benefits to participants in future employment outcomes and improvements in implicit skills.[38] Career academies attendance is associated with positive impacts in earnings and employment even without improving educational attainment or test scores.[39] The following are a few examples of current programs that build implicit skills on the job and assist individuals from disadvantaged backgrounds to succeed in today's workforce.

WORKADVANCE In 2011, the WorkAdvance workforce development program was established to provide a sector-based employment strategy for low-income and unemployed adults in fields with strong workforce demand.[40] While WorkAdvance offered sector-specific technical skills training, it also developed a strategy for tackling implicit skills. In response to employer feedback that employees most often failed due to a lack of appropriate workplace behavior rather than technical deficiency, WorkAdvance programs implemented a "work readiness" curriculum focusing on workplace culture, career readiness, communication, employee etiquette, and basic job interview preparation. An evaluation by MDRC noted that many participants said the training on soft skills was crucial to their career readiness.[41]

A three-year randomized controlled evaluation showed that participants in WorkAdvance-funded programs had higher rates of employment and wages compared to the control group.[42] Across all tested sites, WorkAdvance resulted in increased participation in vocational training in a targeted sector (e.g., information technology and health care) and increased employment by a range of 12 to 41 percentage points. In addition, three of the four sites reported statistically significant increases in earnings, with one site, Per Scholas, finding a substantial 26 percent ($3,700) increase in earnings among participants.[43]

FEDERATION FOR ADVANCED MANUFACTURING EDUCATION The well-regarded Federation for Advanced Manufacturing Education (FAME; http://fame-usa.com/) program, which originated in Louisville, Kentucky, incorporates soft-skills professional training into its advanced manufacturing curriculum to prepare workers for jobs in the auto manufacturing sector. Students learn professional behaviors, engage in collaborative exercises to build teamwork, and are evaluated on their communication, initiative, and interpersonal abilities, spending as much as 25 percent of program time developing these skills. Similar to WorkAdvance, FAME recognizes that many of its participants are not aware of the employer's expectations for professional behavior and etiquette. Since implementation, FAME has seen rapid uptake in regional economies and has expanded to eight states and fourteen programs.[44]

Remedial Interventions

Individuals from low-income and disadvantaged backgrounds commonly arrive in adulthood with implicit-skill deficits manifesting in executive functioning impairment that inhibits employability and fosters dependence on public programs.[45] Remediating these deficits among adults is crucial not only for improving employment and other economic outcomes but also for interrupting the intergenerational cycle of poverty.

PROJECT QUEST Established in 1992, Project QUEST (https://www.questsa.org/history/) is a sectoral training program for low-income individuals in San Antonio, Texas, that has a long history of positive impact in the lives of its participants. A recent randomized controlled evaluation of the program found annual wage increases of more than $5,000 for program participants nine years after program completion.[46] Particularly germane to this discussion, the study found that the participants who experienced the largest benefits from the program were individuals older than age thirty-four or with children.

While a majority of the program's training takes place in partnership with local community colleges, Project QUEST places a strong emphasis on intensive case management services for participants. This includes weekly VIP (Vision, Initiative, and Perseverance) sessions where counselors meet with students to discuss the myriad implicit skills that will be demanded from them on the job and in the classroom.[47] Counselors take participants through mock interviews, offer support for the highs and lows of daily life, and provide coaching on time management and communication, among other things. Trainees and instructors point to the importance of these sessions in preparing students with the implicit skills that allow for a remarkable level of success in the workforce.[48] As one student said, "My QUEST counselor helps teach us so many different kinds of things about life. We learn how to work with people at all different levels. We learn how personality plays into the equation—all sorts of things we would never learn if QUEST were just giving us financial aid. We learn how to interact with our peers and with authority."[49]

ECONOMIC MOBILITY PATHWAYS   One innovative program working to assist adults in improving their noncognitive skills is the Economic Mobility Pathways (EMPath) Intergenerational Mobility Project (IMP).[50] IMP provides an interesting example of programs that combine behavioral interventions with typical workforce, welfare, and education services. EMPath takes a comprehensive, long-term approach to its clients as it helps them reach financial self-sufficiency. To reach these goals, EMPath targets participants' executive functioning skills, recognizing that an individual's past may have impaired his or her ability to control emotions, avoid setbacks, and plan ahead. EMPath management, coaching, and human service interventions are designed to improve executive functioning in both work and nonwork contexts and remove many of the stress-related barriers common for people from vulnerable backgrounds.

While no formal studies have been conducted yet, an EMPath-Intergen report on families with an average of four months' participation in the program shows promising results. Seventy-one percent of families involved in the project improved their scores on an externally validated Confusion, Hubbub, and Order Scale measure (a survey used to measure parents' reporting on environmental confusion) of household functioning.[51] Sixty-four percent of adults were working, compared to the state average for low-income households of 40 percent. Children also improved on an index of education, health, and self-control outcomes.

The program notes that 86 percent of participating households made progress toward self-sufficiency goals such as saving more money, getting new jobs, or enrolling in educational programs.[52] While the findings from EMPath-Intergen are new and still being tested, the program offers ideas and models of interventions that address intergenerational poverty factors rooted in an understanding of the crucial role of implicit skills in building a successful life.

CONCLUSION

Implicit skills have always been a critical component of success in the workplace. As artificial intelligence, automation, and machine learning absorb increasing amounts of routine, pattern-driven tasks, workers will be expected to bring even more of these skills to bear in their day-to-day tasks. Increasingly, workers will be expected to interact with and leverage new technologies (the so-called "co-bot" phenomenon) while also becoming more adept in inherently "human" skills like collaboration, communication, teamwork, and critical thinking. These changes bode well for productivity and innovation, but they will require a significant shift away from a siloed, "either explicit or implicit skill" learning approach and toward one that values and seeks to integrate both.

In the world of human capital development, we are doing learners a disservice if we narrowly focus on one side of the ledger (in most cases, technical skills) while ignoring the other side. In a recent interview, a local chamber of commerce executive told us, "Employers hire for technical skills, but they fire for soft skills." Even if they are not fired, employees with impaired implicit-skill sets tend to lack opportunities for advancement. While this may be a simple framing of the issue, the statement illustrates an important point. Both implicit and explicit skills are necessary but insufficient on their own. It is not one or the other, but a healthy mix of both, that provides the foundation for career success.

CHAPTER 9

Social Capital and the Social Construction of Skills

– NANCY HOFFMAN AND MARY GATTA –

New graduates are entering a working world that is pitched as never before in favor of the well-connected, the socially knowledgeable, and the rich.[1]

The preceding statement is the conclusion of a news story about a young man in Britain, the son of a low-income single mother. "Joe" graduated from an elite university (the Harvard/Yale equivalent) and found himself unable to access the job market for which he had prepared. The reasons: affluent graduates had families who set them up in London, helped with rent, introduced them to family and work friends, and paid their living expenses during their job searches. They had had prestigious unpaid internships during university vacations, and had connected with potential employers, while Joe worked during vacations and still had a huge college loan debt he was paying off. The fairy tale end of Joe's story is that a wealthy friend's parents stepped in to set him up just as they had their own child. But most such stories don't end this way.

As Michael Lawrence Collins and Pam Eddinger point out in their essays at the beginning of this volume, older youth and adult students from low-income backgrounds make enormous sacrifices to attend community college. Most are like Joe, working part or full time while studying. They arrive at college with a commitment to gaining new knowledge and skills that will launch them into better jobs. Most have gained, as Eddinger observes, "basic work literacies in their prior or current workplaces," and so intend to "[focus] on skills in their field of study and . . . the potential for job placement." Basic work literacies are, of course, the foundation for all that follows, but what these students may not fully comprehend is the degree to which getting a better-paying and more satisfying job may require reaching out to and forming relationships or connections with strangers and acquaintances who can help. And they may conclude—given their responsibilities at home, at work, and at college—that an internship that can launch a new career is simply not possible. As Eddinger notes in chapter 2, community colleges are struggling to figure out how to provide well-designed, paid internships for their students as valuable as those available to students with fewer life obligations and more free time.

Reaching out, whether through an internship or simply by strategizing ways to meet new and well-connected people, falls under the ubiquitous term *networking*. In today's world, where job openings are posted for all to see on online job sites, the system may seem fairer than it once was. However, despite easy access to online job sites, job seekers are increasingly advised to make personal connections with a hiring manager or someone who can get to such a person. Ironically, whom you know has become even more important than it was in the days when information about jobs passed mainly by word of mouth.[2] And for those who hope to move into new fields or get a higher salary with a freshly minted degree, just finding out what jobs exist, what various companies or organizations do, and how they are run requires a much different kind of knowledge than what one finds in a job description. This chapter takes a look at the factors underlying the common advice to "network": why is networking important; what is the value of actively seeking relationships outside of one's community and friendship circle; and how do class, race, and gender impact one's ability to successfully build a relationship with a "connector" or link to a company or sector of interest? The chapter also takes a look at what underlies that pervasive complaint of many hiring managers and employers: that prospective hires don't have the requisite and all-important professional or "soft" skills.

COLLEGE AND CAREER OUTCOMES

As the data shows, the income level of one's family of origin is associated not only with level of education, but also with post-graduation earnings—lower-income graduates earn less than their affluent peers with the same college degrees. The ability of a job seeker to reach out to new networks, to make connections, may be a partial explanation for this phenomenon. An extensive 2018 study, *Degrees of Poverty: The Relationship Between Family Income Background and the Returns to Education*, by Timothy Bartik and Brad Hershbein of Upjohn Institute, stratifies earning levels by family income during adolescence. Their research shows that bachelor's degree recipients from families at 185 percent of the poverty rate and above during the graduate's high school career get a return on their degree that is 65 percentage points higher than those whose family income during high school was below 185 percent of the poverty rate.[3] In addition, Bartik and Hershbein looked at earning trajectories between the ages of twenty and forty in relation to family income during adolescence. While higher-income workers increased their salaries by about $5,200 every two years, the comparable figure for low-income workers was $2,300, with the consequence that "the average college graduate who grew up in a low-income family earns about as much at the peak of the career as the average college graduate from a higher-income family whose career is just beginning."[4]

Such differentials have an impact on lifetime earnings. It is important to note that these findings pertain to white males. The returns for lower-income and higher-income African Americans with bachelor's degrees are much closer to each other—in other words, where you start out has less impact on African Americans in this research. This finding should not be construed to mean that African American bachelor's holders do well in the economy, but rather that—whether a salary bump is large or small—family income of origin makes less difference for African Americans than for the population at large.

The Georgetown Center on Education and the Workforce has done research looking at the highest-paying college majors and then comparing incomes of African American and white graduates with the same majors.[5] This is a different slice of the data than that of Bartik and Hershbein and shows that, in all cases except the STEM fields, African Americans earn lower wages than their similarly educated white peers. For example, African American architecture and engineering graduates earn on average $68,000; white graduates earn $90,000.

We should not interpret this data to suggest that college isn't worthwhile for low-income people. The wage premium is worth it, along with the many other factors that accrue from getting a college degree. But the bottom line is not surprising: while there is a premium for low-income people getting a bachelor's degree rather than stopping at high school, it's not as high as that for people who start out with substantial economic advantages. It's just a case of the rich getting richer—especially the richest. Indeed, Bartik and Hershbein show that those who begin in the highest wealth categories and gain graduate degrees push the returns for whites substantially higher than they would be without this group. So while those at that bottom gain, they don't gain as much as those nearer the top. *And that means if you start out low-income to gain higher-than-predicted returns, other factors need to come into play, as we note in the following discussion.*

There are various hypotheses as to why people with similar degrees might earn more or less depending on the income, race, or ethnicity of the family from which they come. Most of the explanations for earnings differentials are drawn from the stories of individuals; this is not an area where there is much empirical research. Bartik and Hershbein summarize their hypotheses: fewer professional connections and networks, less polished mainstream professional skills, lack of a sense of entitlement, biases of employers, lack of knowledge about potential earnings or available career ladders as they choose majors, lower risk tolerance, and lower likelihood of self-promotion.[6] A recent book by Julia Freedman Fisher, *Who You Know: Unlocking Innovations That Expand Students' Networks*, focuses on access to a variety of relationships from childhood through adolescence. She explains "the vastly different webs of relationships" between low-income and affluent children. The latter have tutors, music lessons, and enrichment activities of all kinds, and their parents can "buy" time to spend with them. In addition, affluent children have access to their parents' professional and social networks. Freedman Fisher calls relationships "the best-hidden asset" of the privileged.[7]

SOCIAL CAPITAL

Many of the dynamics noted above can be explained by a lack of the right kind of *social capital*. What is social capital? Let's begin with the premise that all people have social capital, but some kinds of social capital are more useful than others in specific situations. The social capital we focus on here is specific to accessing the labor market. As with many abstract concepts or theories—and social capital is both—there are many definitions and a substantial defining literature. In addition, there are many examples of putting social capital to work as an analytic tool. We draw on some key studies here.

For the purposes of this chapter, three definitions will serve the purpose. Nan Lin defines social capital as "resources embedded in one's social networks, resources that can be accessed or mobilized through ties in the networks. Through such social relations or through social networks . . . an actor may borrow or capture other actors' resources (e.g., their wealth, power, or reputation). Those social resources can then generate a return for the actor. The general premise that social capital is network based is acknowledged by all scholars who have contributed to the discussion."[8]

Lin's work on social capital is generally admired and his definition frequently cited. What his definition does well is translate the word *capital* meaning "financial assets" into a metaphor for social relations. *Social* capital returns value through human rather than financial assets, mainly through connecting one person with another or one network with another, as we will see. Lin also emphasizes networks, and his subsequent research theorizes how networks function and how their power can be measured, especially in regard to work and the job search. And, important for those looking to move from a lower-paying and perhaps lower-status job to a better one, Lin defines resources to be mobilized as the wealth, power, and reputation of the helping individual or network, and asserts based on numerous research studies, his and others, that a contact's "superior status" makes a positive difference in the job search.

These additional definitions of social capital are also useful; the first is from Paul Adler and Seok-Woo Kwon, and the second from Giorgos Cheliotis:

[Social capital] is the goodwill available to individuals or groups. Its source lies in the structure and content of the actor's social relations. Its effects flow from the information, influence, and solidarity it makes available to the actor.[9]

The term [social capital] broadly refers to resources that accrue to individual or groups through the maintenance of a network of social ties. It is more often associated with intangible resources representative of social cohesion (e.g. trust, reciprocity, mutual support). A social group's or individual's stock of social capital can be thought of as a reservoir of social trust and support that they can tap into in their daily lives and especially in times of need.[10]

Adler and Kwon and Cheliotis add the terms *goodwill, trust,* and *reciprocity* to our definition of social capital. None of these is a financial asset, but each has high value in originating, activating, and sustaining social relations. When I ask someone I know to call her hiring manager to put in a good word for me after I have submitted my résumé for a job, I am drawing on her goodwill toward me, as well as her trust that I would be a superior employee—that she at minimum would not be embarrassed by my performance and at best would get points for recommending an outstanding hire. The Cheliotis definition adds the metaphor of a *reservoir,* or store that can be tapped into as needed. Just as reservoirs generally replenish, a strong relationship can withstand numerous requests for help with the understanding that the person being helped would reciprocate if asked. Even when there is the assumption of goodwill and trust, however, it takes courage and a certain set of social skills for a job seeker to ask for a favor.

NETWORKS

Today we think of social networks first as online platforms or communities where people sharing interests come together and those seeking connections can find friends or at least like-minded others. But the term *social network* was borrowed by the tech world from a sociological tradition that studied networks long before the internet. In network theory, social networks are the vehicles through which social capital is accrued. Networks provide access to the resources embedded in social capital. And, as this chapter will discuss, the networking that helps someone find a job and remain employed demands a set of "soft skills" that are context dependent; there are different self-presentation requirements in a retail position than there are in an engineering firm or government office.

In the literature, social capital comes in two distinct but interrelated forms: the resources that accrue to membership in a tight network or community with which one shares values, versus the resources that accrue when a person serving as a broker or connector links a job seeker to a new network in which s/he is not known. In 2000, Robert Putnam published the book *Bowling Alone: The Collapse and Revival of American Community,* which got substantial attention for its findings that the store of such qualities as trust, reciprocity, goodwill, and simple neighborliness were in steep decline with negative consequences for civic life and engagement. Putnam's cry of alarm about the decline of trust in government and the collapse of civic institutions such as church membership, parent-teacher associations, and clubs of various sorts (e.g., bowling leagues) put the term *social capital* as a measure of community health into wide circulation.

Networks such as those Putnam and others study have both positive and negative aspects. To the degree to which a network is closed—that it admits only like-minded people who share values, and even identity (a fraternity, a religious or ethnic group, a social club)—it is exclusive, and with exclusivity comes a variety of advantages. Members enjoy affiliation, or *homophily*, meaning that similar people have more contact and connections with one another than do people who differ. The best common phrase is "birds of a feather flock together." As the authors of an article with that name observe: "Similarity breeds connection. This principle—the homophily principle—structures network ties of every type, including marriage, friendship, work, advice, support, information transfer, exchange, comembership, and other types of relationship. The result is that people's personal networks are homogeneous with regard to many sociodemographic, behavioral, and intrapersonal characteristics."[11]

But the researchers go on to say that "homophily limits people's social worlds in a way that has powerful implications for the information they receive, the attitudes they form, and the interactions they experience. Homophily in race and ethnicity creates the strongest divides in our personal environments, with age, religion, education, occupation, and gender following in roughly that order."[12]

The negative side of closed networks, then, is that people within the network often want affiliation because they prefer to exclude others, those who are different from them. And even if the intention or aim is not exclusion explicitly, as anyone who has attempted to break into a new group (remember high school cliques) knows, learning the norms and behaviors to gain acceptance is challenging, can take time, and is sometimes close to impossible. Certainly if exclusion is based on observable race, ethnicity, gender, or language, then entry may be unattainable, although the mechanisms of exclusion may not be explicit.

Today's tech world uses *closed* and *open* to refer to networks too, but whether relating to a platform (LinkedIn, Facebook, or your work intranet) or an actual physical grouping of people (a book club, a soccer league, a community neighborhood watch), these are relative terms. Bringing to mind the phrase "six degrees of separation," networks come in layers or concentric circles. The densest or primary network is that of family and intimates, those with whom one shares confidences and personal information. This circle comes with mutual obligations and the expectation of reciprocity and is "more closed" than the second layer. Lin calls the relationships in this first network "binding." A second layer, again following Lin, is a "bonding" network with weaker ties but with people sharing social values and perhaps spending work or leisure time together—for example, a recreational sports team or a topical discussion group. Members of a bonded network have fewer expectations of each other. Finally, Lin defines a network that generates "belongingness"; that is, one feels some affiliation, but there may be little to no direct interaction.[13] This kind of network is characteristic of the many internet groupings to which one may belong, but with which there is never any personal, face-to-face interaction.

Each of these networks has its own resources, valuable uses, ways of interacting—and disadvantages. A body of research focused on how people find and get jobs suggests that the more closed the network to which one belongs, the more likely it is for members to have the same information. Thus, for our focus on labor market access, it is important to understand not only how networks create bonds between people and groups, but also how bridges or links *between* networks enable access to and mobilization of the kind of social capital that is required in the job search. As Putnam puts it in *Bowling Alone*, bonding networks are good for "getting by," while bridging networks are good for "getting ahead."[14] So we have four Bs: binding, bonding, belonging, and bridging.

Bridging is important as we talk about networking. Several decades before *Bowling Alone*, Mark Granovetter upset the tradition that Putnam drew upon with an article entitled "The Strength of Weak Ties." Until that moment, sociologists had focused on the analysis of interpersonal ties (their intensity, duration, etc.) within networks. But trust or goodwill between people can serve to connect an actor—in this case, someone wanting to learn about career opportunities—with someone in a second unfamiliar network with a higher level of societal power. Granovetter's contribution was to study the links *between* networks or the relationship between the micro and the macro.[15] The question he asked in his book on the topic, *Getting a Job: A Study of Contacts and Careers*, was: How do people find jobs, or in his words, "How [do] people become aware of the opportunities they take?"[16] Until he asked this question, most research assumed that people found jobs through formal search processes. Granovetter's studies showed that most jobs did not come as a result of a formal search process, but rather through information passed from a member of one network to a member of another. Most often, information was passed between people who were not members of the same network and did not know each other well.

To put the process in lay terms, most of the people Granovetter studied learned about jobs through someone they did not know well—a former colleague, a college acquaintance, a friend of a friend. As Granovetter recapped in the 1995 afterword to a new edition of *Getting a Job*, his initial research

> proposed that "weak ties" were strong in connecting people to information beyond what they typically had access to through their strong ties, since our acquaintances are less likely than our close friends to know one another, and more likely to move in circles different from and beyond our own. Although close friends and relatives might be more motivated to help us with job information, [the first edition] argued that "weak ties" were structurally located in such a way as to be more likely to offer help, and suggested that this was one reason why most of [the] respondents had found jobs through contacts they saw only infrequently at the time the job information was passed.[17]

As Granovetter also noted in the 1995 afterword, it was later research done by those following him that asked whether jobs found through weak ties resulted in higher incomes. On this question, he cites Lin's empirical evidence that weak ties yield better jobs "only if those ties linked people to those higher up some hierarchical structure."[18]

ECONOMIC RETURNS ON SOCIAL CAPITAL

There is one final dimension of social capital theory that is important to keep in mind regarding the following question: By what means and under what conditions does social capital produce returns, or more specifically, how do networks used in jobs searches operate? This has to do with the distinction between accessing and mobilizing social capital. Here again we are drawing on Lin. An assessment of the social capital to be accessed tells how much or what kind is available to a job seeker. For a job seeker, the capital to be accessed might consist of linkage with someone who can provide a reference, someone who will make a call on behalf of a candidate, or even someone who might simply provide informal intel about what qualifications and profile the employer is seeking. These are the resources available in general. But accessed capital is of little value unless and until it is mobilized, and mobilization depends on an interaction between actors for a specific end.

To go back to an earlier metaphor, a job seeker draws from the reservoir of goodwill and trust at a specific time for a specific purpose, but unless the contact acts on the request, the mobilization is incomplete and of no value. For example, often people call my (Hoffman's) office asking that I put in a good word about them with our hiring managers. I can politely say, "I'm so pleased you're interested in our organization," but nothing more. I can say, "I think you'd be a terrific candidate; we'd be lucky to have you." And then I can act, or I can do nothing. Or I can say, "Happy to help, I'll call X the minute we hang up" because I know the candidate by reputation and think his résumé brings exactly what we need.

With a focus on social capital in the job search, there are, of course, additional important factors to consider. There is some evidence that while information is always a valuable commodity, it is differentially distributed and depends on the "quality, quantity, and diversity of friendship networks."[19] For a specific example, in her study *Lone Pursuit: Distrust and Defensive Individualism Among the Black Poor*, Sandra Susan Smith argues that "macrostructural changes in society" in the last decades have heightened distrust and noncooperation among members of impoverished communities, a point similar to that presented in *Bowling Alone*. As Smith points out, trust and distrust are learned behaviors, and there are many and complex reasons why such communities should be characterized in this way. Important for this chapter, she goes on to argue that distrust results in job holders' general reluctance to assist the unemployed with job referrals. In other words, they were reluctant to mobilize what social capital they had because they did not trust that the person asking for the referral would perform to the standards required, and that would reflect on the employee. As Smith notes, "job holders are making decisions in a labor market context in which soft skills are growing in significance to employers and cyclical changes in the economy affect employers' hiring practices."[20]

This brings us to tech-based networking platforms, which are intended to simplify, make more efficient, and speed the connection-making process, and thus the job search—think LinkedIn. LinkedIn is good for many things: to find people about whom you already know something, to post business-related updates, and, yes, to collect connections at various degrees of separation. But as Ilana Gershon argues in *Down and Out in the New Economy*, while it is almost obligatory to have a LinkedIn profile, there is little evidence that LinkedIn helps people get better jobs. She also discusses other problematic aspects of LinkedIn: playing the LinkedIn game requires branding yourself and the standout services you can provide to employers, no easy task when employers often receive hundreds of résumés for an attractive opening. Even creating a LinkedIn profile in itself is a confusing and anxiety-provoking exercise, especially for those not experienced in the protocols and behaviors expected.

It speaks directly to the issues raised about who defines "professional" or "soft" skills, and how they are racialized, class-influenced, and gendered. Gershon observes importantly that the underlying assumption of LinkedIn is that users are white-collar professionals already, not workers seeking to enter the professions.[21] For example, to have a profile that ranks as "all star" on the LinkedIn "profile strength meter," the user is expected to supply daunting information that would stymie many, and especially new graduates of community college programs seeking different and better-paying opportunities. "All stars" provide their "industry and location; an up-to-date current position (with a description); two past positions; their education; [their] skills (minimum of three); a profile photo; and at least fifty connections."[22]

A recent positive article about LinkedIn in the *New York Times* differentiates LinkedIn from Facebook and Twitter, calling LinkedIn "a notably minor character in major narratives about the hazards of social media." The article goes on to note that "the site hasn't proved especially useful for mainstreaming disinformation. . . . LinkedIn is not, in the popular imagination, a force for radicalization, a threat to democracy, a haven for predators, an environment that encourages mob behavior, or even a meeting place for pot stirrers."[23] All these are seen as virtues in the world of out-of-control social media, and on balance they are. But it is precisely the safe, professional, noncontroversial, mainstream version of behavior that also confirms Gershon's conclusion that LinkedIn assumes certain norms that make it of limited use for the unemployed or hourly-wage worker wanting to enter a profession.

If you don't already work in an office, how do you enter a LinkedIn conversation in which users "talk on LinkedIn the same way you talk in the office. . . . There are certain boundaries around what is acceptable." LinkedIn is characterized as "a non-office office, with thousands of bosses, none of them yours, all of them potentially watching."[24] Most people use one way of speaking, dressing, and behaving—one mode of self-presentation—with friends and family, and another among work colleagues. They *code switch*, or "shift from one linguistic code (a language or dialect) to another, depending on the social context or conversational setting."[25] One needs to be able to "read" LinkedIn language ("how you talk in an office") and adjust one's self-presentation to expectations. But adjusting one's self-presentation requires office experiences, in the LinkedIn case, that allow one to "perform" mainstream business behaviors. All of this suggests that LinkedIn might be a place to learn or observe professional office behaviors and language, but it is not a place that is hospitable to those who do not already belong.

Gershon and others have recognized biases inherent in the way LinkedIn and other networking and job search tools are set up to benefit those who are already privileged and who have impressive job histories. As Gershon notes in a *Harvard Business Review* article:

> what those hiring value most is a strong recommendation from someone who actually knows the applicant as a worker and can assure them that the person will be a good hire. While these connections are important, it's important to note that they may not change one of the most problematic results of networking: relatively homogenous workplaces. . . . After all, if no one of color or from a working-class background was hired into an office, there were fewer people to

spread the word that the job existed in the first place. Nowadays, the problem is more of an implicit bias in how recommendations function—people tend to recommend their former coworkers whom they liked working with. Relying on workplace ties doesn't solve the problem of how networking creates barriers to creating a more diverse workplace.[26]

A set of tech-based startups are trying to minimize documented biases of hiring managers—for example, against those with black-sounding names, or women in roles stereotypically held by men, or those with skills but without degrees. The intent is to provide greater equity in connection-making. Some startups disguise résumé information that would signal race, prior incarceration, or other such markers that make candidates subject to discrimination. Some provide assessments promoting skills rather than college degrees as signals of a candidate's value. In addition, some address equity by directly advertising their ability to help diversify a company's workforce with highly qualified candidates of color.

But here is the important conclusion: whatever one thinks of these tech-based platforms including LinkedIn and social justice–themed startups, as Gershon concludes, "none of these genres are particularly good at revealing someone's personal qualities."[27] And therein lies the problem. When Granovetter did his study and developed the argument that weak ties provide better access to job-related information and referrals, it was the personal qualities of the job seeker that led a reference to mobilize her social capital on behalf of the candidate. Follow-up research found similarly what a potential employer wants to know is the candidate's character and personal qualities. Technical skill and experience can be documented through a paper résumé or online, but neither will answer these critical questions: What is this person like? Will she fit into my company? Does he understand the company's values and ways of working? While LinkedIn does invite "endorsements" (informal brief statements about the candidate), these are inadequate for the questions most hiring managers want to answer. And while meritocratic in that anyone can list their skills and personal brand for free along with their endorsements, we are back to the much more subjective issue of the way people assess each other, with the attendant problems of race, gender, and class prejudices, assumptions, and biases that are embedded in social capital.

SKILLS

How employers and hiring managers decide whether a candidate is suitable for or fits a particular work environment requires that we understand how workplace soft skills, which are instrumental to securing jobs via less formalized channels, are socially constructed. In popular vernacular, we often see skills as something that either one is born with or one earns. One has "natural" skill in basketball, but one needs to earn the skill required to achieve prominence as a highly credentialed and successful neurosurgeon. The sociological terms are that skills are either *ascribed* or *achieved*. However, this binary hides considerable complexity. Sociologists have suggested that skills cannot be so neatly and objectively conceived. Instead, we must understand the circumstances by which occupations become socially constructed as "skilled," and the ways skills are inextricably tied to social categories such as race, class, and gender.

The literature on the social construction of skill turns on a key distinction between education and training—achieved skill (with qualifications such as degrees, certifications, and licenses as its proxy) and ascribed skill based on social category. Exclusion of certain social groups from certain jobs can result from blocking their access to achieved skills or from ascribing lack of skill to them. And the two exclusionary processes may be linked, as Paul Attewell points out in his article, "What Is Skill?"[28] Moreover, ascription tends to be self-reinforcing: the absence (via exclusion) of a given social group from a given job reinforces the sense that persons of this group are not well suited to the job. So while the relationship between class and achieved skill may seem straightforward—using qualifications as a proxy for skill and occupation as a proxy for class—the reality is less so. Instead, workplace norms and expectations, which are typically set by people in power in that workplace (most often white middle- and upper-middle-class men) align with characteristics and behaviors of people in power. So the skills that are valued often represent the ability of those not in power to behave in ways that align with the behavior of those in power; as noted, on LinkedIn you talk the way you talk in a white-collar office.

Increasing reliance on soft skills compounds opportunity for stereotyping, which creates increased opportunities for discriminatory action in the labor market. Mary Gatta's qualitative research with small, high-end American retailers found that they tended to view basic customer service and the required aesthetic and emotion skills as something the prospective worker had or did not have. Building on Malcolm Gladwell's "blink moment," Gatta found that employers judge this possession and accordingly make their hiring decisions in the initial few seconds of meeting a perspective employee. The blink moment, then, has the real potential of reproducing social inequality, as employers can end up relying on cultural capital cues, stereotypes, and prejudices. In many ways the blink moment can obscure race and class bias among employers, as noted earlier.[29] More concrete signifiers of job suitability—such as work-related certifications or years of experience—are seen as less important in hiring decisions.

The idea of skill "fit" plays an important role: employers see particular groups of workers as suited to particular jobs. This may act against workers' interests even when employers ascribe highly sought skills to particular groups. For example, employers often assume that Latinx immigrants are willing to work hard (thus ascribing the highly valued "skill" of a good work ethic), but also assume that they are willing to do so for little pay. (For additional analysis of barriers based on race and ethnicity, see chapter 7, "Work-Related Barriers Experienced by Low-Income People of Color and Indigenous Individuals," in this volume.) Similarly for women, caring labor is often treated as a natural attribute—something women do for its intrinsic satisfaction in providing help rather than for money—and not skilled work. In part, this contributes to the low pay of predominately female jobs in health care and childcare. This subjective aspect of skills, and particularly soft skills, leads to an environment where middle-class white male workers are seen as more skilled than working-class workers, female workers, and workers of color as they enter employment, which accounts for their occupational super-ordination. White male workers continue to acquire more achieved skills as their careers progress. By contrast, marginalized groups are exposed to fewer opportunities for further skill development in their jobs so that they cumulatively acquire fewer skills over their working lives than more socially privileged groups. This differential outcome is not regarded as problematic, because it is, after all, why the working class is defined as working class—they have a lower level of achieved skill. The process of ascribing skills can also limit skill achievement. Students and workers perceived by teachers and supervisors to have few skills are also given access to fewer opportunities to learn and demonstrate new skills. Similarly, workers of color often have less access to social and professional networks because potential mentors see them as less skilled and are therefore less likely to support them.

Moreover, Dennis Nickson and his colleagues found that the skills that employers demand are not just social, but also aesthetic. Compiling survey data from retail, hotels, bars, restaurants, and cafés in Glasgow, they found overwhelmingly that both interpersonal communication and self-presentation were central to service work. Specifically, 99 percent of employers felt that social and interpersonal skills were of significant importance and 98 percent of employers felt the same of self-presentation skills. Conversely, only 48 percent of employers reported that technical skills were important. Indeed, the right appearance and personality took precedence over technical qualifications.[30] Lynne Pettinger found that sales assistants are a critical part of the "branding" of retail stores, and that their social and aesthetic skills are central to their work. One of her interesting conclusions is that "fashion orientation is one facet of brand-strategy [used by the stores] and the ability to present a fashionable appearance is one of the skills needed by sales assistants in many stores."[31]

As Chris Warhurst, Paul Thompson, and Dennis Nickson have noted, much aesthetic labor is about style that an employer is looking to sell.[32] Our presentation of self matters, and we need to not only present the correct self, but also know when to present that self, as business dress is not the same in all occupations. For instance, a job interview for a college professor may involve a different type of attire than a job interview for a Wall Street broker or a Silicon Valley software designer. As one article about the quandary of how to dress as a female Silicon Valley employee pointed out, people are suspicious if you look too nice.[33] One must know when to deploy which aesthetic. Yet, as Pierre Bourdieu has noted, social class (among other things) is manifested through aesthetics providing visual cues about one's social standing.[34] As a result, poverty is often embodied. For example, the lack of access to health care contributes to physical markers of poverty, such as poor teeth. Such indicators are impossible to cover up or "mask for the task." So while soft skills training can help blunt the blink moment and enhance some opportunities, it will not eliminate the potential biases in the blink moment, nor will it alter the ways this labor market works.

CONCLUSION

In sum, what is particularly problematic is that the middle-class and white populations continue to both define soft skills and benefit disproportionally from those definitions. Not only does the middle class acquire more achieved skill through education and training but, with this broadening, *being* middle class is ascribed as a skill. This development partly reflects how the characterization of "skill" now includes both achieved skills—that is, for the most part, qualifications—but also the ascribed soft skills formerly constituting "personality" or "culture," as we have seen in the case of workers of color.[35] In part it also reflects the shift to service-dominated economies in which jobs involve face-to-face or voice-to-voice interactions between worker and customer. With these jobs, the articulation of education and employment has become loosened.[36] In these jobs, workers' productivity is aligned with ascribed, not just achieved, skills; with socialization rather than education the source of skill formation.

While it is absolutely clear that middle-class soft skills are important to advancement in the labor market, it is equally clear that educators and others working with students owe them help in understanding what will be expected of them. How to employ social capital, enter helpful social networks, and demonstrate appropriate soft skills—these things must first be understood, then learned and practiced.

NOTES

INTRODUCTION

1. Anthony Carnevale and Nicole Smith, *Balancing Work and Learning: Implications for Low-Income Students* (Washington, DC: Georgetown University Center on Education and the Workforce, 2018).
2. Equitable Futures, Bill & Melinda Gates Foundation, "American Narratives About Occupational Identity and Future Careers: Narrative Analytics Presentation," https://equitablefutures.org/american-narratives-about-occupational-identity-and-future-careers/.
3. For additional analysis of this topic, see Anthony P. Carnevale et al., *African Americans: College Majors and Earnings* (Washington, DC: Georgetown University Center on Education and the Workforce, 2016), https://cew.georgetown.edu/cew-reports/african-american-majors/; Anthony P. Carnevale and Megan L. Fasules, *Latino Education and Economic Progress: Running Faster but Still Behind* (Washington, DC: Georgetown University Center on Education and the Workforce, 2017).
4. Occupational Employment Statistics, Bureau of Labor Statistics, "Occupational Employment and Wages, May 2017," https://www.bls.gov/oes/2017/may/oes211093.htm.
5. See Amy K. Glasmeier and the Massachusetts Institute of Technology, "MIT Living Wage Calculator," http://livingwage.mit.edu.
6. See Lauren Weber, "U.S. Workers Report Highest Job Satisfaction Since 2005," *Wall Street Journal*, August 29, 2018, https://on.wsj.com/2wrfXpU.
7. Weber, "U.S. Workers"; Jim Harter, "Employee Engagement on the Rise in the US," *Gallup*, August 26, 2018, https://news.gallup.com/poll/241649/employee-engagement-rise.aspx.
8. Annamarie Mann and Jim Harter, "The Worldwide Employee Engagement Crisis," *Gallup*, January 7, 2016, https://www.gallup.com/workplace/236495/worldwide-employee-engagement-crisis.aspx.

9. Malcolm Gladwell, *Blink: The Power of Thinking Without Thinking* (New York: Little Brown, 2005).

10. Arlie Hochschild, *The Managed Heart: Commercialization of Human Feeling* (Oakland: University of California Press, 1983), 97.

11. Fabian T. Pfeffer, "Growing Wealth Gaps in Education," *Demography* 55, no. 3 (2018): 1033–1068, https://doi.org/10.1007/s13524-018-0666-7.

CHAPTER 1

1. Anthony Carnevale, Stephen Rose, and Ban Cheah, *The College Payoff: Education, Occupations, Lifetime Earnings* (Washington, DC: Georgetown University Center on Education and the Workforce, 2011).

2. Raj Chetty et al., *Mobility Report Cards: The Role of Colleges in Intergenerational Mobility* (Cambridge, MA: Opportunity Insights, 2017), https://opportunity insights.org/paper/mobilityreportcards/.

3. Clair Gilbert and Donald Heller, "The Truman Commission and Its Impact on Federal Higher Education Policy from 1947 to 2010" (paper presented at the Association for the Study of Higher Education annual meeting, Indianapolis, Indiana, November 2010).

4. Gilbert and Heller, "The Truman Commission," 2.

5. Angelica Cervantes et al., *Opening the Doors to Higher Education: Perspectives on the Higher Education Act 40 Years Later* (Round Rock, TX: Texas Guaranteed Student Loan Corporation, 2005), https://files.eric.ed.gov/fulltext/ED542500.pdf.

6. National College Access Network, "Strengthen Pell: Restore the Purchasing Power of the Pell Grant," https://collegeaccess.org/page/Pell.

7. Thomas R. Bailey, Shanna S. Jaggars, and Davis Jenkins, *Redesigning America's Community Colleges: A Clearer Path to Student Success* (Cambridge, MA: Harvard University Press, 2015), 4.

8. S.580, "Student Right to Know and Campus Security Act," 101st Congress (1989–1990) amended the Higher Education Act of 1965 (HEA) to require all institutions participating under HEA Title IV to disclose the completion or graduation rates of certificate- or degree-seeking students entering into those institutions. It would be ten years before higher education institutions worked through the technical, analytic, and human capacity challenges to disclose comparable data.

9. US Census Bureau, 1947–2015, Current Population Survey and 1947 Decennial Census.

10. Bailey et al., *Redesigning America's Community Colleges*, 5.

11. The White House, President Barack Obama, "Below are excerpts of the President's remarks in Warren, Michigan today and a fact sheet on the American Graduation Initiative," Office of the Press Secretary, July 14, 2009, https://bit.ly/33CN5ta/.

12. The White House, President Barack Obama, "Remarks by the President on the American Graduation Initiative in Warren, MI," Briefing Room, July 14, 2009, https://bit.ly/2EUUooA.

13. MDC, "Developmental Education Initiative," https://www.mdcinc.org/home/projects/education/developmental-education-initiative/.

14. "Completion by Design," https://www.completionbydesign.org/s/.

15. JFF, *Joining Forces: How Student Success Centers Are Accelerating Statewide Community College Improvement Efforts* (Boston: JFF, 2013), https://www.jff.org/resources/joining-forces-how-students-success-centers-are-accelerating-statewide-community/.

16. For more information on guided pathways, see https://www.pathwaysresources.org.

17. Timothy J. Bartik and Brad Hershbein, *Degrees of Poverty: The Relationship Between Family Income Background and the Returns to Education*, W. E. Upjohn Institute Working Paper 18-284 (Kalamazoo, MI: W.E. Upjohn Institute for Employment Research, 2018), https://doi.org/10.17848/wp18-284.

18. Anthony P. Carnevale, Ban Cheah, and Andrew R. Hanson, *The Economic Value of College Majors* (Washington, DC: Georgetown University Center on Education and the Workforce, 2015), 4.

19. Anthony P. Carnevale et al., *African Americans: College Majors and Earnings* (Washington, DC: Georgetown University Center on Education and the Workforce, 2016).

20. Anthony P. Carnevale et al., *Our Separate & Unequal Public Colleges* (Washington, DC: Georgetown University Center on Education and the Workforce, 2018).

21. Sarah Turner and John Bound, *Closing the Gap or Widening the Divide: The Effects of the G.I. Bill and World War II on the Educational Outcomes of Black Americans*, Working Paper 9044 (Cambridge, MA: National Bureau of Economic Research, 2002).

22. Nick Kotz, "'When Affirmative Action Was White': Uncivil Rights," *New York Times*, August 28, 2005, https://nyti.ms/2IWBIo6.

23. Jack A. Taylor III, "War," in *The Jim Crow Encyclopedia, Vol. 2*, ed. Nikki L. M. Brown and Barry M. Stentiford (Westport, CT: Greenwood Publishing Group, 2008).

24. National College Access Network, "Strengthen Pell: Restore the Purchasing Power of the Pell Grant," https://collegeaccess.org/page/Pell.

25. Anthony P. Carnevale and Ben Cheah, *Five Rules of the College and Career Game* (Washington, DC: Georgetown University Center on Education and the Workforce, 2015), 3.

26. Davis Jenkins and John Fink, *What We Know About Transfer* (New York: Columbia University, Teachers College Community College Research Center, 2015), 1.

27. Janelle Jones and John Schmitt, *A College Degree Is No Guarantee* (Washington, DC: Center For Economic and Policy Research, 2014).

28. Jones and Schmitt, *College Degree*, 2.

29. Jones and Schmitt, *College Degree*, 6.

30. Devah Pager and Hana Shepherd, "The Sociology of Discrimination: Racial Discrimination in Employment, Housing, Credit, and Consumer Markets,"*Annual Review of Sociology* 34 (2008): 187, doi:10.1146/annurev.soc.33.040406.131740.

31. Marianne Bertrand and Sendhil Mullainathan, *Are Emily and Greg More Employable Than Lakisha and Jamal? A Field Experiment on Labor Market Discrimination*, Working Paper 9873 (Cambridge, MA: National Bureau of Economic Research, 2003).

CHAPTER 2

1. For more on the topic of social connections and social capital, see chapter 9, "Social Capital and the Social Construction of Skills."

2. Richard Kazis and Nancy Snyder, *Uncovering Hidden Talent: Community College Internships That Pay and Pay Off for Students and Employers* (Boston: The Boston Foundation, 2019).

3. AACC 21st Century Center, "A Quick Look at Community College Fast Facts," July 25, 2017, http://www.aacc21stcenturycenter.org/article/a-quick-look-at -community-college-fast-facts/.

4. Kathryn Larin et al., *Food Insecurity: Better Information Could Help Eligible College Students Access Federal Food Assistance Benefits, Report to Congressional Requesters* (Washington, DC: United States Government Accountability Office, 2018), https://www.gao.gov/assets/700/696254.pdf.

5. See chapter 3, "Ethnographies of Work: A Transformative Framework for Career Learning," for a more extensive description of this course and its impact.

CHAPTER 3

1. Debra Humphreys, "Next-Generation Quality Assurance for Tomorrow's Talent," *News & Views*, September 19, 2017, https://www.luminafoundation.org /news-and-views/qa-commons.

2. George Kuh, *High-Impact Educational Practices: What They Are, Who Has Access to Them, and Why They Matter* (Washington, DC: AAC & U, 2008); Susan Scrivener et al., *Doubling Graduation Rates: Three-Year Effects of CUNY's Accelerated Study in Associate Programs (ASAP) for Developmental Education Students* (New York: MDRC, 2015).

3. Parts of this section are based on Mary Gatta and Nancy Hoffman, *Putting Vocation at the Center of the Curriculum* (Boston: JFF, 2018); Nancy Hoffman and Mary Gatta, "Putting Work at the Heart of Learning: An Approach to Student

Economic Mobility," *Essays on Employer Engagement in Education* (New York: Routledge, 2018).

4. Melinda Mechur Karp et al., "Revising a College 101 Course for Sustained Impact: Early Outcomes," *Community College Journal of Research and Practice* 41, no. 1 (2016): 42–55.

5. Karp et al., "Revising a College 101 Course."

6. Nancy Hoffman and Robert Schwartz, *Learning for Careers: The Pathways to Prosperity Network* (Cambridge, MA: Harvard Education Press, 2017).

7. Robert Putnam, *Our Kids: The American Dream in Crisis* (New York: Simon & Schuster, 2015), 255.

8. Putnam, *Our Kids*, 125.

9. Annette Lareau, *Unequal Childhoods: Class, Race and Family Life* (Berkeley: University of California Press, 2003); Annette Lareau, *Unequal Childhoods: Class, Race, and Family Life, with an Update a Decade Later* (Berkeley: University of California Press, 2011).

10. Lareau, *Childhoods*; Lareau, *Childhoods Update*, 30.

11. Lareau, *Childhoods Update*, 29.

12. Kevin A. Tate et al., "An Exploration of First-Generation College Students' Career Development Beliefs and Experiences," *Journal of Career Development* 42, no. 4 (2015): 294–310.

13. Mark Granovetter, "The Strength of Weak Ties," *American Journal of Sociology* 78, no. 6 (1973): 1360–80.

14. Excerpts of this section were included in Gatta and Hoffman, *Vocation at the Center.*

15. Nathalie Saltikoff, "The Positive Implications of Internships on Early Career Outcomes," *NACE Journal* (May 2017), https://www.naceweb.org/job-market/internships/the-positive-implications-of-internships-on-early-career-outcomes.

16. Geneva Gay, *Culturally Responsive Teaching: Theory, Research, and Practice*, 2nd ed. (New York: Teachers College Press, Columbia University, 2010), 31.

17. Yolanda Sealey-Ruiz, "Building Racial Literacy in First-Year Composition," *Teaching English in the Two-Year College* 40, no. 4 (2013): 386.

CHAPTER 4

1. Accenture, *It's Learning. Just Not as We Know It. How to Accelerate Skills Acquisition in the Age of Intelligent Technologies* (New York: Accenture, 2018), https://accntu.re/2MqS7Ty. An excellent and comprehensive annotated bibliography summarizing the extensive body of research on the future of work and changing skill requirements has been produced by Canada's Labour Market Information Council, "Annotated Bibliography: Future of Work," Version 2.4, Labour Market Information Council, August 2019, https://bit.ly/2MsmGIR. A useful

literature review is Thereza Balliester and Adam Elsheikhi, *The Future of Work: A Literature Review* (Geneva: International Labour Office, 2018), https://bit
.ly/2YcmhwR.

2. Accenture, *It's Learning.* See also David Deming, "The Growing Importance of Social Skills in the Labor Market," *Quarterly Journal of Economics* 132, no. 4 (2017): 1593–1640.

3. David J. Deming and Kadeem Noray, "STEM Careers and the Changing Skill Requirements of Work" (working paper, Harvard Kennedy School, Cambridge, MA, 2019), https://scholar.harvard.edu/ddeming/publications/stem-careers-and
-technological-change.

4. Deming, "Growing Importance."

5. This section is adapted directly from Sara Lamback, Carol Gerwin, and Dan Restuccia, *When Is a Job Just a Job—And When Can It Launch a Career?* (Boston: JFF, 2018), https://www.jff.org/resources/when-job-just-joband-when-can-it
-launch-career/.

6. The authors of the study defined middle-skill jobs as those that require some education beyond high school but not a four-year degree. The study focused upon those roles that pay at least $15 per hour and in which at least 20 percent of online job postings indicate a preference for a sub-baccalaureate degree or credential. See Lamback, Gerwin, and Restuccia, *When Is a Job*, for additional information on each of the metrics related to job transitions and the study methodology.

7. Lamback, Gerwin, and Restuccia, *When Is a Job.*

8. According to the study, 60 percent of middle-skill manufacturing workers are employed in static jobs. Further, manufacturing workers are 3.5 times more likely than the average worker to be employed as a temporary worker, illustrating the challenging dynamics that face a significant proportion of workers in this career area.

9. For an overview of labor sheds, or the region from which a city or other employment center draws workers, see US Department of Labor, Bureau of Labor Statistics, Employment and Training Administration, "Data on Commuting Patterns Helps Identify Labor Sheds," Workforce GPS, LMI Central, https://
lmi.workforcegps.org/resources/2015/06/18/11/22/Commuting_Patterns.

10. US Census Bureau, Center for Economic Studies, "OnTheMap," https://
onthemap.ces.census.gov.

11. For additional information on industries and how they are classified, see the "2017 NAICS Classification System" manual, produced by the US Census Bureau, at https://www.census.gov/eos/www/naics/. An overview of the Standard Occupational Classification (SOC) system is available through the US Department of Labor, Bureau of Labor Statistics, https://www.bls.gov/soc/.

12. US Department of Labor, Bureau of Labor Statistics, "Employment Projections," https://www.bls.gov/data/#projections.

13. A list of state labor market agencies, along with links, is available through the US Department of Labor, Bureau of Labor Statistics: https://www.bls.gov/bls/ofolist.htm.

14. US Department of Labor, Employment and Training Administration, "O*Net OnLine," https://www.onetonline.org.

15. Amy K. Glasmeier and the Massachusetts Institute of Technology, "MIT Living Wage Calculator," http://livingwage.mit.edu.

16. A crosswalk between the Classification of Instructional Programs (CIP) and the Standard Occupational Classification (SOC) codes is available through the US Department of Education's Institute for Education Sciences, National Center for Educational Statistics; see https://nces.ed.gov/ipeds/cipcode/resources.aspx?y=55. In some cases, states also create their own CIP-to-SOC Crosswalks.

17. Kevin Doyle, *Employer Engagement Toolkit: From Placement to Partners* (Boston: JFF, 2015), https://www.jff.org/resources/employer-engagement-toolkit-placement-partners/.

18. Elisa Rassen et al., *Using Labor Market Data to Improve Student Success* (Washington, DC: Aspen Institute, 2014).

19. Anthony P. Carnevale, Tanya I. Garcia, and Artem Gulish, *Career Pathways: Five Ways to Connect College and Careers* (Washington, DC: Center on Education and the Workforce, 2017).

20. Davis Jenkins et al., *What We Are Learning About Guided Pathways* (New York: Community College Research Center, Teachers College, Columbia University, 2018), https://ccrc.tc.columbia.edu/publications/what-we-are-learning-guided-pathways.html.

21. Jenkins et al., *Guided Pathways.* For more on the history and key features of guided pathways, see "Guided Pathways Resource Center," Pathways Collaborative, https://www.pathwaysresources.org.

22. Carnevale, Garcia, and Gulish, *Career Pathways.* See also Nancy Hoffman and Robert B. Schwartz, *Learning for Careers: The Pathways to Prosperity Network* (Cambridge, MA: Harvard Education Press, 2017).

23. Michel Grosz, *Do Postsecondary Training Programs Respond to Changes in the Labor Market?* (Rockville, MD: Abt Associates, 2019).

24. Michelle R. Weise et al., *Robot-Ready: Human+ Skills for the Future of Work* (Indianapolis: Strada Institute for the Future of Work and Emsi, 2018), https://www.economicmodeling.com/robot-ready-reports/.

25. See, for example, Scott Hartley, *The Fuzzy and the Techie: Why the Liberal Arts Will Rule the Digital World* (New York: Houghton Mifflin Harcourt, 2017) and

Christian Madsbjerg, *Sensemaking: The Power of Humanities in the Age of the Algorithm* (New York: Hachette Books, 2017).

26. Theo Pippens, Clive Belfield, and Thomas Bailey, *Humanities and Liberal Arts Education Across America's Colleges: How Much Is There?* (New York: Community College Research Center, Teachers College, Columbia University, 2019), https://ccrc.tc.columbia.edu/publications/humanities-liberal-arts-education-how-much.html.

27. Weise et al., *Robot-Ready*.

28. Weise et al., *Robot-Ready*, 38.

29. Susan White, Raymond Chu, and Roman Czujko, "The 2012–13 Survey of Humanities Departments at Four-Year Institutions" (College Park, MD: Statistical Research Center, American Institute of Physics, 2014).

30. Samina Sattar, *Evidence Scan of Work Experience Programs* (Oakland, CA: Mathematica Policy Research, 2010), https://bit.ly/2BmpRLI.

31. Charlotte Cahill, *Making Work-Based Learning Work* (Boston: JFF, 2016), https://www.jff.org/resources/making-work-based-learning-work/.

CHAPTER 5

1. US Bureau of Labor Statistics, "May 2018 National Occupational Employment and Wage Estimates," https://www.bls.gov/oes/current/oes_nat.htm.

2. US Bureau of Labor Statistics, "Occupational Outlook Handbook. Fastest Growing Occupations," https://www.bls.gov/ooh/fastest-growing.htm. We exclude jobs that employ fewer than twenty thousand individuals; US Bureau of Labor Statistics, "Labor Force Statistics from the Current Population Survey," https://www.bls.gov/cps/cpsaat11b.htm.

3. Pronita Gupta et al., *Paid Family and Medical Leave Is Critical for Low-Wage Workers and Their Families* (Washington, DC: CLASP, 2018).

4. Pew Charitable Trust, *Retirement Plan Access and Participation Across Generations* (chartbook) (Philadelphia: Pew Charitable Trust, 2017).

5. Good Jobs Institute, "What Is a 'Good' Job?" https://goodjobsinstitute.org/what-is-a-good-job/.

6. Amy K. Glasmeier and the Massachusetts Institute of Technology, "MIT Living Wage Calculator," http://livingwage.mit.edu; Economic Policy Institute, "Family Budget Calculator," https://www.epi.org/resources/budget/.

7. Monique Morrissey, *The State of American Retirement: How 401(k)s Have Failed Most American Workers* (Washington, DC: Economic Policy Institute, 2016).

8. Daniel Schneider and Kristen Harknett, "The Brutal Psychological Toll of Erratic Work Schedules," *Washington Post*, June 27, 2019, https://wapo.st/32AnLUx.

9. Sarah Todd, "The Short but Destructive History of Mass Layoffs," *Quartz*, July 12, 2019, https://qz.com/work/1663731/mass-layoffs-a-history-of-cost-cuts-and-psychological-tolls/.

10. Henry Reeve et al., *Spotlight on Statistics: 25 Years of Worker Injury, Illness, and Fatality Case Data* (Washington, DC: Bureau of Labor Statistics, 2019).

11. Randall Beck and Jim Harter, "Managers Account for 70% of Variance in Employee Engagement," *Gallup Business Journal*, April 21, 2015, https://news.gallup.com/businessjournal/182792/managers-account-variance-employee-engagement.aspx.

12. Zeynep Ton, *The Good Jobs Strategy* (Boston: Houghton Mifflin Harcourt, 2014).

13. J. Richard Hackman and Greg Oldham, *Work Redesign* (Reading, MA: Addison-Wesley, 1980).

14. Carrie Leana, "The Cost of Financial Precarity," *Stanford Social Innovation Review* (Spring 2019), https://ssir.org/articles/entry/the_cost_of_financial_precarity.

15. MetLife, *Financial Wellness Programs Foster a Thriving Workforce* (New York: MetLife, 2019).

16. Joan C. Williams et al., *Stable Scheduling Increases Productivity and Sales: The Stable Scheduling Study* (San Francisco: University of California Hastings College of the Law, University of Chicago School of Social Service Administration, and University of North Carolina Kenan-Flagler Business School, 2018).

17. Good Jobs Institute, "Good Jobs Institute Scorecard," https://goodjobsinstitute.org/good-jobs-scorecard/.

18. Donald Sull, Charles Sull, and Andrew Chamberlain, "Measuring Culture in Leading Companies: Introducing the MIT SMR/Glassdoor Culture 500," *MIT Sloan Management Review*, June 24, 2019, https://sloanreview.mit.edu/projects/measuring-culture-in-leading-companies.

19. Portia Crowe, "The World's Largest Investor Is Trying to Break Down the Wall Between You and Your Money," *Business Insider*, June 18, 2016, https://www.businessinsider.com/how-blackrock-uses-alternative-data-for-impact-investing-2016-6; Barclay Leib, "Big Data Big Future," *Institutional Investor's Alpha* 10 (Winter 2005), http://www.sandspring.com/altinv/BigData-BarclayLeib-IIA-winter2015.pdf; Hema Parmer, "From Fitbits to Rokus, Hedge Funds Mine Data for Consumer Habits," *Bloomberg*, July 24, 2019, https://www.bloomberg.com/news/articles/2019-07-24/from-fitbits-to-rokus-hedge-funds-mine-data-for-consumer-habits.

20. The wages on these crowdsourced sites are imperfect (they are an average over time, may not reflect recent wage raises, average across regions that may have different wage rates, etc.), but they are a guide.

21. Sull, Sull, and Chamberlain, "Measuring Culture."

22. MIT Sloan Management Review/Glassdoor, "Culture 500," https://sloanreview
.mit.edu/culture500/.

23. Yaryna Serkez and Theo Francis, "See How Your Salary Compares," *Wall Street
Journal*, March 5, 2019, https://www.wsj.com/graphics/how-does-your-pay
-stack-up/.

24. Ranita Jain and Amy Blair, *Now Jobs in Young Adult Workforce Programming*
(Washington, DC: Aspen Institute, 2018).

CHAPTER 6

1. Correspondence concerning this chapter should be addressed to David L. Blustein, Department of Counseling, Developmental, and Educational Psychology,
Campion-315, Boston College, Chestnut Hill, MA 02467; email: David.Blustein
@bc.edu.

2. David L. Blustein, *The Importance of Work in an Age of Uncertainty: The Eroding
Work Experience in America* (New York: Oxford University Press, 2019).

3. David L. Blustein, "Integrating Theory, Research, and Practice: Lessons Learned
from the Evolution of Vocational Psychology," in *Integrating Theory, Research,
and Practice in Vocational Psychology: Current Status and Future Directions*, ed. J. P.
Sampson et al. (Tallahassee: Florida State University Libraries, 2017), 179–87.

4. Steven D. Brown and Robert W. Lent, eds., *Career Development and Counseling:
Putting Theory and Research to Work*, 2nd ed. (New York: Wiley, 2013).

5. David L. Blustein, *The Psychology of Working: A New Perspective for Career Development, Counseling, and Public Policy* (New York: Routledge, 2006); Ryan D.
Duffy et al., "The Psychology of Working Theory," *Journal of Counseling Psychology* 63, no. 2 (2016): 127–48, http://dx.doi.org/10.1037/cou0000140.

6. Blustein, "Integrating."

7. Blustein, *Psychology of Working*; David L. Blustein, ed., *The Oxford Handbook of
the Psychology of Working* (New York: Oxford University Press, 2013); Duffy et al.,
"Psychology of Working Theory."

8. Blustein, *Psychology of Working*; Blustein, *Oxford Handbook*; Duffy et al., "Psychology of Working Theory."

9. David L. Blustein et al., "Expanding the Impact of the Psychology of Working: Engaging Psychology in the Struggle for Decent Work and Human Rights,"
Journal of Career Assessment 27, no. 1 (2019): 5, https://doi.org/10.1177
/1069072718774002.

10. The interplay of predictors, moderators, and outcomes is illustrated in figure 1
in Duffy et al., "Psychology of Working Theory."

11. International Labor Organization, "Report of the Director-General: Decent
Work" (presented at the International Labour Conference, 87th Session, Geneva, Switzerland, June 10, 2008), https://bit.ly/2AVToiI.

12. Duffy et al., "Psychology of Working Theory."

13. Blustein et al., "Expanding the Impact."

14. Duffy et al., "Psychology of Working Theory."

15. Duffy et al., "Psychology of Working Theory."

16. Mark L. Savickas, "Career Construction," *Career Choice and Development* 149 (2002): 205.

17. Duffy et al., "Psychology of Working Theory."

18. David L. Blustein, "A Relational Theory of Working," *Journal of Vocational Behavior* 79, no. 1 (2011): 1–17, https://doi.org/10.1016/j.jvb.2010.10.004.

19. Blustein et al., "Expanding the Impact;" Duffy et al., "Psychology of Working Theory."

20. Blustein, *Psychology of Working*; Blustein, *Oxford Handbook*.

21. Brown and Lent, *Career Development*; Mark L. Savickas, *Theories of Psychotherapy Series: Career Counseling*, 2nd ed. (Washington, DC: American Psychological Association, 2019).

22. Blustein, *Importance of Work*; Blustein, *Psychology of Working*.

23. Duffy et al., "Psychology of Working Theory."

24. David L. Blustein et al., "Psychology of Working in Practice: A Theory of Change for a New Era," *Career Development Quarterly* 67, no. 3 (2019): 236–54; Maureen E. Kenny et al., "Applying the Psychology of Working Theory for Transformative Career Education," *Journal of Career Development* 46, no. 6 (2018): 623–36, https://doi.org/10.1177/0894845319827655.

25. Blustein et al., "Psychology of Working in Practice."

26. Kenny et al., "Applying the Psychology of Working Theory"; Lisa (Leigh) Patel, "Literacy, Capital, and Education: A View from Immigrant Youth," *Theory into Practice* 50, no. 2 (2011): 133–40, https://doi.org/10.1080/00405841.2011.558441.

27. Blustein et al., "Psychology of Working in Practice."

28. Blustein et al., "Psychology of Working in Practice."

29. Roderick J. Watts, Derek M. Griffith, and Jaleel Abdul-Adil, "Sociopolitical Development as an Antidote for Oppression—Theory and Action," *American Journal of Community Psychology* 27, no. 2 (1999): 255–71, https://doi.org/10.1023/A:1022839818873.

30. Matthew A. Diemer et al., "Critical Consciousness: A Developmental Approach to Addressing Marginalization and Oppression," *Child Development Perspectives* 10, no. 4 (2016): 216–21, https://doi.org/10.1111/cdep.12193.

31. Duffy et al., "Psychology of Working Theory."

32. Maureen E. Kenny et al., "Combatting Marginalization and Fostering Critical Consciousness for Decent Work," *Interventions in Career Design and Education* (2018): 55–73.

33. Kenny et al., "Combatting Marginalization."

34. Saliha Kozan et al., "Awakening, Efficacy, and Action: A Qualitative Inquiry of a Social Justice–Infused, Science Education Program," *Analyses of Social Issues and Public Policy* (ASAP) 17, no. 1 (2017): 205–34, https://doi.org/10.1111/asap.12136.

35. Mary Gatta and Nancy Hoffman, *Putting Vocation at the Center of Work: The Student Experience in CUNY's Ethnographies of Work Course* (Boston: JFF, 2018), https://www.jff.org/resources/vocation-center-curriculum.

36. Lisa (Leigh) Patel, "Contact Zones, Problem Posing and Critical Consciousness," *Pedagogies: An International Journal* 7, no. 4 (2012): 333–46, https://doi.org/10.1080/1554480X.2012.715738; Lisa (Leigh) Patel et al., "Re/imaging Existing Structures of Schooling: Immigrant Youth, Community Partners, and Dynamic Learning Through Internship," in *Cultural Transformation: Youth and Pedagogies of Possibility*, ed. Korina M. Jocson (Cambridge, MA: Harvard Education Press, 2013), 97–114.

37. Roderick J. Watts, Matthew A. Diemer, and Adam M. Voight, "Critical Consciousness: Current Status and Future Directions," *New Directions for Child and Adolescent Development* 2011, no. 134 (2011): 43–57, https://doi.org/10.1002/cd.310.

38. Roderick J. Watts and Carlos Hipolito-Delgado, "Thinking Ourselves to Liberation?: Advancing Sociopolitical Action in Critical Consciousness," *Urban Review* 47, no. 5 (2015): 847–67.

39. Emily J. Ozer, "Youth-Led Participatory Action Research: Overview and Potential for Enhancing Adolescent Development," *Child Development Perspectives* 11, no. 3 (2017): 173–77, https://doi.org/10.1111/cdep.12228; Sánchez Carmen et al., "Revisiting the Collective in Critical Consciousness: Diverse Sociopolitical Wisdoms and Ontological Healing in Sociopolitical Development," *Urban Review* 47, no. 5 (2015): 824–46.

40. Blustein et al., "Psychology of Working in Practice."

CHAPTER 7

1. Nadya A. Fouad and Angela M. Byars-Winston, "Cultural Context of Career Choice: Meta-Analysis of Race/Ethnicity Differences," *Career Development Quarterly* 53, no. 3 (2005): 223–33; Maureen E. Kenny et al., "Urban Adolescents' Constructions of Supports and Barriers to Educational and Career Attainment," *Journal of Counseling Psychology* 54, no. 3 (2007): 336–43; Ellen Hawley McWhirter et al., "Perceived Barriers and Postsecondary Plans in Mexican American and White Adolescents," *Journal of Career Assessment* 15, no. 1 (2007): 119–38.

2. Saba Rasheed Ali and Kristen A. Menke, "Rural Latino Youth Career Development: An Application of Social Cognitive Career Theory," *Career Development Quarterly* 62, no. 2 (2014): 175–86; Fouad and Byars-Winston, "Cultural Context"; McWhirter et al., "Perceived Barriers."

3. Ellen Hawley McWhirter, Karina Ramos, and Cynthia Medina, "¿Y ahora que? Anticipated Immigration Status Barriers and Latina/o High School Students' Future Expectations," *Cultural Diversity and Ethnic Minority Psychology* 19, no. 3 (2013): 288–97.

4. Ellen Hawley McWhirter, Marina Valdez, and Alisia R. Caban, "Latina Adolescents' Plans, Barriers, and Supports: A Focus Group Study," *Journal of Latina/o Psychology* 1, no. 1 (2013): 35–52.

5. Fouad and Byars-Winston, "Cultural Context"; Lisa Y. Flores, Rachel L. Navarro, and S. Joseph Dewitz, "Mexican American High School Students' Post-Secondary Educational Goals: Applying Social Cognitive Career Theory," *Journal of Career Assessment* 16, no. 4 (2008): 489–501.

6. Steven D. Brown et al., "Relationships Among Supports and Barriers and Career and Educational Outcomes: A Meta-Analytic Investigation," *Journal of Career Assessment* 26, no. 3 (2018): 395–412; Madonna G. Constantine, Barbara C. Wallace, and Mai M. Kindaichi, "Examining Contextual Factors in the Career Decision Status of African American Adolescents," *Journal of Career Assessment* 13, no. 3 (2005): 307–19; Lisa Y. Flores and Karen M. O'Brien, "The Career Development of Mexican American Adolescent Women: A Test of Social Cognitive Career Theory," *Journal of Counseling Psychology* 49, no. 1 (2002): 14–27; Lourdes M. Rivera et al., "The Effects of Perceived Barriers, Role Models, and Acculturation on the Career Self-Efficacy and Career Consideration of Hispanic Women," *Career Development Quarterly* 56, no. 1 (2007): 47–61; Brown et al., "Supports and Barriers"; Margo A. Jackson et al., "Constructively Challenging Diverse Inner-City Youth's Beliefs About Educational and Career Barriers and Supports," *Journal of Career Development* 32, no. 3 (2006): 203–18; Nancy E. Hill, Cynthia Ramirez, and Larry E. Dumka, "Early Adolescents' Career Aspirations: A Qualitative Study of Perceived Barriers and Family Support Among Low-Income, Ethnically Diverse Adolescents," *Journal of Family Issues* 24, no. 7 (2003): 934–59; Maureen E. Kenny et al., "The Role of Perceived Barriers and Relational Support in the Educational and Vocational Lives of Urban High School Students," *Journal of Counseling Psychology* 50, no. 2 (2003): 142–55; Cristina M. Risco et al., "A Meta-Analysis of the Correlates of Educational and Vocational Goals for Latina/o Students," *Journal of Career Assessment* 27, no. 1 (2019): 29–46.

7. George V. Gushue et al., "Self-Efficacy, Perceptions of Barriers, Vocational Identity, and the Career Exploration Behavior of Latino/a High School Students," *Career Development Quarterly* 54, no. 4 (2006): 307–17; Brown et al., "Supports and Barriers"; Ali and Menke, "Rural Latino Youth"; Mindi N. Thompson, "Career Barriers and Coping Efficacy Among Native American Students," *Journal of Career Assessment* 21, no. 2 (2012): 311–25.

8. Brown et al., "Supports and Barriers"; Risco et al., "Meta-Analysis."

9. Jeff Davis, The First-Generation Student Experience: Implications for Campus Practice, and Strategies for Improving Persistence and Success (Sterling, VA: Stylus Publishing, LLC, 2010).

10. Patton O. Garriott, Lisa Y. Flores, and Matthew P. Martens, "Predicting the Math/Science Career Goals of Low-Income Prospective First-Generation College Students," Journal of Counseling Psychology 60, no. 2 (2013): 200–9; Melinda M. Gibbons and L. DiAnne Borders, "Prospective First-Generation College Students: A Social-Cognitive Perspective," Career Development Quarterly 58, no. 3 (2010): 194–208; Trisha L. Raque-Bogdan and Margaretha S. Lucas, "Career Aspirations and the First Generation Student: Unraveling the Layers with Social Cognitive Career Theory," Journal of College Student Development 57, no. 3 (2016): 248–62.

11. Ernest T. Pascarella et al., "First-Generation College Students: Additional Evidence on College Experiences and Outcomes," Journal of Higher Education 75, no. 3 (2004): 249–84.

12. Gibbons and Borders, "First-Generation College Students"; Neeta Kantamneni et al., "Contextual Factors in the Career Development of Prospective First-Generation College Students: An Application of Social Cognitive Career Theory," Journal of Career Assessment 26, no. 1 (2018): 183–196; Steven D. Brown et al., "Social Cognitive Career Theory, Conscientiousness, and Work Performance: A Meta-Analytic Path Analysis," Journal of Vocational Behavior 79, no. 1 (2011): 81–90; Robert W. Lent et al., "Predictors of Science, Technology, Engineering, and Mathematics Choice Options: A Meta-Analytic Path Analysis of the Social-Cognitive Choice Model by Gender and Race/Ethnicity," Journal of Counseling Psychology 65, no. 1 (2018): 17–35; Hung-Bin Sheu et al., "Testing the Choice Model of Social Cognitive Career Theory Across Holland Themes: A Meta-Analytic Path Analysis," Journal of Vocational Behavior 76 (2010): 252–64.

13. Joann S. Olson, "Opportunities, Obstacles, and Options: First-Generation College Graduates and Social Cognitive Career Theory," Journal of Career Development 41, no. 3 (2014): 199–217.

14. Evelyn Nakano Glenn, Unequal Freedom: How Race and Gender Shaped American Citizenship and Labor (Cambridge, UK: Harvard University Press, 2009); Michael Omi and Howard Winant, Racial Formation in the United States (New York: Routledge, 2014); David R. Roediger, The Wages of Whiteness: Race and the Making of the American Working Class (New York: Verso, 2007).

15. Bill Fletcher and Fernando Gapasin, Solidarity Divided: The Crisis in Organized Labor and a New Path Toward Social Justice (Berkeley: University of California Press, 2008); Glenn, Unequal Freedom; Alyosha Goldstein, Poverty in Common: The Politics of Community Action During the American Century (Durham, NC:

Duke University Press, 2012); Jeffrey Helgeson, "American Labor and Working-Class History, 1900–1945," in *Oxford Research Encyclopedia of American History*, ed. Jon Butler (New York: Oxford University Press, 2017), https://bit.ly/2JdZnAy; Lisa Phillips, *A Renegade Union: Interracial Organizing and Labor Radicalism* (Urbana: University of Illinois Press, 2012); Roediger, *Wages of Whiteness*.

16. Richard M. Lee and Brooke L. Dean, "Middle-Class Mythology in an Age of Immigration and Segmented Assimilation: Implication for Counseling Psychology," *Journal of Counseling Psychology* 51, no. 1 (2004): 19–24.

17. Karl Alexander, Doris Entwisle, and Linda Olson, *The Long Shadow: Family Background, Disadvantaged Urban Youth, and the Transition to Adulthood* (New York: Russell Sage Foundation, 2014).

18. Dennis L. Gilbert, *The American Class Structure in an Age of Growing Inequality* (Thousand Oaks, CA: Sage Publications, 2017); Margaret C. Simms, Karina Fortuny, and Everett Henderson, *Racial and Ethnic Disparities Among Low-Income Families* (New York: Urban Institute, 2009).

19. Arne L. Kalleberg, "Job Quality and Precarious Work: Clarifications, Controversies, and Challenges," *Work and Occupations* 39, no. 4 (2012): 427–48; Brian C. Thiede and Shannon M. Monnat, "The Great Recession and America's Geography of Unemployment," *Demographic Research* 35, no. 30 (2016): 891–928; Jake Rosenfeld and Patrick Denice, "What Do Government Unions Do? Public Sector Unions and Nonunion Wages, 1977–2015," *Social Science Research* 78 (2019): 41–56; Christian E. Weller and Angela Hanks, "The Widening Racial Wealth Gap in the United States After the Great Recession," *Forum for Social Economics* 47, no. 2 (2018): 237–52.

20. Simms et al., *Disparities*.

21. Daniel T. Lichter, Domenico Parisi, and Michael C. Taquino, "The Geography of Exclusion: Race, Segregation, and Concentrated Poverty," *Social Problems* 59, no. 3 (2012): 364–88; Simms et al., *Disparities*.

22. John M. Pascoe et al., "Mediators and Adverse Effects of Child Poverty in the United States," *Pediatrics* 137, no. 4 (2016): e20160340.

23. Kevin J. A. Thomas and Catherine Tucker, "Child Poverty During the Years of the Great Recession: An Analysis of Racial Differences Among Immigrants and US Natives," *Race and Social Problems* 7, no. 4 (2015): 300–14.

24. Lauren Musu-Gillette et al., *Status and Trends in the Education of Racial and Ethnic Groups 2017* (NCES 2017-051). (Washington, DC: US Department of Education, National Center for Education Statistics, 2017), https://nces.ed.gov /pubs2017/2017051.pdf.

25. Salvatore Saporito and Deenesh Sohoni, "Mapping Educational Inequality: Concentrations of Poverty Among Poor and Minority Students in Public Schools," *Social Forces* 85, no. 3 (2007): 1227–53.

26. Eve L. Ewing, Ghosts in the Schoolyard: Racism and School Closings on Chicago's South Side (Chicago: University of Chicago Press, 2018); Jonathan Kozol, Savage Inequalities: Children in America's Schools (New York: Broadway Books, 2012).

27. Sarah Burd-Sharps and Rebecca Rasch, *Impact of the US Housing Crisis on the Racial Wealth Gap Across Generations* (New York: Social Science Research Council, 2015), https://bit.ly/2od8jic; Jacob S. Rugh and Douglas S. Massey, "Racial Segregation and the American Foreclosure Crisis," *American Sociological Review* 75, no. 5 (2010): 629–51.

28. Julia B. Isaacs and Phillip Lovell, *The Impact of the Mortgage Crisis on Children and Their Education* (Washington, DC: Brookings Institution, 2008); Vicki Been et al., "Does Losing Your Home Mean Losing Your School?: Effects of Foreclosures on the School Mobility of Children," *Regional Science and Urban Economics* 41, no. 4 (2011): 407-414.

29. Linda van den Bergh et al., "The Implicit Prejudiced Attitudes of Teachers: Relations to Teacher Expectations and the Ethnic Achievement Gap," *American Educational Research Journal* 47, no. 2 (2010): 497–527; Natasha Warikoo et al., "Examining Racial Bias in Education: A New Approach," *Educational Researcher* 45, no. 9 (2016): 508–14.

30. Keith C. Herman and Wendy M. Reinke, "Improving Teacher Perceptions of Parent Involvement Patterns: Findings from a Group Randomized Trial," *School Psychology Quarterly* 32, no. 1 (2017): 89–104.

31. E. R. Peterson et al., "Teachers' Explicit Expectations and Implicit Prejudiced Attitudes to Educational Achievement: Relations with Student Achievement and the Ethnic Achievement Gap," *Learning and Instruction* 42 (2016): 123–40; van den Bergh et al., "Implicit Prejudiced Attitudes"; John B. Diamond, Antonia Randolph, and James P. Spillane, "Teachers' Expectations and Sense of Responsibility for Student Learning: The Importance of Race, Class, and Organizational Habitus," *Anthropology and Education Quarterly* 35, no. 1 (2004): 75–98; McWhirter et al., "Latina Adolescents' Plans"; Anne Gregory, Russell J. Skiba, and Kavitha Mediratta, "Eliminating Disparities in School Discipline: A Framework for Intervention," *Review of Research in Education* 41, no. 1 (2017): 253–78; Monique W. Morris, *Pushout: The Criminalization of Black Girls in Schools* (New York: The New Press, 2016)

32. Kozol, *Savage Inequalities*; Theresa Perry, Claude M. Steele, and Asa Hilliard III, *Young, Gifted, and Black: Promoting High Achievement Among African American Students* (Boston: Beacon Press, 2003).

33. Joel McFarland et al., *The Condition of Education 2019* (Washington, DC: National Center for Education Statistics, Institute of Education Sciences, US Department of Education, 2019), https://nces.ed.gov/pubsearch/pubsinfo.asp?pubid=2019144.

34. Musu-Gillette et al., *Education of Racial and Ethnic Groups 2017*; Jason Fletcher and Marta Tienda, "Race and Ethnic Differences in College Achievement: Does High School Attended Matter?" *Annals of the American Academy of Political and Social Science* 627, no. 1 (2010): 144–66.

35. Erik C. Ness and Richard Tucker, "Eligibility Effects on College Access: Under-Represented Student Perceptions of Tennessee's Merit Aid Program," *Research in Higher Education* 49, no. 7 (2008): 569; Benjamin L. Castleman, Karen Arnold, and Katherine Lynk Wartman, "Stemming the Tide of Summer Melt: An Experimental Study of the Effects of Post–High School Summer Intervention on Low-Income Students' College Enrollment," *Journal of Research on Educational Effectiveness* 5, no. 1 (2012): 1–17.

36. Anthony P. Carnevale and Jeff Strohl, *Separate & Unequal: How Higher Education Reinforces the Intergenerational Reproduction of White Racial Privilege* (Washington, DC: Georgetown University on Education and the Workforce, 2013), https://cew.georgetown.edu/cew-reports/separate-unequal/; Tressie McMillan Cottom, *Lower Ed: The Troubling Rise of For-Profit Colleges in the New Economy* (New York: The New Press, 2017).; James L. Stephan, Jennifer E. Rosenbaum, and Ann E. Person, "Stratification in College Entry and Completion," *Social Science Research* 38, no. 3 (2009): 572–93.

37. Christopher Newfield, *Unmaking the Public University: The Forty-Year Assault on the Middle Class* (Cambridge, MA: Harvard University Press, 2008).

38. Katharine C. Lyall and Kathleen R. Sell, "The De Facto Privatization of American Public Higher Education," *Change: The Magazine of Higher Learning* 38, no. 1 (2006): 6–13; John Quinterno and Viany Orozco, *The Great Cost Shift: How Higher Education Cuts Undermine the Future Middle Class* (Washington, DC: Dēmos, 2012).

39. Leisy J. Abrego and Roberto G. Gonzales, "Blocked Paths, Uncertain Futures: The Postsecondary Education and Labor Market Prospects of Undocumented Latino Youth," *Journal of Education for Students Placed at Risk* 15, no. 1–2 (2010): 144–57; Mark Huelsman, *The Debt Divide: The Racial and Class Bias Behind the "New Normal" of Student Borrowing* (Washington, DC: Dēmos, 2015).

40. Jason N. Houle and Fenaba R. Addo, "Racial Disparities in Student Debt and the Reproduction of the Fragile Black Middle Class," *Sociology of Race and Ethnicity* 5, no. 4 (2018): 562–77; Huelsman, *Debt Divide*; Louise Seamster and Raphaël Charron-Chénier, "Predatory Inclusion and Education Debt: Rethinking the Racial Wealth Gap," *Social Currents* 4, no. 3 (2017): 199–207.

41. Castleman, Arnold, and Wartman, "Stemming the Tide"; Benjamin L. Castleman and Lindsay C. Page, "A Trickle or a Torrent? Understanding the Extent of Summer 'Melt' Among College-Intending High School Graduates," *Social Science Quarterly* 95, no. 1 (2014): 202–20; Rachel E. Dwyer, Laura McCloud,

and Randy Hodson, "Debt and Graduation from American Universities," *Social Forces* 90, no. 4 (2012): 1133–55; Cliff A. Robb, Beth Moody, and Mohamed Abdel-Ghany, "College Student Persistence to Degree: The Burden of Debt," *Journal of College Student Retention: Research, Theory & Practice* 13, no. 4 (2012): 431–56; Jennifer Logan, Traci Hughes, and Brian Logan, "Overworked? An Observation of the Relationship Between Student Employment and Academic Performance," *Journal of College Student Retention: Research, Theory & Practice* 18, no. 3 (2016): 250–62; Jesse Rothstein and Cecilia Elena Rouse, "Constrained After College: Student Loans and Early-Career Occupational Choices," *Journal of Public Economics* 95, no. 1–2 (2011): 149–63; Lei Zhang, "Effects of College Educational Debt on Graduate School Attendance and Early Career and Lifestyle Choices," *Education Economics* 21, no. 2 (2013): 154–75.

42. Mark Chesler, Amanda E. Lewis, and James E. Crowfoot, *Challenging Racism in Higher Education: Promoting Justice* (Lanham, MD: Rowman & Littlefield Publishers, 2005); Drew S. Jacoby-Senghor, Stacey Sinclair, and J. Nicole Shelton, "A Lesson in Bias: The Relationship Between Implicit Racial Bias and Performance in Pedagogical Contexts," *Journal of Experimental Social Psychology* 63 (2016): 50–55.

43. Alexander S. Browman and Mesmin Destin, "The Effects of a Warm or Chilly Climate Toward Socioeconomic Diversity on Academic Motivation and Self-Concept," *Personality and Social Psychology Bulletin* 42, no. 2 (2016): 172–87; James M. Ellis et al., "Examining First-Generation College Student Lived Experiences with Microaggressions and Microaffirmations at a Predominately White Public Research University," *Cultural Diversity and Ethnic Minority Psychology* 25, no. 2 (2018): 266–79; Patton O. Garriott, "A Critical Cultural Wealth Model of First-Generation and Economically Marginalized College Students' Academic and Career Development," *Journal of Career Development* (2019), https://doi.org/10.1177/0894845319826266; Sarah D. Herrmann and Michael E. W. Varnum, "Integrated Social Class Identities Improve Academic Performance, Well-Being, and Workplace Satisfaction," *Journal of Cross-Cultural Psychology* 49, no. 4 (2018): 635–63.

44. Guy A. Boysen et al., "Incidents of Bias in College Classrooms: Instructor and Student Perceptions," *Journal of Diversity in Higher Education* 2, no. 4 (2009): 219–31; Derald Wing Sue et al., "How White Faculty Perceive and React to Difficult Dialogues on Race: Implications for Education and Training," *Counseling Psychologist* 37, no. 8 (2009): 1090–1115.

45. Chesler et al., *Challenging Racism in Higher Education*; Garriott, "Cultural Wealth Model."

46. Anthony P. Carnevale and Andrew R. Hanson, "Learn & Earn: Career Pathways for Youth in the 21st Century," *E-Journal of International and Comparative*

Labour Studies 4, no. 1 (2015): 2–16; Jessica L. Curiale, "America's New Glass Ceiling: Unpaid Internships, the Fair Labor Standards Act, and the Urgent Need for Change," *Hastings Law Journal* 61 (2009): 1531–60; Samantha Rae Powers and Karen K. Myers, "Vocational Anticipatory Socialization: College Students' Reports of Encouraging/Discouraging Sources and Messages," *Journal of Career Development* 44, no. 5 (2017): 409–24.

47. Elizabeth A. Armstrong and Laura T. Hamilton, *Paying for the Party* (Cambridge, UK: Harvard University Press, 2013).

48. Anthony Abraham Jack, "Crisscrossing Boundaries: Variation in Experiences with Class Marginality Among Lower-Income, Black Undergraduates at an Elite College," in *College Students' Experiences of Power and Marginality*, ed. Elizabeth M. Lee and Chaise LaDousa (New York: Routledge, 2015), 91–109; Garriott, "Cultural Wealth Model"; Deborah M. Warnock and Allison L. Hurst, "'The Poor Kids' Table': Organizing Around an Invisible and Stigmatized Identity in Flux," *Journal of Diversity in Higher Education* 9, no. 3 (2016): 261; Amy C. Wilkins, "Race, Age, and Identity Transformations in the Transition from High School to College for Black and First-Generation White Men," *Sociology of Education* 87, no. 3 (2014): 171–87.

49. Shouping Hu and Gregory C. Wolniak, "College Student Engagement and Early Career Earnings: Differences by Gender, Race/Ethnicity, and Academic Preparation," *Review of Higher Education* 36, no. 2 (2013): 211–33; Kevin Stainback, "Social Contacts and Race/Ethnic Job Matching," *Social Forces* 87, no. 2 (2008): 857–86.

50. George Wilson et al., "Particularism and Racial Mobility into Privileged Occupations," *Social Science Research* 78 (2019): 82–94.

51. Joan Acker, "Inequality Regimes: Gender, Class, and Race in Organizations," *Gender & Society* 20, no. 4 (2006): 441–64; Eric Arce and Denise A. Segura, "Stratification in the Labor Market," in *The Wiley Blackwell Encyclopedia of Race, Ethnicity, and Nationalism*, ed. John Stone et al. (Chichester, West Sussex, UK: Wiley Blackwell, 2015).

52. Richard Florida and Charlotta Mellander, *Segregated City: The Geography of Economic Segregation in America's Metros* (Toronto: Martin Prosperity Institute, 2015), http://martinprosperity.org/content/segregated-city/; Richard Florida and Charlotta Mellander, "The Geography of Economic Segregation," *Social Sciences* 7, no. 8 (2018): 123; Sara McLafferty and Valerie Preston, "Who Has Long Commutes to Low-Wage Jobs? Gender, Race, and Access to Work in the New York Region," *Urban Geography* (2019): 1–21, https://doi.org/10.1080/027236 38.2019.1577091; Stainback, "Social Contacts"; Wilson et al., "Particularism"; John L. Cotton, Bonnie S. O'Neill, and Andrea Griffin, "The 'Name Game': Affective and Hiring Reactions to First Names," *Journal of Managerial Psychology*

23, no. 1 (2008): 18–39; Joyce C. He et al., "Stereotypes at Work: Occupational Stereotypes Predict Race and Gender Segregation in the Workforce," *Journal of Vocational Behavior* 115 (2019), https://doi.org/10.1016/j.jvb.2019.103318; Janelle Jones and John Schmitt, *A College Degree Is No Guarantee* (Washington, DC: Center for Economic and Policy Research, 2014); André Ndobo et al., "The Ethno-Racial Segmentation Jobs: The Impacts of the Occupational Stereotypes on Hiring Decisions," *Journal of Social Psychology* 158, no. 6 (2018), 663–79.

53. Jones and Schmitt, *College Degree*; Thomas Luke Spreen, "Recent College Graduates in the US Labor Force: Data from the Current Population Survey," *Monthly Labor Review* 136 (2013): 3–13; Thompson, "Career Barriers."

54. Acker, "Inequality Regimes"; Arce and Segura, "Stratification"; Carolyn A. Liebler, Jacob Wise, and Richard M. Todd, "Occupational Dissimilarity Between the American Indian/Alaska Native and the White Workforce in the Contemporary United States," *American Indian Culture and Research Journal* 42, no. 1 (2018): 41–70; Wilson et al., "Particularism."

55. He et al., "Stereotypes at Work"; Elizabeth Hirsh and Christopher J. Lyons, "Perceiving Discrimination on the Job: Legal Consciousness, Workplace Context, and the Construction of Race Discrimination," *Law & Society Review* 44, no. 2 (2010): 269–98; Anna M. Kallschmidt and Asia A. Eaton, "Are Lower Social Class Origins Stigmatized at Work? A Qualitative Study of Social Class Concealment and Disclosure Among White Men Employees Who Experienced Upward Mobility," *Journal of Vocational Behavior* 113 (2018); Young Hwa Kim and Karen M. O'Brien, "Assessing Women's Career Barriers Across Racial/Ethnic Groups: The Perception of Barriers Scale," *Journal of Counseling Psychology* 65, no. 2 (2018): 226–38; Adia Harvey Wingfield, "The Modern Mammy and the Angry Black Man: African American Professionals' Experiences with Gendered Racism in the Workplace," *Race, Gender & Class* 14, no. 1/2 (2007): 196–212.

56. Alison Cook and Christy Glass, "The Power of One or Power in Numbers? Analyzing the Effect of Minority Leaders on Diversity Policy and Practice," *Work and Occupations* 42, no. 2 (2015): 183–215; Seval Gündemir et al., "The Impact of Organizational Diversity Policies on Minority Employees' Leadership Self-Perceptions and Goals," *Journal of Leadership & Organizational Studies* 24, no. 2 (2017): 172–88.

57. Cook and Glass, "Power of One?"; Orlando C. Richard et al., "The Impact of Supervisor-Subordinate Racial-Ethnic and Gender Dissimilarity on Mentoring Quality and Turnover Intentions: Do Positive Affectivity and Communal Culture Matter?" *International Journal of Human Resource Management* (2017): 1–28, http://dx.doi.org/10.1080/09585192.2017.1344288; Acker, "Inequality Regimes"; Kevin Stainback and Donald Tomaskovic-Devey, "Intersections of Power and

Privilege: Long-Term Trends in Managerial Representation," *American Sociological Review* 74, no. 5 (2009): 800–20.

58. Wilson et al., "Particularism."

59. Brigid Schulte, "The US Ranks Last in Every Measure When It Comes to Family Policy, in 10 Charts," *Washington Post*, June 23, 2014, https://wapo.st/35 ZDlLu.

60. Evangelina Holvino, "Intersections: The Simultaneity of Race, Gender and Class in Organization Studies," *Gender, Work & Organization* 17, no. 3 (2010): 248–77; Annette Lareau, *Unequal Childhoods: Class, Race, and Family Life* (Berkeley: University of California Press, 2011).

61. Steven D. Brown and Nancy E. Ryan Krane, "Four (or Five) Sessions and a Cloud of Dust: Old Assumptions and New Observations About Career Counseling," in *Handbook of Counseling Psychology*, 3rd ed., ed. Steven D. Brown and Robert W. Lent (Hoboken, NJ: Wiley, 2000), 740–66.

62. Kimberly A. Howard and Mary E. Walsh, "Children's Conceptions of Career Choice and Attainment: Model Development," *Journal of Career Development* 38, no. 3 (2011): 256–71.

63. Saba Rasheed Ali and Jodi L. Saunders, "College Expectations of Rural Appalachian Youth: An Exploration of Social Cognitive Career Theory Factors," *Career Development Quarterly* 55, no. 1 (2006): 38–51; Mindi N. Thompson et al., "The Transmission of Social Class and World of Work Information in Parent-Adolescent Dyads," *Journal of Career Assessment* 26, no. 4 (2018): 697–716; Susan C. Whiston and Briana K. Keller, "The Influences of the Family of Origin on Career Development: A Review and Analysis," *Counseling Psychologist* 32, no. 4 . (2004): 493–568; Julie Bettie, *Women Without Class: Girls, Race, and Identity* (Berkeley: University of California Press, 2014); Moin Syed, Margarita Azmitia, and Catherine R. Cooper, "Identity and Academic Success Among Underrepresented Ethnic Minorities: An Interdisciplinary Review and Integration," *Journal of Social Issues* 67, no. 3 (2011): 442–68.

64. Mindi N. Thompson, Pa Her, and Rachel S. Nitzarim, "Personal and Contextual Variables Related to Work Hope Among Undergraduate Students from Underrepresented Backgrounds," *Journal of Career Assessment* 22, no. 4 (2014): 595–609; Mindi N. Thompson et al., "A Grounded Theory Exploration of Undergraduate Experiences of Vicarious Unemployment," *Journal of Counseling Psychology* 60, no. 3 (2013): 421; Ellen Gutowski et al., "How Stress Influences Purpose Development: The Importance of Social Support," *Journal of Adolescent Research* 33, no. 5 (2018): 571–97.

65. Caroline S. Clauss-Ehlers et al., "APA Multicultural Guidelines Executive Summary: Ecological Approach to Context, Identity, and Intersectionality," *American Psychologist* 74, no. 2 (2019): 232–44; Henri Tajfel, "Introduction," in *Social*

Identity and Intergroup Relations, Vol. 7, ed. Henri Tajfel (Cambridge, UK: Cambridge University Press, 2010).

66. Syed et al., "Identity and Academic Success."

67. Samuel T. Beasley, Collette Chapman-Hilliard, and Shannon McClain, "Linking the Emancipatory Pedagogy of Africana/Black Studies with Academic Identity Outcomes Among Black Students Attending PWIs," *Journal of Pan African Studies* 9, no. 8 (2016): 9–25; Roderick J. Watts, Matthew A. Diemer, and Adam M. Voight, "Critical Consciousness: Current Status and Future Directions," *Youth Civic Development: Work at the Cutting Edge, New Directions for Child and Adolescent Development* 134 (2011): 43–57.

68. Bryana H. French et al., "Toward a Psychological Framework of Radical Healing in Communities of Color," *Counseling Psychologist* (2019), https://doi.org/10 .1177/0011000019843506; Jioni A. Lewis and Patrick R. Grzanka, "Applying Intersectionality Theory to Research on Perceived Racism," in *The Cost of Racism for People of Color: Contextualizing Experiences of Discrimination*, ed. Alvin N. Alvarez, Christopher T. H. Lang, and Helen A. Neville (Washington, DC: American Psychological Association, 2016), 31–54.

69. Clauss-Ehlers et al., "APA Multicultural Guidelines"; Katrina M. Walsemann, Bethany A. Bell, and Debeshi Maitra, "The Intersection of School Racial Composition and Student Race/Ethnicity on Adolescent Depressive and Somatic Symptoms," *Social Science & Medicine* 72, no. 11 (2011): 1873–83.

70. Erin B. Godfrey, Carlos E. Santos, and Esther Burson, "For Better or Worse? System-Justifying Beliefs in Sixth-Grade Predict Trajectories of Self-Esteem and Behavior Across Early Adolescence," *Child Development* 90, no. 1 (2019): 180–95; Carlos P. Hipolito-Delgado, "Internalized Racism, Perceived Racism, and Ethnic Identity: Exploring Their Relationship in Latina/o Undergraduates," *Journal of College Counseling* 19, no. 2 (2016): 98–109; Syed et al., "Identity and Academic Success."

71. Maureen E. Kenny et al., "Setting the Stage: Career Development and the Student Engagement Process," *Journal of Counseling Psychology* 53, no. 2 (2006): 272–79.

72. Frederick T. L. Leong and Mei Tang, "Career Barriers for Chinese Immigrants in the United States," *Career Development Quarterly* 64 (2016): 259–71.

73. Gushue et al., "Self-Efficacy."

74. In Heok Lee and Jay W. Rojewski, "Development of Occupational Aspiration Prestige: A Piecewise Latent Growth Model of Selected Influences," *Journal of Vocational Behavior* 75, no. 1 (2009): 82–90; Mary E. M. McKillip, Anita Rawls, and Carol Barry, "Improving College Access: A Review of Research on the Role of High School Counselors," *Professional School Counseling* 16, no. 1 (2012), https://doi.org/10.1177/2156759X1201600106.

75. Robert W. Lent et al., "Testing Social Cognitive Interest and Choice Hypotheses Across Holland Types in Italian High School Students," *Journal of Vocational Behavior* 62, no. 1 (2003): 101–18.

76. Jennifer Brown, *Inclusion: Diversity, the New Workplace & the Will to Change* (Hartford, CT: Publish Your Purpose Press, 2017), 34.

77. Vivian Hunt, Dennis Layton, and Sara Prince, *Diversity Matters* (New York: McKinsey & Company, 2015), 15–29.

78. Andrew A. Helwig, "A Test of Gottfredson's Theory Using a Ten-Year Longitudinal Study," *Journal of Career Development* 28, no. 2 (2001): 77–95.

79. There are free curricula that are available to support youth career exploration. For example, JFF, a national workforce development nonprofit organization, offers the Possible Futures curriculum at no cost. Possible Futures provides students (grades 6–10) access to quality information about college and career opportunities to make informed decisions about their future. In short, Possible Futures provides youth a rich, learner-centered, career exploration and readiness experience that helps young people develop a future-ready mind-set with a skill set to match. For more, see https://www.jff.org/what-we-do/impact-stories/possible-futures/.

80. James E. Rosenbaum, Shazia Rafiullah Miller, and Melinda Scott Krei, "Gatekeeping in an Era of More Open Gates: High School Counselors' Views of Their Influence on Students' College Plans," *American Journal of Education* 104, no. 4 (1996): 257–79.

81. American School Counselor Association (ASCA), "About ASCA," https://www.schoolcounselor.org.

82. McKillip, Rawls, and Barry, "Improving College Access."

83. Keith MacAllum et al., *Deciding on Postsecondary Education: Final Report. NPEC 2008-850* (Washington, DC: National Postsecondary Education Cooperative, 2007).

84. American School Counselor Association (ASCA), "Careers/Roles," https://www.schoolcounselor.org/school-counselors-members/careers-roles.

85. Brown et al., "Social Cognitive Career Theory"; Lent et al., "Predictors"; Sheu et al., "Testing the Choice Model."

86. Lent et al., "Predictors."

87. Albert Bandura, *Social Foundations of Thought and Action: A Social Cognitive Theory* (Englewood Cliffs, NJ: Prentice Hall, Inc., 1986).

88. Angela Byars-Winston et al., "Unique Effects and Moderators of Effects of Sources on Self-Efficacy: A Model-Based Meta-Analysis," *Journal of Counseling Psychology* 64, no. 6 (2017): 645–58.

89. Margo A. Jackson et al., "Constructively Challenging Diverse Inner-City Youth's Beliefs About Educational and Career Barriers and Supports," *Journal of Career Development* 32, no. 3 (2006): 203–18; Maureen E. Kenny, "Preparing Youth to

Meet the Challenges of an Uncertain Future: A New Direction of Prevention," *Prevention and Health Promotion: Research, Social Action, Practice, and Training* 10, no. 2 (2017): 23–30.

90. Yiwen Zhang et al., "Promotion- and Prevention-Focused Coping: A Meta-Analytic Examination of Regulatory Strategies in the Work Stress Process," *Journal of Applied Psychology* (2019).

91. Brown and Ryan Krane, "Four (or Five) Sessions."

92. Whiston and Keller, "Influences of the Family of Origin."

93. Diemer and Blustein, "Critical Consciousness"; Ellen Hawley McWhirter and Benedict T. McWhirter, "Critical Consciousness and Vocational Development Among Latina/o High School Youth: Initial Development and Testing of a Measure," *Journal of Career Assessment* 24, no. 3 (2016): 543–58.

94. Mark B. Scholl, "The Career Path Tournament: Developing Awareness of Sociological Barriers to Career Advancement," *Career Development Quarterly* 47, no. 3 (1999): 230–42.

95. Kevin A. Tate et al., "An Exploration of First-Generation College Students' Career Development Beliefs and Experiences," *Journal of Career Development* 42, no. 4 (2015): 294–310.

96. Jackson et al., "Constructively Challenging."

97. Brown, "Inclusion," 24.

CHAPTER 8

1. Iain McGilchrist, *The Master and His Emissary: The Divided Brain and the Making of the Western World* (New Haven, CT: Yale University Press, 2009).

2. See, for example, Kate Davidson, "Employers Find 'Soft Skills' Like Critical Thinking in Short Supply," *Wall Street Journal,* August 30, 2016, https://on.wsj.com/31F6jNs; Jeffrey Salingo, "Forget Coding. It's the Soft Skills, Stupid. And That's What Schools Should Be Teaching," *Washington Post,* April 20, 2018, https://wapo.st/2qHovpX; and Jill Casner-Lotto and Linda Barrington, *Are They Really Ready to Work? Employers' Perspectives on the Basic Knowledge and Applied Skills of New Entrants to the 21st Century US Workforce* (New York: The Conference Board, Inc., the Partnership for 21st Century Skills, Corporate Voices for Working Families, and the Society for Human Resource Management, 2006).

3. Margaret Andrews, "What Do Employers Want?," *Inside Higher Ed,* June 30, 2015, https://www.insidehighered.com/blogs/stratedgy/what-do-employers-want.

4. Benjamin Spar et al., "2018 Workplace Learning Report," LinkedIn Learning, 2018, https://bit.ly/2t7VWFA; Davidson, "'Soft Skills' in Short Supply."

5. David Deming, *The Growing Importance of Social Skills in the Labor Market,* NBER Working Paper No. 21473 (Cambridge, MA: National Bureau of Economic Research, 2017), https://www.nber.org/papers/w21473.pdf.

6. Diane Whitmore Schanzenbach et al., *Seven Facts on Noncognitive Skills from Education to the Labor Market* (Washington, DC: The Hamilton Project, 2016).

7. David Autor, *Work of the Past, Work of the Future*, NBER Working Paper No. 25588 (Cambridge, MA: National Bureau of Economic Research, 2019), https://www.nber.org/papers/w25588.pdf.

8. Centre for the New Economy and Society, *The Future of Jobs Report 2018* (Geneva: World Economic Forum, 2018), http://www3.weforum.org/docs/WEF_Future_of_Jobs_2018.pdf.

9. Strada Institute for the Future of Work and Emsi, *Robot-Read: Human+ Skills for the Future of Work* (Indianapolis: Strada Education Network, 2018), https://www.economicmodeling.com/robot-ready-reports/.

10. Jacques Bughin et al., *Skill Shift: Automation and the Future of the Workforce* (Washington, DC: McKinsey Global Institute, 2018), https://mck.co/2MBBlzg.

11. Project Lead the Way and Burning Glass Technologies, *The Power of Transportable Skills* (Boston: Burning Glass Technologies), https://bit.ly/2pQpOoI.

12. Nikki Graf, Richard Fry, and Gary Funk, "7 Facts About the STEM Workforce," Pew Research Center *FactTank*, January 9, 2018, https://www.pewresearch.org/fact-tank/2018/01/09/7-facts-about-the-stem-workforce/.

13. Claudia Goldin and Lawrence Katz, *The Race Between Education and Technology*, NBER Working Paper No. 12984 (Cambridge, MA: National Bureau of Economic Research, 2007), http://www.nber.org/papers/w12984.

14. Sally C. Curtin, Stephanie J. Ventura, and Gladys M. Martinez, "Recent Declines in Nonmarital Childbearing in the United States," National Center for Health Statistics, August 2014, https://www.cdc.gov/nchs/data/databriefs/db162.pdf; Sheela Kennedy and Steven Ruggles, "Breaking Up Is Hard to Count: The Rise of Divorce in the United States, 1980–2010," *Demography* 51, no. 2 (2014): 587–98, https://www.ncbi.nlm.nih.gov/pmc/articles/PMC3972308/.

15. Anthony Walsh, "Illegitimacy, Child Abuse and Neglect, and Cognitive Development," *Journal of Genetic Psychology* 151, no. 3 (1990): 279–85, https://www.ncbi.nlm.nih.gov/pubmed/2266355; Randal D. Day et al., "Marital Quality and Outcomes for Children and Adolescents: A Review of the Family Process Literature," US Department of Health and Human Services, May 2009, https://aspe.hhs.gov/system/files/pdf/76006/index.pdf; Susan L. Brown, "Marriage and Child Well-Being: Research and Policy Perspectives," *Journal of Marriage and Family* 72, no. 5 (2010): 1059–77, https://www.ncbi.nlm.nih.gov/pmc/articles/PMC3091824/.

16. Joyce A. Martin et al., "Births Final Data for 2017," *National Vital Statistics Report* 67, no. 8 (2018), https://www.cdc.gov/nchs/data/nvsr/nvsr67/nvsr67_08-508.pdf; Centers for Disease Control and Prevention, "Number and Percent of Births to Unmarried Women, by Race and Hispanic Origin: United States,

1940–2000," https://www.cdc.gov/nchs/data/statab/t001x17.pdf; Joseph Chamie, "Out-of-Wedlock Births Rise Worldwide," *YaleGlobal Online*, March 16, 2017, https://yaleglobal.yale.edu/content/out-wedlock-births-rise-worldwide.

17. Flavio Cunha and James Heckman, *Investing in Our Young People*, NBER Working Paper No. 16201 (Cambridge, MA: National Bureau of Economic Research, 2010), http://www.nber.org/papers/w16201.

18. Holly Brophy-Herb et al., "Longitudinal Connections of Maternal Supportiveness and Early Emotion Regulation to Children's School Readiness in Low-Income Families," *Journal of the Society for Social Work and Research* 4, no. 1 (2013): 2–19; Clancy Blair et al., "Poverty, Stress, and Brain Development: New Directions for Prevention and Intervention," *Academic Pediatrics* 16, no. 3 (2016): 30–6.

19. Pamela Scorza et al., "Towards Clarity in Research on 'Non-Cognitive' Skills: Linking Executive Functions, Self-Regulation, and Economic Development to Advance Life Outcomes for Children, Adolescents and Youth Globally," *Human Development* 58, no. 6 (2016): 313–17.

20. Blair et al., "Poverty, Stress, and Brain Development."

21. Katharine B. Stevens, "Social from Birth," American Enterprise Institute *AEIdeas*, October 15, 2018, http://www.aei.org/publication/social-from-birth/.

22. Administration for Children and Families, Office of Family Assistance, "Healthy Marriage & Responsible Fatherhood," https://www.acf.hhs.gov/ofa/programs /healthy-marriage.

23. Quinn Moore et al., *Parents and Children Together: Effects of Two Healthy Marriage Programs for Low-Income Couples*, OPRE Report 2018-58 (Washington, DC: Mathematica Policy Research, 2018), https://bit.ly/32RI0gJ.

24. Office of Planning, Research and Evaluation, Administration for Children and Families, "Federally-Funded Research and Evaluation on Healthy Marriage Programs" (presentation, October 9, 2018).

25. Alan J. Hawkins, *Are Federally Supported Relationship Education Programs for Lower-Income Individuals and Couples Working? A Review of Evaluation Research* (Washington, DC: American Enterprise Institute, 2019), https://bit.ly/32HhEhd.

26. Nurse-Family Partnerships, https://www.nursefamilypartnership.org/.

27. US Department of Health and Human Services, Administration for Children and Families, "Nurse-Family Partnership," May 2016.

28. Lynn A. Karoly, *Investing in the Early Years: The Costs and Benefits of Investing in Early Childhood in New Hampshire* (Santa Monica: RAND Corporation, 2017), https://www.rand.org/pubs/research_reports/RR1890.html.

29. Flavio Cunha et al., "Interpreting the Evidence on Life Cycle Skill Formation," in *Handbook of the Economics of Education, Vol. 1*, ed. Eric Hanushek and Finis Welch (Amsterdam: Elsevier, 2006), http://jenni.uchicago.edu/papers/Cunha _Heckman_etal_2006_HEE_v1_ch12.pdf.

30. James J. Heckman et al., *An Analysis of the Memphis Nurse-Family Partnership Program*, NBER Working Paper No. 23610 (Cambridge: National Bureau of Economic Research, 2017), https://heckmanequation.org/assets/2017/07/NFP_Final-Paper.pdf.

31. Lynn A. Karoly, M. Rebecca Kilburn, and Jill S. Cannon, *Early Childhood Interventions* (Santa Monica: RAND Corporation, 2005), https:// www.rand.org /content/dam/rand/pubs/monographs/2005/RAND_MG341.pdf.

32. James J. Heckman, Rodrigo Pinto, and Peter Savelyev, "Understanding the Mechanisms Through Which an Influential Early Childhood Program Boosted Adult Outcomes," *American Economic Review* 103, no. 6 (2013): 2052–86, http://europepmc.org/backend/ptpmcrender.fcgi?accid=PMC3951747&blobtype=pdf.

33. Heckman, Pinto, and Savelyev, "Influential Early Childhood Program."

34. David Deming, "Early Childhood Intervention and Life-Cycle Skill Development: Evidence from Head Start," *American Economic Journal: Applied Economics* 1, no. 3 (2009): 111–34, http://www.people.fas.harvard.edu/~deming/papers/Deming_ HeadStart.pdf.

35. Diane Whitmore Schanzenbach and Lauren Bauer, "The Long-Term Impact of the Head Start Program," Brookings Institution, August 19, 2016, https://www .brookings.edu/research/the-long-term-impact-of-the-head-start-program/.

36. J. Mark Eddy et al., "A Randomized Controlled Trial of a Long-Term Professional Mentoring Program for Children at Risk: Outcomes Across the First 5 Years," *Prevention Science* 18 (2017): 899–910.

37. Tim Kautz et al., *Fostering and Measuring Skills: Improving Cognitive and Non-Cognitive Skills to Promote Lifetime Success* (Paris: Organisation for Economic Co-operation and Development, 2015), https://bit.ly/2uUbawv.

38. Robert Lerman, "Are Employability Skills Learned in U.S. Youth Education and Training Programs?," *IZA Journal of Labor Policy* 2, no. 6 (2013), https://izajolp .springeropen.com/track/pdf/10.1186/2193-9004-2-6.

39. James J. Kemple, *Career Academies: Long-Term Impacts on Work, Education, and Transitions to Adulthood* (New York: MDRC, 2008), https://www.mdrc.org /publication/career-academies-long-term-impacts-work-education-and-transitions -adulthood.

40. MDRC, "Project Overview: WorkAdvance," https://www.mdrc.org/project /workadvance#overview.

41. Betsy L. Tessler et al., *Meeting the Needs of Workers and Employers* (New York: MDRC, 2014), https://bit.ly/2JhrpLw.

42. Kelsey Schaberg, *Can Sector Strategies Promote Longer-Term Effects? Three-Year Impacts from the WorkAdvance Demonstration* (New York: MDRC, 2017), https:// bit.ly/32F4Uru.

43. Schaberg, *Sector Strategies*.

44. US Chamber of Commerce Foundation Talent Pipeline Management, https:// www.uschamberfoundation.org/talent-pipeline-management.

45. *Executive functioning skills* refer to capacities for attention, self-regulation, mental flexibility, and managing multiple tasks.

46. Anne Roder and Mark Elliott, *Nine Year Gains: Project QUEST's Continuing Impact*, New York: Economic Mobility Corporation, 2019), https://bit.ly/2pSewQT.

47. Project QUEST, "Skills Training," https://www.questsa.org/skills-training/; Nelson D. Schwartz, "Job Training Can Change Lives. See How San Antonio Does It," *New York Times,* August 19, 2019, https://nyti.ms/30glJaJ.

48. Schwartz, "Job Training."

49. Ida Rademacher, Marshall Bear, and Maureen Conway, *Project QUEST: A Case Study of a Sectoral Employment Development Approach* (Washington, DC: Aspen Institute, 2001), 47, https://assets.aspeninstitute.org/content/uploads/files/content /docs/PQCASESTUDY.PDF.

50. EMPath, "Intergenerational Mobility Project," https://www.empathways.org /direct-services/intergen-project.

51. Elisabeth Babcock and Nicki Ruiz de Luzuriaga, *Families Disrupting the Cycle of Poverty: Coaching with an Intergenerational Lens* (Boston: Economic Mobility Pathways, 2016); Adam P. Matheny et al., "Bringing Order Out of Chaos: Psychometric Characteristics of the Confusion, Hubbub, and Order Scale," *Journal of Applied Developmental Psychology* 16, no. 3 (1995): 429–44, https://doi.org/10 .1016/0193-3973(95)90028-4.

52. Matheny et al., "Order Out of Chaos."

CHAPTER 9

1. Jenni Russell, "Britain's Broken Ladder of Social Mobility," *New York Times,* June 27, 2017, https://nyti.ms/2tg6iSU.

2. Ilana Gershon, "Getting Off the Screen and into Networks," *Down and Out in the New Economy* (Chicago: University of Chicago Press, 2017), 89–120.

3. Timothy J. Bartik and Brad Hershbein, "Degrees of Poverty: The Relationship Between Family Income Background and the Returns to Education," *W.E. Upjohn Institute Working Paper* 18-284 (Kalamazoo, MI: W.E. Upjohn Institute for Employment Research, 2018), https://doi.org/10.17848/wp18-284. See also Timothy J. Bartik and Brad Hershbein, *College Grads Earn Less If They Grew Up Poor* (Kalamazoo, MI: W.E. Upjohn Institute for Employment Research, 2016).

4. Bartik and Hershbein, "Degrees of Poverty," 12.

5. Anthony Carnevale et al., *African Americans: College Majors and Earnings* (Washington, DC: Georgetown University Center on Education and the Workforce, 2016).

6. Brad Hershbein, "So, Why Is a College Degree Worth Less If You Are Raised Poor? A Response to Readers' Comments," *Social Mobility Memos*, Brookings Institute, March 4, 2016, https://brook.gs/35YEhzT.

7. Julia Freeland Fisher, with Daniel Fisher, *Who You Know: Unlocking Innovations That Expand Students' Networks* (San Francisco: Jossey-Bass, 2018).

8. Nan Lin, "Building a Network Theory of Social Capital," in *Social Capital: Theory and Research*, ed. Nan Lin, Karen S. Cook, and Ronald S. Burt (New York: Aldine de Gruyter, 2001), 4.

9. Paul Adler and Seok-Woo Kwon, "Social Capital: Prospects for a New Concept," *Academy of Management Review* 27, no. 1 (2002): 17, 23.

10. Giorgos Cheliotis, "Assessing CC Growth" (PowerPoint presentation, CC Summit, National University of Singapore, 2011), https://www.slideshare.net/gcheliotis.

11. Miller McPherson, Lynn Smith-Lovin, and James M. Cook, "Birds of a Feather: Homophily in Social Networks," *Annual Review of Sociology* 27 (2001): 415–44.

12. McPherson et al., "Birds of a Feather," 415.

13. Nan Lin, Karen S. Cook, and Ronald S. Burt, *Social Capital: Theory and Research* (New York: Aldine de Gruyter, 2001).

14. Tristan Claridge makes this comment in "What Is the Difference Between Bonding and Bridging Social Capital," *Social Capital Research and Training*, January 2, 2018, https://www.socialcapitalresearch.com/difference-bonding-bridging-social-capital.

15. Mark Granovetter, "The Strength of Weak Ties," *American Journal of Sociology* 78, no. 6 (1973): 1360–80.

16. Mark Granovetter, *Getting a Job: A Study of Contacts and Careers* (Chicago: University of Chicago Press, 1974), 3.

17. Mark Granovetter, *Getting a Job: A Study of Contacts and Careers*, 2nd ed. (Chicago: University of Chicago Press, 1995), 148.

18. Granovetter, *Getting a Job*, 2nd ed., 150.

19. Michael Bernabé Aguilera, "The Impact of Social Capital on Labor Force Participation: Evidence from the 2000 Social Capital Benchmark Survey," *Social Science Quarterly* 83, no. 3 (2002): 872.

20. Sandra Susan Smith, *Lone Pursuit: Distrust and Defensive Individualism Among the Black Poor* (New York: Russell Sage Foundation, 2007), 94–5.

21. Ilana Gershon, "Didn't We Meet on LinkedIn?" *Down and Out in the New Economy* (Chicago: University of Chicago Press, 2017), 121–58.

22. Peggy McKee, "LinkedIn's Profile Strength Indicator—How Do You Measure Up?" https://careerconfidential.com/linkedins-profile-strength-indicator-how-do-you-measure-up/.

23. John Herrman, "Why Aren't We Talking About LinkedIn?" *New York Times*, August 8, 2019, https://nyti.ms/31yiaxb.

24. Herrman, "Why?"

25. Carlos D. Morrison, "Code-Switching, Linguistics," https://www.britannica.com/topic/code-switching.

26. Ilana Gershon, "'A Friend of a Friend' Is No Longer the Best Way to Find a Job," *Harvard Business Review*, June 2, 2017, https://hbr.org/2017/06/a-friend-of-a-friend-is-no-longer-the-best-way-to-find-a-job.

27. Gershon, *Down and Out*, 167.

28. Paul Attewell, "What Is Skill?" *Work and Occupations*, 17, no. 4 (1990): 422–48.

29. Mary Gatta, "In the 'Blink' of an Eye: American High-End Small Retail Businesses and the Public Workforce System," *Retail Work*, ed. Irena Grugulis and Ödül Bozkurt (Basingstoke, UK: Palgrave Macmillan, 2011), 49–67.

30. Dennis Nickson et al., *Journal of Education and Work* 16, no. 2 (2003): 185–203.

31. Lynne Pettinger, "Brand Culture and Branded Workers: Service Work and Aesthetic Labour in Fashion Retail," *Consumption Markets & Culture* 7, no. 2 (2004): 165–84.

32. Chris Warhurst, Paul Thompson, and Dennis Nickson, "Labor Process Theory: Putting the Materialism Back into the Meaning of Service Work," in *Service Work: Critical Perspectives*, ed. Marek Korczynski and Cameron Lynne Macdonald (New York: Routledge, 2009), 91–112.

33. Aimee Groth, "The Subtle Sexism of Hoodies: Women in Silicon Valley Have No Idea What to Wear to Work," *Quartz*, January 6, 2016, https://bit.ly/2BGD6XO.

34. Pierre Bourdieu, *Distinction: A Social Critique of the Judgement of Taste* (Abingdon, UK: Routledge, 1984).

35. Irena Grugund, Chris Warhurst, and Ewart Keep, "What's Happening to 'Skill'?" in *The Skills That Matter*, ed. Irena Grugund, Chris Warhurst, and Ewart Keep (London: Palgrave, 2004), 1–18.

36. John Goldthorpe, "The Myth of Education-Based Meritocracy," *IPPR Progressive Review* 10, no. 4 (2003): 234–39.

ABOUT THE EDITORS
AND CONTRIBUTORS

KATIE BACH is managing director of the Good Jobs Institute, and has spent most of her career focused on job creation, access, and quality. Prior to joining the Good Jobs Institute, Katie was a Director of Global Strategy at Starbucks, where she led the development of the company's annual strategic plan. Previously, she spent nearly five years in management consulting, first with McKinsey & Company and then at a Nairobi-based firm, advising clients on strategy, organizational structure, and human capital management. While at McKinsey, Katie was also on the founding team of Generation, McKinsey's global youth employment program.

Katie has an undergraduate degree in Politics, Philosophy, and Economics from the University of Oxford. She was valedictorian of her master's program in Global Politics at the London School of Economics and received her MBA from MIT Sloan School of Management. At MIT Sloan, she won a Siebel Scholarship, McKinsey Award, and Forte Fellowship, all for outstanding academic and leadership contributions.

DAVID L. BLUSTEIN is a professor in the Department of Counseling, Developmental, and Educational Psychology at the Lynch School of Education at Boston College. David is the author of *The Psychology of Working: A New Perspective for Career Development, Counseling, and Public Policy* (Erlbaum) and a new book entitled *The Importance of Work in an Age of Uncertainty: The Eroding Experience of Work in America* (Oxford University Press). He also has contributed numerous articles and book chapters on the psychology of working theory, unemployment, work-based counseling/career development education, decent work, precarious work, relationships and work, and other aspects of the role of work in people's lives. David has consulted with national and international organizations, such as the International Labor Organization and the United Nations Development Program. In addition, David has worked as a practicing counseling psychologist for over three decades providing relationally oriented psychotherapy and work-based counseling.

CHARLOTTE CAHILL is a senior associate director at JFF and director of its Pathways to Prosperity initiative. In this role, she collaborates with states and regions to develop college and career pathway systems that expand opportunities for young people and support economic growth. Charlotte leads state policy and strategy development for the Pathways to Prosperity Network and oversees the Pathways to Prosperity asset mapping process. She also conducts research on topics that include work-based learning, labor market information, economic development, and pathways-related federal and state policies to support the development of career pathways systems. Charlotte also works with JFF's Center for Apprenticeship and Work-Based Learning on projects focused on developing work-based learning tools and resources and on scaling youth apprenticeship.

Prior to joining JFF, Charlotte worked at the Council for Adult and Experiential Learning (CAEL), where she did policy research and facilitated a peer-learning network of colleges and universities focused on strengthening postsecondary programs and career pathways for student veterans. Charlotte has taught at both two- and four-year postsecondary institutions, including Northwestern University, DePaul University, and the College of Lake County in Grayslake, Illinois. She holds a bachelor's degree in history from Boston College and a master's degree and PhD in the history of US public policy from Northwestern University.

MICHAEL LAWRENCE COLLINS is vice president at JFF, a national nonprofit working to transform the workforce and education systems to accelerate economic advancement for all. For over a decade, he has led a multistate postsecondary reform network committed to increasing the success of students from low-income backgrounds through connecting colleges and state systems to evidence-based practices and policies and supporting their implementation through nationally recognized initiatives such as Achieving the Dream, Completion by Design, and the Student Success Center Initiative. He serves as Chair of the Board for the National Student Clearinghouse Research Center and serves on the boards of the National Student Clearinghouse, the National Center for Higher Education Management Systems, and the advisory board for Guttman Community College. He is the Pahara-Aspen Education Fellow. Michael is a graduate of the LBJ School of Public Affairs at the University of Texas at Austin. He lives in Shaker Heights, Ohio, with his wife, Dana, and son, Dashel.

PAM EDDINGER is president of Bunker Hill Community College (BHCC), the largest of fifteen community colleges in Massachusetts. Pam began her tenure at BHCC in 2013, and previously served as president of Moorpark College in Southern California from 2008.

Pam's service in the community college movement spans more than twenty-five years, with senior posts in academics and student affairs, communications and policy, and executive leadership. In addition to the chairpersonship of the community college reform network Achieving the Dream, Pam serves on a number of boards and commissions, including the New England Commission of Higher Education, WGBH Boston, the Boston Foundation, the Massachusetts Workforce Development Board, and Boston Private Industry Council. Pam was honored in 2016 by the Obama White House as a Champion of Change. She earned a bachelor's degree in English from Barnard College in New York City and her master's and doctorate in Japanese Literature from Columbia University.

LISA Y. FLORES is a professor and the Norm C. Gysbers Faculty Fellow in Counseling Psychology at the University of Missouri. She has expertise in the career development of women and Latinxs and the integration of Latinx immigrants in rural communities. She has published ninety-seven journal articles and book chapters and presented over two hundred conference presentations in these areas. She has been PI and co-PI on grants totaling $3.6 million from the NSF, USDA, and US Department of Education to support her research. She is editor of the *Journal of Career Development* and past associate editor of the *Journal of Counseling Psychology*, and has served on the editorial boards of the *Journal of Vocational Behavior*, *The Counseling Psychologist*, *Journal of Counseling Psychology*, and *Career Development Quarterly*. She is a Fellow of the American Psychological Association (Divisions 17, 35, 45) and has received several honors for her work, including the Distinguished Career Award from the Society of Vocational Psychology, the Shining Star Award from the National Multicultural Conference and Summit, the John Holland Award for Outstanding Achievement in Career or Personality Research from the Society of Counseling Psychology, and early career professional awards from both the Society of Counseling Psychology and the National Latina/o Psychological Association.

MARY GATTA has been an associate professor of sociology at Stella and Charles Guttman Community College at CUNY since 2015. Prior to her appointment at CUNY, Mary served as a Senior Scholar at Wider Opportunities for Women in Washington, DC, and as Director of Gender and Workforce Policy at the Center for Women and Work, and assistant professor of Labor Studies at Rutgers University. At Guttman, Mary teaches social science courses and served as the faculty coordinator of *Ethnographies of Work*, described in this volume.

Mary recently served on New Jersey Governor Phil Murphy's Labor and Workforce Development Transition Team. Mary has also led evaluations of workforce and education programs including US Department of Labor programs, New Jersey Department of Labor and Workforce Development programs, and various education and workforce programs.

Mary is a leader in research related to job quality, such as workplace flexibility for low-wage workers, workforce development programs, and nontraditional job training for women. Her books include *Waiting on Retirement: Aging and Economic Insecurity in Low Wage Work* (2018), a study of the experiences of older low-wage workers, and *All I Want Is a Job! Unemployed Women Navigating the Public Workforce System* (2014); both were published by Stanford University Press. She is also the author of *Not Just Getting By: The New Era of Flexible Workforce Development* and *Juggling Food and Feelings: Emotional Balance in the Workplace* (both from Lexington Books) and is the editor of *A US Skills System for the 21st Century: Innovations in Workforce Education and Development*.

NANCY HOFFMAN is senior advisor at JFF, a national nonprofit based in Boston. Nancy is the cofounder, with Bob Schwartz, of the Pathways to Prosperity State Network, a collaboration between the Harvard Graduate School of Education, JFF, sixteen states, and sixty economic regions with the goal of building pathways to careers for low-income young people. Nancy also led JFF's work to develop early college high schools and expand opportunities for college-level work in high school to a wide range of students.

Nancy's most recent book, coauthored with Bob Schwartz, is *Learning for Careers: The Pathways to Prosperity Network (2017)*. She is also the author of *Schooling in the Workplace: How Six of the World's Best Vocational Education Systems Prepare Young People for Jobs and Life* (2011). She edited three JFF books: *Double the Numbers: Increasing Postsecondary Credentials for Underrepresented Youth*; *Minding the Gap: Why Integrating High School with College Makes Sense and How to Do It*; and *Anytime, Anywhere: Student-Centered Learning for Schools and Teachers*. Nancy is also the author of *Women's True Profession: Voices from the History of Teachin*g. These books are all published by the Harvard Education Press. Nancy serves on the Massachusetts Board of Higher Education as well as the boards of North Bennet Street School, Adult and Continuing Education Martha's Vineyard, and BuildUP Birmingham. She holds a BA and PhD in comparative literature from University of California, Berkeley, and has held teaching and administrative posts at Brown, Temple, Harvard, MIT, and elsewhere.

SARAH KALLOCH is executive director of the Good Jobs Institute, whose mission is to help companies thrive by creating good jobs. She builds partnerships with companies looking to implement the Institute's Good Jobs Strategy, and creates tools and resources to guide the transformation process. Sarah previously spent more than a decade in international policy and operations. At Oxfam America, she built global partnerships to support socially responsible corporate supply chain policy. At Physicians for Human Rights, Sarah served on the executive management team, cofounding two health and human rights organizations in East Africa and advocating for billions of dollars in global health/workforce investment.

Sarah graduated magna cum laude with a degree in Social Studies from Harvard. She received her MBA from MIT Sloan School of Management, where she studied sustainable operations and won the Seley Scholarship for leadership and academic achievement. She is a 2018–2019 Aspen Institute Job Quality Fellow and has guest lectured on good jobs and sustainable operations in MIT Sloan's Executive Education and MBA programs.

RICHARD KAZIS, a nonresident senior fellow at the Brookings Institution Metropolitan Policy Program and a senior consultant to MDRC, partners with organizations and foundations to advance education and workforce development reform. Richard was previously senior vice president of JFF, where he led the organization's research and advocacy agenda. Current projects focus on community colleges and the future of work, state policies to promote work-based learning, and strengthening mathematics pathways for community college students. Richard has written widely on low-wage worker advancement, community college student success, and college and career readiness. Recent publications include: *Uncovering Hidden Talent: Community College Internships That Pay and Pay Off for Students and Employers* (coauthored with Nancy Snyder for The Boston Foundation) and The Right Math at the Right Time for Michigan (with Jenny Schanker for the Charles A. Dana Center at the University of Texas at Austin). A graduate of Harvard College and MIT, Richard has also taught social studies at an alternative high school, helped organize fast-food workers, and built labor-environmental jobs coalitions. Richard currently serves as board chair of the Institute for College Access and Success.

MAUREEN E. KENNY is a professor in the Department of Counseling, Developmental and Educational Psychology in the Boston College Lynch School, where she also held the positions of Dean and Associate Dean for Faculty and Academics. Maureen completed her PhD in counseling and school psychology at the University of Pennsylvania and is a Fellow of Division 17, Society of Counseling Psychology, of the American Psychological Association. Maureen is the author of more than fifty articles in referred journals, seven books, and twenty-five book chapters. Her research interests focus on prevention and positive youth development, especially as related to student career development, work-based learning, school engagement, and the development of social-emotional competencies. She is the recipient of the

Lifetime Achievement Award in Prevention by the APA Division 17 Section on Prevention.

SARA LAMBACK is an associate director at JFF. She provides leadership and program management on a range of projects that help low-income adults train for and succeed in jobs with career advancement potential, with a particular focus on workforce development programs in the technology sector. Sara also leads JFF's labor market information practice. Sara recently coauthored the JFF report "When Is a Job Just a Job—And When Can It Launch a Career?" which is highlighted in chapter 4 of this volume.

Before joining JFF, Sara conducted research at Harvard's Achievement Gap Initiative, where she coauthored the report *Creating Pathways to Prosperity: A Blueprint for Action*, with Professor Ronald Ferguson. She serves on the industry advisory board of the Dearborn STEM Academy in Boston. Sara holds a Master of Arts in French literature from Middlebury College and earned her Master of Education in education policy and management from the Harvard Graduate School of Education.

GLORIA G. MCGILLEN is a PhD student in counseling psychology at the University of Missouri and a graduate clinician at the University of Missouri Counseling Center. Her research explores economic justice issues as they relate to vocational psychology and career development, as well as racial-ethnic identity development and experiences of classism, racism, and racial privilege among the US working class and poor.

BRENT ORRELL is a resident fellow at the American Enterprise Institute, where he researches job training, workforce development, and criminal justice reform. For over twenty years, Brent worked in the executive and legislative branches of the US government. He was nominated by President George W. Bush to lead the Employment and Training Administration of the US Department of Labor and was Deputy Assistant Secretary for Policy at the Administration for Children and Families (HHS). His research focuses on expanding opportunity for all Americans through improved work readiness and job training and improving the performance of the criminal justice system through rehabilitation and prisoner re-entry programs.

GREGORY SEATON is an associate director at JFF and works with the Pathways to Prosperity team. He supports state, regional, and local organizations in building better systems to transition young people from high school to post-secondary credentials to careers. Gregory blends practical work experiences in urban schools and communities with academic experience. His research primarily focuses on the developmental and academic outcomes of youth, particularly urban males.

Previously, he served as associate professor at the College of New Jersey in the Department of Education Administration and Secondary Education, and as senior researcher at the University of Pennsylvania's Center for Health, Achievement, Neighborhood, Growth, and Ethnic Studies; the New Jersey Department of Education; Center for Disease Control; and the Environment Protection Agency. He also served as a youth outreach worker for the Orlando Housing Authority, and prior to that as executive director for Teacher Education for America's Minorities (TEAM) at the University of Central Florida, where he recruited and trained minority teachers to provide high-quality instruction in urban and poorly funded schools.

Gregory has a master's degree from Harvard University and a PhD in educational leadership and human development from the University of Pennsylvania.

CALEB SEIBERT is a research assistant at the American Enterprise Institute, where his work focuses on workforce development and criminal justice reform. Caleb received a Bachelor of Business Administration from Baylor University and a Master of Public Affairs from the LBJ School of Public Affairs at the University of Texas.

NIESHA ZIEHMKE, Associate Dean of Academic Affairs, works to promote educational equality for the students of Guttman Community College, CUNY, where she oversees academic majors, the Center for Career Preparation and Partnerships, study abroad, experiential learning, strategic planning, and academic assessment. Prior to joining Guttman in 2017, Niesha served as Executive Associate for Academic Affairs at LaGuardia Community College, where she worked collaboratively to strengthen student success and assessment across the institution. From 2009 to 2013, Niesha served as Director for First College Year Programs at Brooklyn College.

Niesha earned her master's in education from the New School for Social Research and taught Spanish in a New York City public high school for six years. She then completed her PhD in linguistics at the CUNY Graduate Center, with a focus on methods for teaching academic English to students who speak nonacademic varieties of English. While working on her doctorate, she administered an educational psychology research program in Self-Regulated Learning (SRL), sponsored by the Center for Advanced Study in Education at the Graduate Center. The SRL program aimed to improve the academic performance of developmental math and writing students at the college level.

INDEX